# Mastering Unity 2D Game Development

## Second Edition

Master everything you need to build a 2D game using Unity 5 by developing a complete RPG game framework!

**Ashley Godbold**
**Simon Jackson**

BIRMINGHAM - MUMBAI

# Mastering Unity 2D Game Development

## Second Edition

First published: August 2014

Second edition: October 2016

Production reference: 1071016

Published by Packt Publishing Ltd.
Livery Place
35 Livery Street
Birmingham
B3 2PB, UK.

ISBN 978-1-78646-345-6

www.packtpub.com

# Credits

**Authors**

Ashley Godbold

Simon Jackson

**Reviewer**

Claudio Scolastici

**Commissioning Editor**

Amarabha Banerjee

**Acquisition Editor**

Smeet Thakkar

**Content Development Editor**

Prashanth G

**Technical Editor**

Sushant S Nadkar

**Copy Editor**

Sameen Siddiqui

**Project Coordinator**

Ulhas Kambali

**Proofreader**

Safis Editing

**Indexer**

Rekha Nair

**Graphics**

Kirk D'Penha

**Production Coordinator**

Aparna Bhagat

# About the Authors

**Dr. Ashley Godbold** is a programmer, game designer, artist, mathematician, and teacher. She holds a Bachelor of Science in Mathematics, a Master of Science in Mathematics, a Bachelor of Science in Game Art and Design, and a Doctor of Computer Science in Emerging Media, where her dissertation research focused on educational video game design. She works full-time as a game developer and also runs a small indie/passion studio. She teaches college courses in Unity, 3ds Max, Adobe Flash, game design, and mathematics.

*I would like to thank my husband, Kyle, and my daughter, Claire, for supporting me after I made the crazy decision to write a book and a dissertation at the same time. I would also like to thank my good friend, Danny Rich, for being the person with whom I initially set out to learn Unity and for helping me with character art in this book.*

*I'd also like to thank everyone at Packt Publishing for helping me through this process, particularly Smeet Thakkar, Prashanth G Rao, and Sushant Nadkar for all of their help through this process.*

**Simon Jackson** has been a tinkerer, engineer, problem solver, and solution gatherer ever since his early years. In short, he loves to break things apart, figure out how they work, and then put them back together; usually better than before.

He started way back when with his first computer, the Commodore Vic20. It was simple, used a tape deck, and forced you to write programs in Basic or assembly language; those were fun times. From there, he progressed through the ZX Spectrum +2 and the joyous days of modern graphics, but still with the 30-minute load times from a trusty tape deck. Games were his passion even then, which led to many requests for another gaming machine, but Santa brought him an Amstrad 1640, his first PC. From there, his tinkering and building exploded, and that machine ended up being a huge monstrosity with so many add-ons and tweaked fixes. He was Frankenstein, and this PC became his own personal monster crafted from so many parts. Good times.

This passion led him down many paths, and he learned to help educate others on the tips and tricks he learned along the way; these skills have equipped him well for the future.

Today, he would class himself as a game development generalist. He works with many different frameworks, each time digging down and ripping them apart, and then showing whoever would listen through his biog, videos, and speaking events how to build awesome frameworks and titles. This has been throughout many generations of C++, MDX, XNA (what a breath of fresh air that was), MonoGame, Unity3D, The Sunburn Gaming Engine, HTML, and a bunch of other proprietary frameworks—he did them all. This gives him a very balanced view of how to build and manage many different types of multiplatform titles.

He didn't stop there as he regularly contributed to the MonoGame project, adding new features and samples, and publishing on NuGet. He also has several of his own open source projects and actively seeks any new and interesting ones to help with.

By day, he is a lowly lead technical architect working in the healthcare industry, seeking to improve patients' health and care through better software (a challenge to be sure). By night, he truly soars! Building, tinkering, and educating while trying to push game titles of his own. One day they will pay the bills, but until then, he still leads a double life.

*I would like to thank my family above all, my wife, Caroline and my four amazing children (Alexander, Caitlin, Jessica, and Nathan), for putting up with me and giving me the space to write this title as well as my other extravagances—they truly lift me up and keep me sane. They are my rock, my shore, my world.*

*I would also like to thank Jamie Hales of PixelBalloon who generously donated some content for the Appendix and gave me new ideas and insights to look into.*

*A big shout out to all the guys who ran and helped me out with the Unity porting events, which I supported throughout the course of this book, namely Lee Stott, Simon Michael, Riaz Amhed, Louis Sykes, Ben Beagley, Josh Naylor, Mahmud Chowdhury, and Michael Cameron. Also, the Unity evangelists who were badgered throughout the events and were pumped for hidden details: Joe Robins and Andy Touch. Truly a great crowd to get game developers energized and their titles onto as many platforms as possible. Lots of weekends lost to writing, but the book was better, for they led to so many different experiences.*

*Finally, thanks to the reviewers of this title who kept me grounded and on target, although that didn't help to keep the page count low—thanks for your support guys.*

# About the Reviewer

**Claudio Scolastici** is a game designer with a background in Psychology, Cognitive Science and AI. He is currently a game designer for the video game and VR/AR developer SpinVector, author of cool games such as *From Cheese* and *Artusi Cooking Time*.

He is also a guest tutor at Digital Tutors/Pluralsight and a book author for Packt.

# www.PacktPub.com

## eBooks, discount offers, and more

Did you know that Packt offers eBook versions of every book published, with PDF and ePub files available? You can upgrade to the eBook version at www.PacktPub.com and as a print book customer, you are entitled to a discount on the eBook copy. Get in touch with us at customercare@packtpub.com for more details.

At www.PacktPub.com, you can also read a collection of free technical articles, sign up for a range of free newsletters and receive exclusive discounts and offers on Packt books and eBooks.

https://www.packtpub.com/mapt

Get the most in-demand software skills with Mapt. Mapt gives you full access to all Packt books and video courses, as well as industry-leading tools to help you plan your personal development and advance your career.

## Why subscribe?

- Fully searchable across every book published by Packt
- Copy and paste, print, and bookmark content
- On demand and accessible via a web browser

# Table of Contents

# Preface

The Unity engine has revolutionized the gaming industry, by making it easier than ever for indie game developers to create quality games on a budget. Hobbyists and students can use this powerful engine to build 2D and 3D games, to play, distribute, and even sell for free! Unity 4.3 dramatically reformed the way developers could create 2D games when they included sprite rendering, 2D physics, and sprite key-frame animation. Unity 4.6 further shook the gaming world by adding a new and elegant UI system that perfectly complimented the 2D games developers began creating. Now, Unity 5 has arrived! And this text will explore all the wonderful features it has to offer for 2D game development.

In this book, you will learn how to build an RPG game framework, learning lots of tips and tricks along the way. You will start by making a character and a village for the character to interact with NPCs. Then you will develop an overworld map for the character to explore that will be loaded with enemies who randomly attack her. After that, you'll cover the process involved in setting up a turn based battle system along with all of the necessary steps for creating a functional GUI. Following that, you'll develop a shop and inventory system and then implement sound and music. By the end of this book, you will be able to architect, create, deploy, your game as well as have the knowledge to build and customize the Unity editor.

## What this book covers

Chapter 1, *Overview*. This chapter gives a basic overview of the 2D features provided within Unity 5. It also provides general guidance for finding free assets to use within 2D projects. Lastly, it points out key differences between Unity 5 and Unity 4.

Chapter 2, *Building your Project and Character*. This chapter covers the steps necessary to start building a project. It describes object oriented programming, how it is used in Unity, and the basic structure of a class in C# using MonoDevelop. This chapter also describes the process of importing, editing, and implementing, 2D sprites into the Unity engine, as well as the programming required to move the sprite around the screen with the player's interaction.

Chapter 3, *Getting Animated*. This chapter introduces animation in Unity by utilizing the various animation components. It describes the process of converting a sprite sheet to an animation clip and implementing the Animator component. It also describes the process of setting up the Animator Controller and explains how to implement animation parameters using scripting.

Chapter 4, *The Town View*. This chapter explains the process of setting up the town in which the character will walk around. It also explains the process of working with the camera and how to program the functionality necessary for the character to interact with her environment.

Chapter 5, *Working with Unity's UI System*. This chapter gives a general overview of the UI system implemented in Unity 4.6.

Chapter 6, *NPCS and Interactions*. This chapter covers the overall structure of interacting with non-player characters within an RPG. It then describes the process of writing and implementing the code necessary to allow the player to speak with the NPCs, and displaying the conversation utilizing the UI system.

Chapter 7, *The World Map*. This chapter discusses the process of building a map for the player to navigate and allowing the player character to exit the initial town.

Chapter 8, *Encountering Enemies and Running Away*. This chapter discusses the process of creating a battle scene that contains randomly spawning enemies. It then covers the programming required to have the player character transition in to random battles and transition back to the map by selecting the option to run away.

Chapter 9, *Getting Ready to Fight*. This chapter discusses the process of developing a battle introduction animation and the GUI that will allow the player to interact with the battle.

Chapter 10, *The Battle Begins*. This chapter further develops the battle system, by implementing the code that allows the player to select various attacks, incorporating particle systems to represent attacks, and utilizing an event system.

Chapter 11, *Shopping for Items*. This chapter discusses the process of creating a shop in which the player can buy items and an inventory system in which the player can save the purchased items.

Chapter 12, *Sound and Music*. This chapter covers the basics of sound integration utilizing audio listeners and sources, by adding background music and a sound effect when the player purchases an item.

Chapter 13, *Putting a Bow on It*. This chapter covers the finishing touches necessary to create a complete game. This includes packaging the game, implementing a splash screen and menu system, extending the editor, and adding a system to save the player's data.

Chapter 14, *Deployment and Beyond*. This final chapter discusses how to convert the final game to a playable game.

# What you need for this book

In order to follow this book, you will need the Unity game engine available at `https://unity3d.com/get-unity/download`.

You will need to download version 5.3 or higher. This text was written using 5.3.4. If for some reason, you want to get Unity 5.3.4 instead of the most recent version, you can get archived versions from `https://unity3d.com/get-unity/download/archive`.

To get the art assets and code discussed within the book, you should download the book's support files.

# Who this book is for

This book is intended for anyone looking to get started in developing 2D games with Unity 5 or anyone already familiar with Unity 2D wishing to expand or supplement their current Unity knowledge. A basic understanding of programming logic is needed to begin learning with this book, but intermediate and advanced programming topic are explained thoroughly so that coders of any level can follow along. Previous programming experience in C# is not required.

# Conventions

In this book, you will find a number of text styles that distinguish between different kinds of information. Here are some examples of these styles and an explanation of their meaning.

Code words in text, database table names, folder names, filenames, file extensions, pathnames, dummy URLs, user input, and Twitter handles are shown as follows: "This is done by calling `DontDestroyOnLoad` when you initialize the class."

A block of code is set as follows:

```
//Set the public property of the singleton
MySingletonManager.Instance.MyTestProperty = "World Hello";

//Run the public method from the singleton
MySingletonManager.Instance.DoSomethingAwesome();
```

**New terms** and **important words** are shown in bold. Words that you see on the screen, for example, in menus or dialog boxes, appear in the text like this: "After selecting **Create project**, you'll be brought to the **Editor** Window"

Warnings or important notes appear in a box like this.

Tips and tricks appear like this.

# Reader feedback

Feedback from our readers is always welcome. Let us know what you think about this book—what you liked or disliked. Reader feedback is important for us as it helps us develop titles that you will really get the most out of.

To send us general feedback, simply e-mail feedback@packtpub.com, and mention the book's title in the subject of your message.

If there is a topic that you have expertise in and you are interested in either writing or contributing to a book, see our author guide at www.packtpub.com/authors.

# Customer support

Now that you are the proud owner of a Packt book, we have a number of things to help you to get the most from your purchase.

## Downloading the example code

You can download the example code files for this book from your account at http://www.packtpub.com. If you purchased this book elsewhere, you can visit http://www.packtpub.com/support and register to have the files e-mailed directly to you.

You can download the code files by following these steps:

1. Log in or register to our website using your e-mail address and password.
2. Hover the mouse pointer on the **SUPPORT** tab at the top.
3. Click on **Code Downloads & Errata**.
4. Enter the name of the book in the **Search** box.
5. Select the book for which you're looking to download the code files.
6. Choose from the drop-down menu where you purchased this book from.
7. Click on **Code Download**.

You can also download the code files by clicking on the **Code Files** button on the book's webpage at the Packt Publishing website. This page can be accessed by entering the book's name in the **Search** box. Please note that you need to be logged in to your Packt account.

Once the file is downloaded, please make sure that you unzip or extract the folder using the latest version of:

- WinRAR / 7-Zip for Windows
- Zipeg / iZip / UnRarX for Mac
- 7-Zip / PeaZip for Linux

The code bundle for the book is also hosted on GitHub at `https://github.com/PacktPubl ishing/Mastering-Unity-2D-Game-Development-Second-Edition`. We also have other code bundles from our rich catalog of books and videos available at `https://github.com/P acktPublishing/`. Check them out!

# Downloading the color images of this book

We also provide you with a PDF file that has color images of the screenshots/diagrams used in this book. The color images will help you better understand the changes in the output. You can download this file from `https://www.packtpub.com/sites/default/files/down loads/MasteringUnity2DGameDevelopmentSecondEdition_ColorImages.pdf`.

# Errata

Although we have taken every care to ensure the accuracy of our content, mistakes do happen. If you find a mistake in one of our books—maybe a mistake in the text or the code—we would be grateful if you could report this to us. By doing so, you can save other readers from frustration and help us improve subsequent versions of this book. If you find any errata, please report them by visiting http://www.packtpub.com/submit-errata, selecting your book, clicking on the **Errata Submission Form** link, and entering the details of your errata. Once your errata are verified, your submission will be accepted and the errata will be uploaded to our website or added to any list of existing errata under the Errata section of that title.

To view the previously submitted errata, go to https://www.packtpub.com/books/content/support and enter the name of the book in the search field. The required information will appear under the **Errata** section.

# Piracy

Piracy of copyrighted material on the Internet is an ongoing problem across all media. At Packt, we take the protection of our copyright and licenses very seriously. If you come across any illegal copies of our works in any form on the Internet, please provide us with the location address or website name immediately so that we can pursue a remedy.

Please contact us at copyright@packtpub.com with a link to the suspected pirated material.

We appreciate your help in protecting our authors and our ability to bring you valuable content.

# Questions

If you have a problem with any aspect of this book, you can contact us at questions@packtpub.com, and we will do our best to address the problem.

# 1
# Overview

Arguably, the most important parts of any project are knowing where to start and what tools you have in your arsenal before setting out to make your game. In this chapter, we will give a brief overview of the 2D tools offered in **Unity 5** and explore the new features available to Unity 5.

Since this is the first chapter, let's cover how this book is structured. The main aim of this book is to build a fully functional, retro-style, **Role-Playing Game (RPG)** framework and cover all the main aspects of any good and well-rounded RPG game, including the following features:

- Character development and setup
- Building your main game view
- A wider world view
- Events and encounters
- Shopping and inventory systems
- Battles

We will be visiting places such as the following:

- Your home town, as shown in the following screenshot:

- The local shop, as shown in the following screenshot:

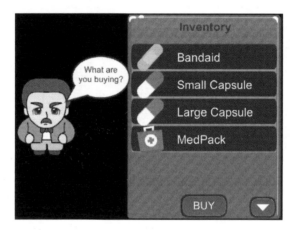

- The outside world, as shown in the following screenshot:

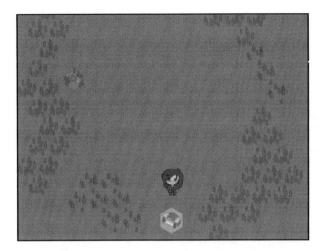

- Battling dragons in the dark forest, as shown in the following screenshot:

In this chapter, we will walk through the key terms used when working in 2D, as well as the big changes made in Unity 5 relevant to 2D game creation. We will kick off the next chapter by building the foundations of our project with some of the best practices in the industry, including guidance from the Unity team themselves (either direct from team members or from responses in the forums).

The following topics will be covered in this chapter:

- Overview of Unity's 2D system
- Rundown of new features provided in Unity 5

# Getting assets

Since creating games can become quite expensive, we'll use some of the best free assets out there. There are plenty of resources available to game developers, either as placement assets for the developer's use, whether they are full assets, or just a framework that you can tweak to get your desired result. There are a multitude of options.

> In the code bundle of this book, you'll get all the assets you need to follow during the creation of the game. The site where it is available online will be listed with the instructions.

Some of the best sites to gather assets are described as follows:

- **Art**: Art, especially 2D art, is generally easy to find on a budget, particularly for the placeholder art, until you buy or create your own for the finished product (although I've seen many games created with some of these assets). Some good sites to start with are `http://opengameart.org/` and `http://open.commonly.cc/`.
- **Audio**: Sound that works for your project is a lot trickier to get. Free sites are okay, but they generally don't have the right sound you will want or you will end up digging through hundreds or more sounds to get a close match. A good website to start with is `http://soundbible.com/`.
- **General**: Some sites just hold a general collection of assets instead of specializing in specific areas. The best site for this, as everything is almost guaranteed to be free, is `http://search.creativecommons.org/`. The Unity **Asset Store** also offers a great deal of free assets from art to code. Some of these assets are available from users, and others are available from the Unity team themselves. Not all of the assets are free, but you can easily sort your search result by price. You can find the Unity Asset Store at `https://www.assetstore.unity3d.com`.

# Unity's 2D features

In 2013, with the release of Unity 4.3, Unity made 2D game development significantly simpler by adding native support for 2D development to the Unity editor environment. Since then, 2D game development has been on the rise among the indie and hobbyist developers. This section will give a general overview the various 2D features and terms as they appear in Unity 5.3.

## 2D mode versus 3D mode

When creating a new Unity project, you can choose between 3D mode and 2D mode, as shown in the following screenshot:

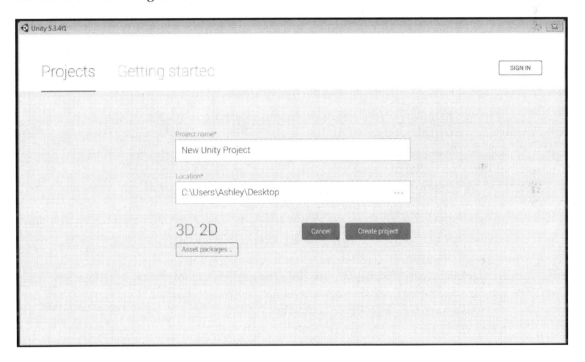

The main differences in the two modes are the way assets will be imported into your project and the default camera view and position. If you select 2D, the default camera will be set to **Orthographic** projection, the camera's position will be set to (0, 0, -10), your scene will be in 2D view, and your and images will be imported as sprites rather than textures.

You can easily swap between the two modes at any time during development by navigating to **Edit** | **Project Settings** | **Editor** and changing the **Default Behavior Mode** option, as shown in the following screenshot:

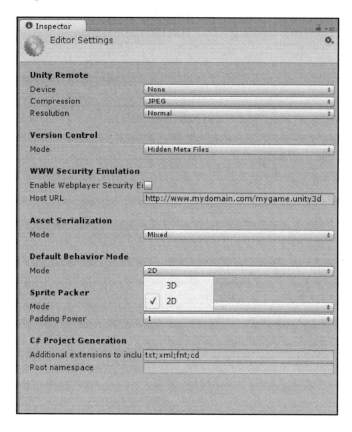

Changing the **Default Behavior Mode** will not affect how your game runs. This setting really only makes the process of importing new assets and creating new cameras quicker, because you will not have to manually change the texture type of images and change the projection of camera.

There are a few other items that are handled differently in 2D mode versus 3D mode, such as lighting, and you can find a list of all the differences at h ttp://docs.unity3d.com/Manual/2DAnd3DModeSettings.html.

# Working with sprites

**Sprites** are 2D images. Sprites can be images that depict a single object (for example, a character) or an entire scene (for example, a background). Several sprites can also be combined to create a single object, as shown in the following screenshot:

A character created by combining multiple sprites; example from Unity's platformer sample

When your project is set to 2D mode, any image you import in to your project folder will automatically be assigned a **Sprite (2D and UI)** texture type. This means that the image is assumed to represent a 2D object or scene rather than an image that will applied to a 3D object.

When a sprite image is dragged from the `Assets` folder to the **Scene** view, a **2D Object-Sprite** will be added to your scene. This object will automatically be given the **Sprite Renderer** component (refer to the following section), making the sprite visible in your game; no additional lighting or work is required.

 It's important to note that if your sprite has transparencies, you want to import your sprite texture as a `.png` formatted image file.

By default, each image is imported as a single sprite; however, by using the **Sprite Editor** (refer to the *Sprite Editor* section), you can change this in various ways.

 While your sprite textures can be any dimension, it is highly recommended that the texture be a perfect square with a power of two pixel height and width (that is 64 px by 64 px, 128 px by 128 px, and so on).

# Sprite Renderer

The **Sprite Renderer** is the component that allows a 2D object to be displayed as a Sprite on the screen. Refer to the following screenshot:

The **Sprite** property selects the image that will be displayed. Any image that is assigned a **Sprite (2D and UI)** texture type can be placed in this property. The **Color** property allows you to change the vertex color of the rendered image as well as the transparency (through the alpha).

**Flip** is a property new to Unity 5.0. This will allow you to flip the sprite in the $X$ or $Y$ planes without having to use **Scale** properties in the transform, as was necessary in previous versions of Unity.

The **Sprite Renderer** component automatically sets the **Material** property of the object to **Sprites-Default**, which uses the default **Shader** property as **Sprite/Default**. The **Sprites/Default** shader does not interact with lights in the scene, so lights are not required to view Sprites with these default settings.

# Sprite Editor

The **Sprite Editor** allows you to manipulate a sprite once it has been imported in to Unity. The **Sprite Editor** is only available for graphics with **Texture Type** set to **Sprite (2D and UI)**. The following is the screenshot of the **Sprite Editor** window showing a single sprite:

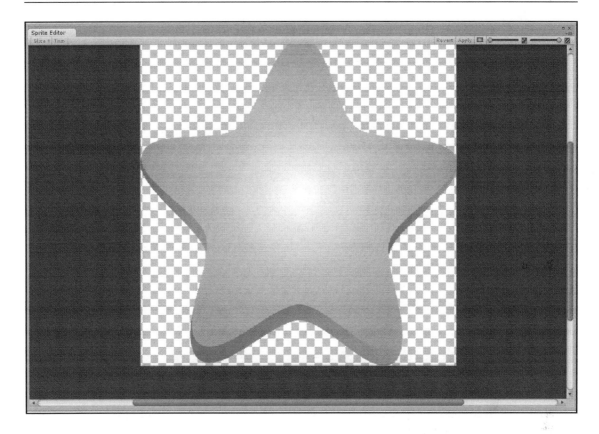

The editor allows some basic manipulations to happen to a sprite, for example:

- Changing the sprite's pixilation (mipmap)
- Altering the sprite's pivot position
- Splicing the texture to identify the sprite region (this is also used for sprite sheets; refer to the next section)

## Sprite sheets

**Sprite sheets** are a core part of any 2D animation system. Sprite sheets are a single texture that contains multiple images that represent individual frames of a 2D animation. Unifying all textures into a single larger texture means greater performance when sending the sprites to the graphic cards, which is a lot faster than sending lots of smaller files. Refer to the following screenshot:

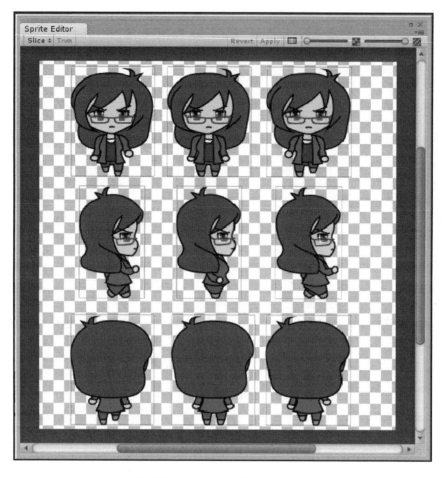

Sprite Editor window showing multiple sprites in a grid

The traditional way of forming sprite sheets is to put sprites into specific regions on a single image and then identify the box regions where the individual sprites lie. These regions form individual frames in the sprite animation. As you can see in the preceding screenshot, nine sprites are arranged in three rows to form a character's walking animation. The sprites could have also been arranged in a single row or a single column; it doesn't matter. It's just how the artist best packs the sprite sheet for the animation. Unity can handle just about any arrangement you wish to throw at it. Just set the width and height of each texture region and the Unity **Sprite Editor** will do the rest. If your individual sprites are non-disjoint images, all of the same size, Unity can also automatically slice the texture in to the appropriate regions.

# Texture atlases

Akin to sprite sheets, texture atlases are a more efficient way of packing textures into a single texture. It can contain various parts of a character (as follows), or a set of weapons, or a set of buttons to be used in your UI—anything really.

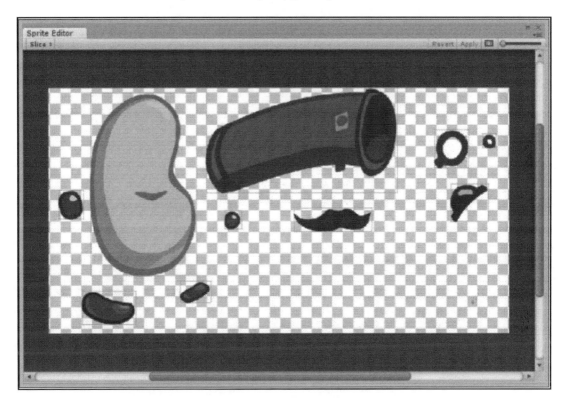

A selection of separate textures that have been automatically packed; example from Unity's platformer sample

Unity has added a very clever texture cutting and edge detection to make this work very well and identify specific regions on the texture for each sprite. You can also change the selection areas if Unity is too optimistic when selecting the texture regions.

The **Sprite Packer** utility provided by Unity can combine all of your sprite textures in to a single tightly packed atlas to help improve the performance of your game.

# Physics 2D

The inclusion of a 2D physics system in Unity 4.3 has made 2D game creation easier than ever. Before the inclusion, these physics had to be either programmed by the developer or faked using 3D physics. However, now, with the use of the **RidgidBody2D** component, the various 2D colliders, physics materials, effectors, and joints, making a 2D game with physics can be achieved with a few simple clicks.

Physics plays an important role in many 2D games. This is particularly true for platformers and certain puzzle games such as Tsum Tsum, Angry Birds, and Cut the Rope.

The **RigidBody2D** component can be added to any object that you want to be affected by the physics engine. For example, you can add the **RigidBody 2D** component to a sprite you want affected by gravity. The various 2D colliders, such as the **Box Collider 2D** and **Polygon Collider 2D**, can be added to any object that you want to check collision on. This can be used to keep objects from passing through one another (refer to the following screenshot) or can be used to check when two objects touch each other.

Example of 2D colliders used in the Unity platformer to surround walkable elements

You can also apply physics materials to your 2D objects using **Physics Material 2D**. This allows greater control over an object's physics interactions, such as friction and bounciness.

An effector is essentially a component that applies a type of force to sprites that interact with the 2D object that has an effector component attached to it. Unity 5 added four effector components to the Physics 2D library: **Area Effector 2D**, **Point Effector 2D**, **Platform Effector 2D**, and **Surface Effector 2D**. When Unity 5.3 released, the **Buoyancy Effector 2D** component was added. **Constant Force 2D** was also included in the Unity 5 update, which allows you to apply a constant force to a sprite.

Joints are also included in the Unity Physics 2D package. Joints allow various 2D game objects to join together in distinct ways. Four new joints were added with Unity 5.3. There are nine joints now included in Unity: **Distance Joint 2D**, **Fixed Joint 2D**, **Friction Joint 2D**, **Hinge Joint 2D**, **Relative Joint 2D**, **Slider Joint 2D**, **Spring Joint 2D**, **Target Joint 2D**, and **Wheel Joint 2D**.

# Changes to Unity 5

If you have been working with Unity 4.x and are now starting out in Unity 5.x, there are a few key differences in the way things behave. Here you will find a general overview of the most relevant changes to 2D game development, other than the ones already discussed concerning 2D physics.

 The following list does not include all of the new features included in Unity 5 and the Unity 5.3 update. For a complete list, visit http://unity3 d.com/unity/whats-new/unity-5. and http://blogs.unity3d.com/215 /12/8/unity-5-3-all-new-features-and-more-platforms/.

# Licensing

Let's start with the best new feature of Unity 5. In previous versions of Unity, certain features were only available in the Pro version and were blocked in the free version. However, in Unity 5, all features are unlocked and can be enjoyed even by developers using the free version, now named **Unity Personal**. If a game you create with Unity Personal makes $100k or more, you will have to pay for the professional version.

# Component access

Another big change to Unity 5 is the removal of quick property accessors within code. This means that a lot of your code written for Unity 4 will need to be rewritten. For example, the use of `.rigidBody2D` and `.collider2D` are no longer permissible. However, if you have code in your game from an older version of Unity, you will be shown the following warning:

Selecting **I Made a Backup. Go Ahead!** will automatically convert all quick property accessors to code containing the `GetComponent` function. For example, take the following code that was previously written as:

```
object.ridgidBody2D.isKinematic=false;
```

Now the preceding code would now be written as follows:

```
object.GetComponent<Rigidbody2D>().isKinematic=false;
```

 Make sure you back up your code before selecting, **I Made a Backup. Go Ahead!** The automatic changes may not be what you expect.

# Animator changes

The most glaring difference when you initially start up the Unity 5 Animator will be the inclusion of an **Entry** node. Unity 5 has now added **Entry** and **Exist** nodes to **StateMachines** (**we will discuss state machines in** `Chapter 8`, *Encountering Enemies and Running Away*). These nodes allow the transition between states machines. For the most part, you animations that were running in Unity 4 should run appropriately in Unity 5, but will include the new **Entry** node, as shown in the following screenshot:

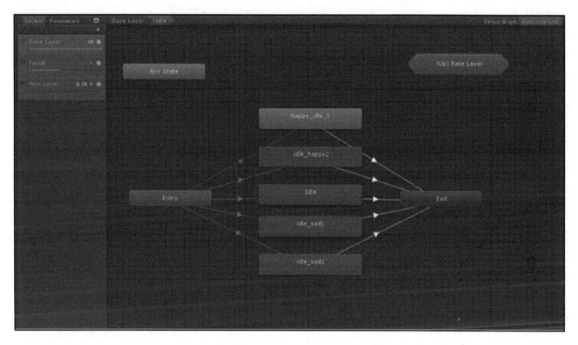

StateMachine Transitions with Entry and Exit nodes provided by Unity

# Audio mixing

Previously, if you had a lot of audio sources in your game, dealing with all of them could be quite a hassle. Unity 5 provide an **Audio Mixer** asset type that now allows you to adjust all of your audio levels more efficiently, as show in the following screenshot:

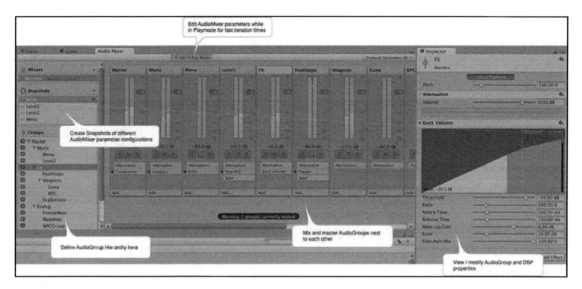

Audio Mixer image provided by Unity

# Summary

2D game development has received a new life with the inclusion of 2D support in Unity 4.3. Since then, many other features have been added, making Unity 5.3 one of the most versatile and user-friendly gaming engines on the market. Never before has it been easier to make a 2D game from start to finish on a budget and within a short amount of time.

In this chapter, we covered the objective of the book, the paths to get the assets needed for the sample project, an overview of the key terms and features related to 2D game development in Unity, and an overview of the most apparent changes implemented in Unity 5 related to 2D game development.

Are you sitting comfortably? Well, keep your arms and legs in the ride at all times and prepare yourself for a high-speed ride!

# 2
# Building Your Project and Character

It's time to start putting the building blocks that will make up your game into Unity. We will start with setting up the project and then move on to building the main character. Setting up the main character is an important first step, as most of your game's core logic and framework generally centers on the main protagonist and highlights exactly how the player will interact with the game.

We will be creating two main locations for the character to explore: a 2.5D town in which she can interact with **Non-Playable Characters** (**NPCs**) and a world map in which she will encounter and battle enemies. To allow our character to interact with and explore these locations, we must first get our character into our project and give her the ability to move around the scenes. We must also get our project started the right way by setting up the project appropriately.

The following topics will be covered in this chapter:

- Designing a good project structure
- Creating a project and scenes
- Importing Sprites
- Working with classes and components
- Planning and designing behaviors
- Setting up user control effectively

# Project overview and structure

Before you start your project, you should consider how you intend to set it up and architect your project in the long term. Far too many developers have created problems for themselves by just diving in rather than designing the outline for the project at the start.

Your game and your assets are not the only things to consider when starting a fresh project. Sure, you can start importing assets, creating scripts, and getting things running; most **Proof of Concept (POC)** projects start this way. Once your project is of a sufficient size and you start expanding on your initial concept, you'll realize that you have issues with regard to picking up items and putting them together. Then, you will start devising new ways to organize your project and eventually find that it's an unmanageable mess; nevertheless, you will stride on, taking longer and longer to produce new content or add new features.

The best advice one can give is to think about your entire project and how you organize it as an asset in itself, and accordingly, design it correctly from the beginning. So, what follows are a few short tricks that you can learn to get started on the right foot.

Architecture is a point that is often missed out in game development and should not be overlooked. What follows are some of the best practices you can use from day one to design your game and thereby save a lot of time to fix or change and reorder things later. These lessons will be used throughout the course of this book, wherever applicable.

# Project overview

Before we can start discussing how to structure our game's project, we need to discuss what features the game we will be creating will actually include.

We will be creating a 2D RPG with the following key attributes:

- A 2.5D town
- A conversation system
- A shop with an inventory system
- A character inventory system
- A top-down overworld with random encounter battles
- A turn-based battle system with character animations

Now that we have a general idea of what type of game we will be creating, we can start structuring our project and implementing some if its features.

# Structure

When you start a new Unity project, Unity places the `Assets` folder within the folder you designate for the project. Many Unity projects have all their assets in the root `Assets` folder or are organized by how the game works. This isn't particularly wrong, but as the project gets larger, this will eventually cause problems.

The best way in which Unity advises you to organize your project (as also shown in all of their own examples) is to group objects by their type in the root `Assets` folder, as shown in the following screenshot:

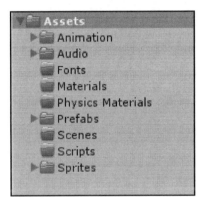

This ensures that you will find assets for your entire project that are ready for reuse in every scene or level according to the type of object. You can then subdivide these appropriately depending on their use, such as the following:

- Separating animation clips from all the controllers that may act on them or on your models:

- Grouping audio by its intended use in your game, such as enemies, special effects, and background music:

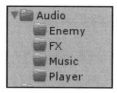

- Grouping prefabs by layer or their intended use:

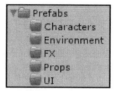

- **Sprites** can also be structured in the same way; you can order them according to how they should be used in your project:

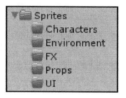

By following the preceding patterns, you are organizing your project effectively in the same way Unity does and guiding yourself to use a more component-based design. Each scene is built up of many assets through the lifetime of your project, so organizing your assets this way will help in the long run.

You can set this level of subgrouping for scripts, scenes, fonts, materials, and so on. However, as these are generally distinct things that apply to every asset, there is no need to divide them further.

# Asset naming

There are no specific patterns for how you should name each of your assets. Generally, this is left to your preference and, more importantly, how you recognize each part of your game. There is no need to give something a really long and complicated name in the preceding structure, only so long that you can find it later.

While it is not required that you follow a naming pattern, some of the more common patterns include the following:

- Prefixing the name with a three letter acronym for its type: scn for a scene, efx for an effect, and so on
- Suffixing an underscore plus the same three letter acronym to the end of an asset's name
- Using a path-like name such as PlayerScene1BounceToWallScript

From experience, these are useful, but my advice is to name things plainly based on what it is. Using the structure mentioned earlier, you have already organized your assets to overcome a lot of the issues that the preceding patterns try to solve.

Plan ahead before you even start your game and set a standard that works for you. You should be able to identify what each asset is and what it does just by looking at the name. However, remember that each asset will most likely be used many times on many different game objects, so plan accordingly. Add prefixes and suffixes only when a script or asset is intended to be limited to a certain type of game object.

The Unity examples are another good place to look for inspiration here. See the following screenshot and decide whether you can tell what these scripts are and what they are used for just by looking at them:

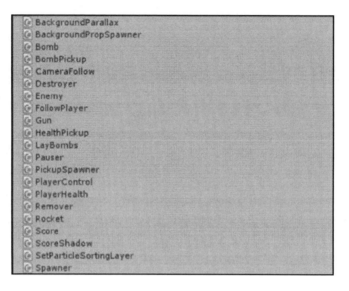

Unity script examples

# Creating the project

Before you can start building the game in Unity, you need to start a new project. Select **New** at the top of Unity's Home Screen. When creating a 2D game, you want to ensure that you start the project in **2D** mode by selecting the appropriate mode in the Unity's home screen, as shown in the following screenshot:

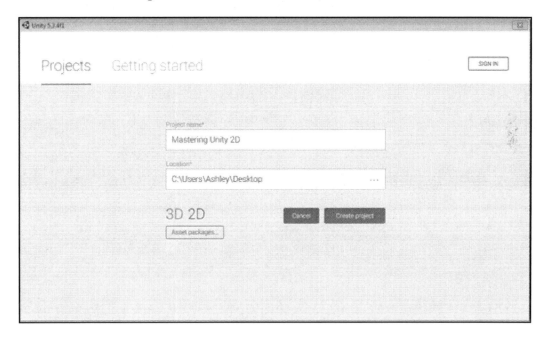

Unity's home screen

 Remember, if you accidentally set the mode to 3D, you can change this at any time for your project through **Editor Settings**, as discussed in the previous chapter.

After selecting **Create project**, you'll be brought to the **Editor** Window, as shown in the following screenshot:

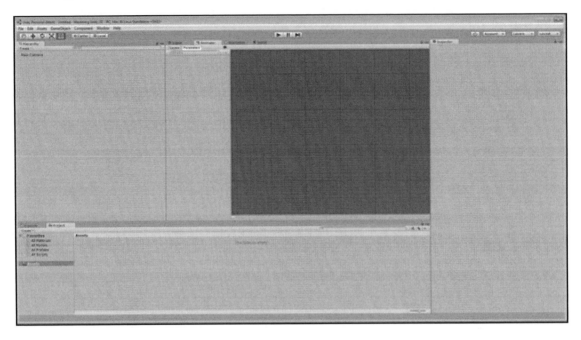

Unity's Editor window

It's important to note that when you create a new project in Unity, you are creating a new folder that can be accessed through File Explorer (Windows) or the Finder (Mac OS X) with the following subfolders:

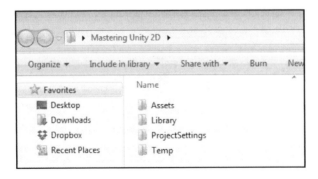

Now that we have created our project, let's create the folder structure for the project, as shown in the following screenshot and discussed previously:

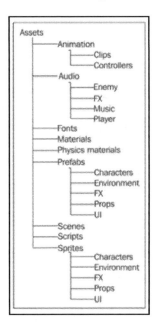

To create a new folder from within Unity, simply select **Create** | **Folder** from the project tab in the bottom left corner of the screen:

When creating folders from within Unity, they will be represented within the `Assets` folder saved to your computer. Alternatively, if you create the folders from within Window's File Explorer (or Mac's Finder), the folders will appear within Unity. In the following screenshot, you will see how the folder structure is mirrored between Unity's **Project** window and Window's File Explorer:

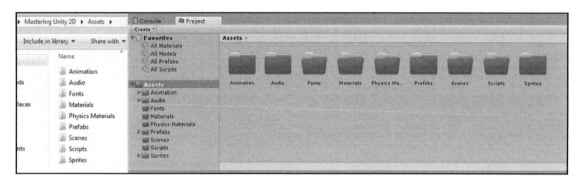

Unity's Project windows and Window's File Explorer

As you can see, these folders created from within Unity are showing up in our project folder saved to our computers.

> At this point, it's important to note that we will most likely not use all of these folders during the course of this book. Nevertheless, it is a good working practice to get these folders set up for every project just so that you have a standard template.

# Creating a scene

Every level or distinct area you create within Unity will be an individual scene. So, the start screen will be a scene, the town will be a scene, the map will be a scene, and so on.

We will have the following scenes in our game:

- Start Screen
- Town
- Shop
- Overworld
- Battle Scene

When you start a new project in Unity, you will be given a blank scene that contains only a camera, as shown in the Hierarchy in the following screenshot:

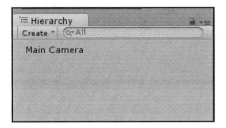

 The Hierarchy displays a list of all the objects within a scene.

The initial scene will be unsaved, as you can see by the word **Untitled** in the area above the toolbar preceding the name of the project:

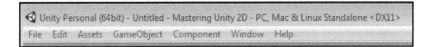

To save the scene, select **File | Save Scene**. The first location we will design will be the town, so let's save the scene as `Town.unity` in the `Scenes` folder we created, as shown in the following screenshot:

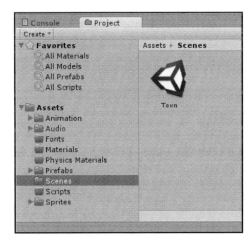

You should now see the scene showing up in your `Assets` folder and you will see the word **Untitled** replaced with **Town**, as shown in the following screenshot:

⊲ Unity Personal (64bit) - Town.unity - Mastering Unity 2D - PC, Mac & Linux Standalone <DX11>

> Save your scenes regularly by using the shortcut keys *Ctrl + S*. You will see an asterisk in the area above the toolbar when you have made changes to your scene and have not saved, as shown in the following screenshot.
>
> ⊲ Unity Personal (64bit) - Town.unity - Mastering Unity 2D - PC, Mac & Linux Standalone* <DX11>

Let's go ahead and create empty scenes for the other five scenes we will have in our game. Select **File** | **Save Scene as...** and save the other five scenes as shown in the following screenshot:

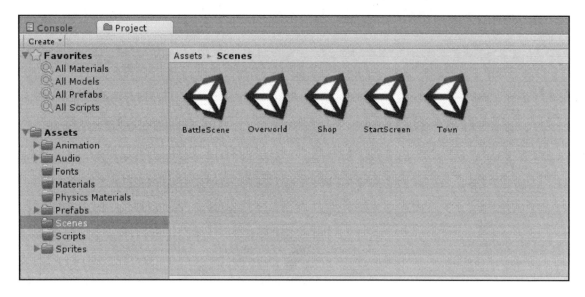

Now that we have the project folders set up appropriately and our scenes created, let's start exploring how to work with 2D objects within Unity.

# Sprite system

It's hard to get excited about a game project until the visual elements are in the scene. We will discuss how to bring our character in the game shortly, but first let's go over how to actually use Sprites in Unity. A brief overview of working with Sprites is given in the previous chapter, but now we will get more technical.

# Importing sprites

The simplest way to import a sprite into a scene is to simply drag it from your File Explorer (Windows) or Finder (Mac OS X) into Unity's **Project** Window. Once the image file is brought into the project, clicking on the image will show its various import settings in the image's **Inspector**, as shown in the following screenshot:

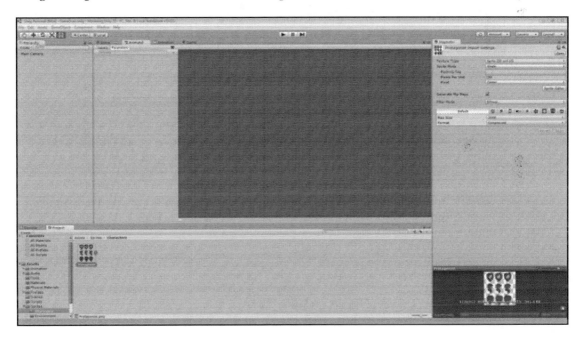

Image Inspector on Project window

Let's take a closer view at the various import settings of an image brought into a 2D project and discuss each of the properties. Here, I will discuss each setting presented in the following screenshot; however, I will discuss the **Sprite Editor** button a later section:

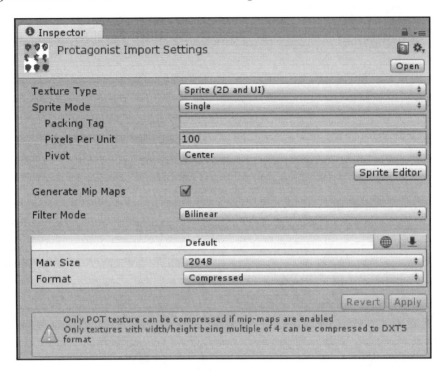

 If you make any changes to the following settings, you must hit **Apply** for the changes to be saved.

# Texture Type – Sprite (2D and UI)

When a Unity project is in 2D Mode, all new images imported into the project are automatically configured as **Sprite (2D and UI)** instead of **Texture**, as they would be if the project were set to 3D Mode.

 The following settings would not appear if the **Texture Type** were changed to something other than **Sprite (2D and UI)**.

## Sprite Mode – Single/Multiple/Polygon

You will leave the **Sprite Mode** set to **Single** if your image contains only a single Sprite and you wish for it to remain on a rectangular plane while being used within your game. If you are importing a sprite sheet or texture atlas (refer to the previous chapter), you will set the **Sprite Mode** to **Multiple**. If you have a single Sprite that you want to be bound by a polygon, rather than the standard rectangle, you will select **Polygon**.

Polygon Sprite Mode will not be discussed further in this text, but its features follow easily from those that are discussed.

## Packing Tag

This is a customizable option that lets you set groups to pack sprites into texture atlases. By putting a name in the **Packing Tag**, it tells Unity to group all the objects with the same tag under a separate texture atlas/sheet together, thereby overriding the default behavior of placing all the assets on the same atlas. Any assets without a tag will be grouped onto the default atlas.

## Pixels Per Units

This option is just a setting that allows you to scale the image asset at import time, the default being 100 pixels per unit (or scaled up to 100 percent).

This setting is important because it sets the relative scale of the assets you will import to your defined game units. Your base game unit guides you on how all the assets will scale appropriately to each other and, more importantly, to the camera.

You can manage the game scale through this setting or you can handle this scale through the original texture's sizes; the choice is up to you.

This is particularly helpful with puzzle games. You can use the **Pixels Per Unit** setting to make a single *block* in your puzzle game count as a unit, thus making your coordinate system easier to deal with.

# Pivot

The pivot point of a sprite determines from where its position will registered. So, if the pivot point is set to **Center**, when a Sprite is positioned to specific coordinate in the scene, the center of the sprite will be positioned at that point. The pivot point also determines the point around which the sprite will be rotated. More options for pivot are available in the Sprite Editor.

# Generate Mip Maps

A **Mip Map** is a smaller version of a texture. Essentially, when **Generate Mip Maps** is selected, an object that is further away from the camera will use a smaller version of the texture. This feature does not change the texture on objects created within the UI.

If you are making a 2D game that is orthographic in view (objects far away from the camera appear the same size as when they are close to the camera), you may want to deselect this option. If you want to have objects in your scene that are further away from the camera appear smaller and will be using a perspective camera, you may want to select this option for performance optimization.

# Filter Mode

Similar to the **Generate Mip Maps** option, the **Filter Mode** will come into play when you are working with a perspective camera and plan on manipulating your objects in 3D space. **Billinear** and **Trilinear** blur the texture as it gets closer to the camera where **Point (no filter)** will make it blocky.

# Default settings and per-platform overrides

The **Max Size** of your texture can be set under the default settings. When an image is initially imported, it is set to 2,048 pixels by 2,048 pixels, as shown in the following screenshot. However, you can change it to any power of two from 32 to 8,192.

When you are developing for different platforms, you may need to consider the resolution size of your textures as each platform has different limitations.

You will get a warning if your image is not using a power of two size texture. This is not critical as Unity will still make best efforts to compress the image:

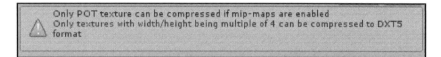

Only POT texture can be compressed if mip-maps are enabled
Only textures with width/height being multiple of 4 can be compressed to DXT5 format

You can find more information about per-platform overrides at: `http://d ocs.unity3d.com/Manual/class-TextureImporter.html`.

# Sprite Editor

The main thing you will likely use the **Sprite Editor** for is identifying the regions of your sprite sheets and texture atlases that represent single sprites. It also allows you to adjust the pivot point of a single sprite (or multiple sprites) and place it in a location not available in the **Pivot Point** drop-down menu. It comes with several simple yet powerful features to control how the individual sprites will be imported, as shown in the following screenshot:

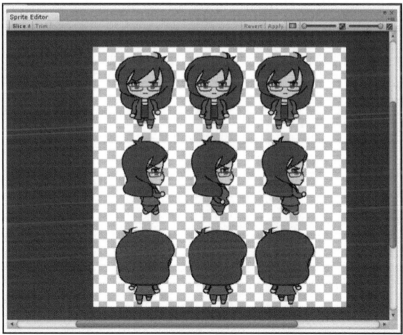

Sprite Editor window

In the editor, you have two sets of functions: the sprite splitter and the view controls. The options available to you will vary depending on the Sprite Mode.

# Sprite slicer

If you have your sprite set to **Multiple**, the **Slice** drop-down menu will be enabled. The slicer has three modes, **Automatic**, **Grid By Cell Size**, and **Grid By Cell Count**, in which it can carve up your sprite sheet to create individual images for use in your game.

## Automatic

Unity has put some very smart logic into its automatic sprite slicing system that can quite easily identify regions in your sprite sheet where your images are packed. Plus, you have some advanced options to guide the system to make it fit for your game, as shown in the following screenshot:

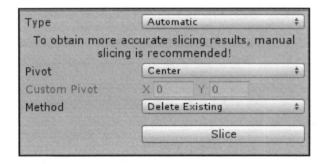

The slicing is based on the alpha regions within the texture, so bear this in mind. The following are the advanced options provided by Unity:

- **Pivot**: As the name suggests, it allows you to set the default pivot position at import time for the sprites that it creates by default.
- **Method**: This option has the following options to guide the selection logic to identify sprites:
    - **Delete existing**: Selecting this option will clear all the existing sprite ranges from the sheet.

 This is the default option and Sprite Editor will not select any sprites until you select one of the sprite identification methods.

- **Smart**: This option will try to identify common patterns in the sprites from the sheet meant for selection. In some cases, it is able to identify groups that make up a single sprite together.
- **Safe**: This option focuses on tighter regions around each element it identifies on the sprite sheet, thereby making the edges as close as possible.

## Grid By Cell Size and Grid By Cell Count (Manual)

The grid options are a lot simpler with no complex logic. **Grid By Cell Size** simply allows you to define (as the name suggests) a grid over the sprite sheet with defined cell sizes by setting the height and width options, as shown in the following screenshot:

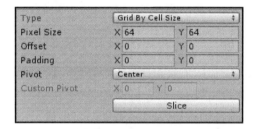

Unity will then automatically identify sprites based on that grid. The **Offset** tells the Sprite Editor where the grids should start relative to the top-left corner and the padding tells the Sprite Editor how much space is in between the various grids.

**Grid By Cell Count** works similarly, except it allows you to state how many columns and rows of Sprites you have rather than how big the Sprites are, as shown in the following screenshot:

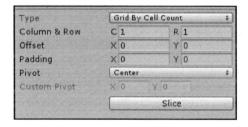

# View controls

The view controls simply change or affect what you are viewing in **Sprite Editor**, as shown in the following screenshot:

The following are the view controls provided by Unity:

- **Revert**: This control simply resets the texture back to the original settings the editor had when it was opened or when the apply option was used to save.

 Note that this is not simply an undo button as it completely resets the editor back to the beginning.

- **Apply**: As the name suggests, this applies any changes you have made in the editor. If you close the editor and keep the changes pending, you will be prompted to apply the changes.

 Note that once you apply your changes, these *cannot* be undone, so when you click on **Apply**, be sure that the changes refer to what you actually want. To undo any of these changes, you would have to restart the sprite editing process.

- **Alpha/Color**: This control simply changes the view between fully textured sprites or just the alpha regions. It is useful if you want to see what the automatic splitting options are using to identify individual sprites.
- **Zoom Slider**: This control is used to zoom in and zoom out. Need I say more?
- **Pixelation Slider**: This slider changes the resolution of the sprite texture. When it is at the rightmost position, it will be at full resolution (based on the import settings). The further to the left the slider is moved, the lower the resolution will be set.

# Sprite region manipulation

Whether you are working with a single sprite or you have your individual regions identified on a sprite sheet, you can change the import settings for each sprite, as shown in the following screenshot:

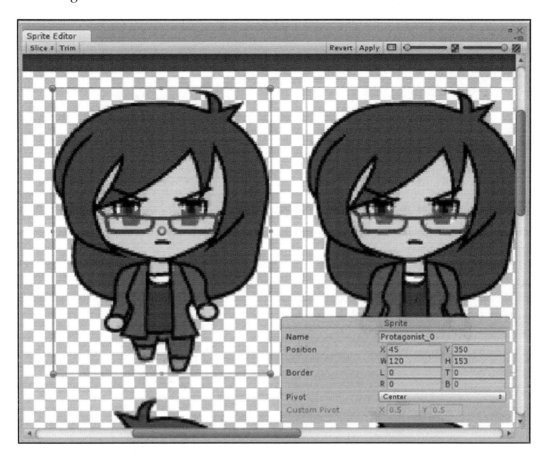

The Sprite Editor zoomed in on a single sprite from the sprite sheet shown earlier

From here, you can alter the following:

- The sprite's name
- The region of the sprite's bounding box by the following methods:
    - Changing the numbers in **Position**
    - Changing the numbers in **Border**
    - Physically adjusting the bounding box with your mouse using the

hook points
- Using the **Trim** button to make the bounding box snap close to the the edges of the sprite
- The pivot point by changing the drop-down option or physical moving it by dragging the pivot circle

The settings you will change with a single sprite selected will only affect that sprite and not the rest that are on the sprite sheet, so keep this in mind if the sprite you are editing is part of an animation.

It is very important to be consistent with pivot point placement with sprite sheets. If pivot points are not placed on the same relative position, the animation with look bouncy.

# Importing our main character

Now that we have discussed how to import and edit a sprite, let us get our main character imported into our game.

Select the image titled `Protagonist.png` from the `characters` folder in the `Art Assets` folder, then drag it to the `Characters` folder under `Assets\Sprites\` in your Unity project, as shown in the following screenshot:

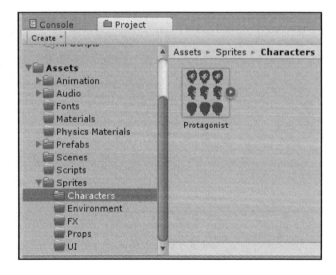

Folder structure in Project window

Next, as our image contains all the frames of the sprite's animation for our main character, we need to break it up. So, select the image from the project view and change **Sprite Mode** in the **Inspector** to **Multiple**, as shown in the following screenshot:

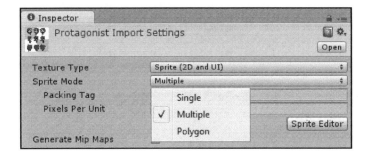

Protagonist Import Settings in Inspector

Click the **Sprite Editor** button to bring up the **Sprite Editor** window and hit **Apply** when prompted. You should see the following:

To separate this sprite sheet into individual images, select **Slice** and change the Type to **Automatic** and change the Pivot to **Bottom**, as shown in the following screenshot:

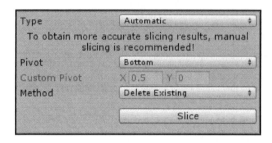

Properties to Slice a Sprite

Click on **Slice** to see all of the sprites now surrounded by appropriate bounding boxes, as shown in the following screenshot:

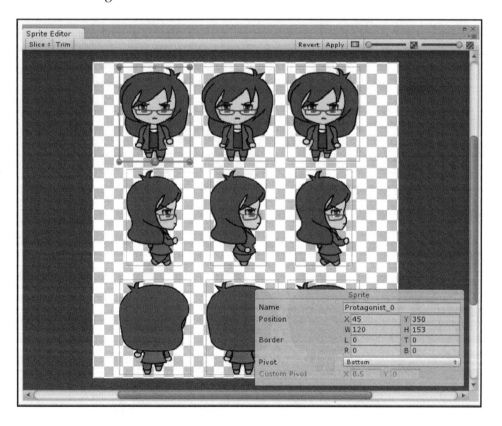

When working with sprite sheets that represent walk cycles, bottom tends to be the best pivot point position.

Now, click on **Apply** and close **Sprite Editor**. Upon returning to the project view, you should see an arrow symbol next to the image asset we imported; clicking on it will show you all the individual Sprites that were identified, as shown in the following screenshot:

Individual Sprites that were identified

Now that we have our character in our project and it is properly imported, let's put our hero into the scene.

# GameObjects and components

In Unity, every object in your scene will be a `GameObject`. A `GameObject` in itself isn't much other than a container for holding a list of `Components`. `Components` are the individual properties that make a `GameObject` unique. When a `GameObject` is selected, you can view each of its `Components` from its **Inspector**.

The most basic GameObject is an empty GameObject, which will contain no components other than a `Transform`. The `Transform` component is essential to each GameObject, as it allows it to have a physical location, rotation, and scale in the scene, as shown in the following screenshot:

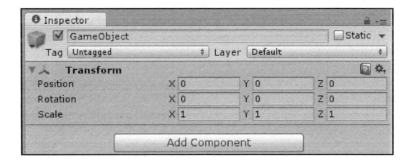

You can create other types of GameObjects by selecting from a list of possible GameObject, starting with and empty one and adding individual components, or adding components to a provided GameObject.

Since we are working in 2D, the majority of our GameObjects will be a Sprite GameObject.

# Sprite GameObjects

To create a Sprite GameObject, select **Create | 2D Object | Sprite,** as shown in the following screenshot:

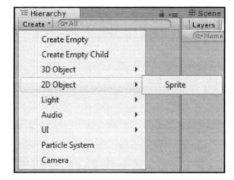

The Sprite GameObject has two components, **Transform** and **Sprite Renderer**, as shown in the following screenshot:

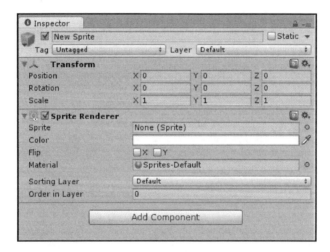

Refer to the previous chapter to see more information concerning the **Sprite Renderer**.

# Bringing our hero into the scene

Earlier, we imported our hero character's sprite sheet into our project and sliced up the sprites from that sheet to ensure they are ready to use. So, now let's bring her into the scene.

As with most things in Unity, there are two ways in which we can do this; first, we'll do this manually, and then we will use a shortcut route. The following steps describe the manual procedure:

1. Create an empty Sprite in our game's Hierarchy for our hero by selecting **Create |
   2D Object | Sprite**.
2. Name it `Player` by changing the name in the inspector:

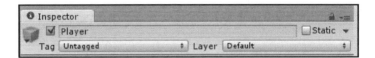

The changes will be reflected in the Hierarchy, as shown the following screenshot:

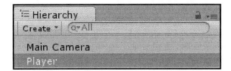

3. You will notice that there is no Sprite assigned to the **Sprite Renderer**. Select the small *circle* next to the **Sprite** slot:

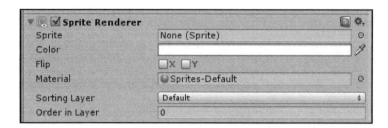

4. Select Protagonist_1 from the list that appears:

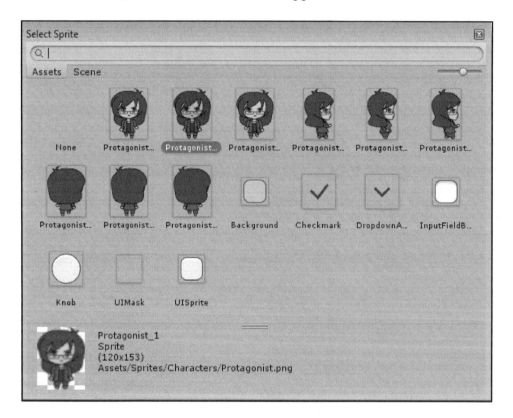

You should now have the same screen as shown in the following screenshot:

Unity's Editor window

A quicker method to create this Sprite is to drag and drop the `Protagonist_1` image from the Project view into the scene and set the Transform Position to (0,0,0).

So, we have a character in a scene, but it's still not very interesting. A game is only truly a game if it has interaction. So let's allow our character to move about. But, before we can do that, we need to discuss some programming caveats.

# Classes

Architecting the core of your game from the beginning is an often-skipped process. Many developers are too eager to build their game and just start placing assets in a scene as they go. This kind of practice is fine for prototypes (mostly, however, even with prototypes, a level of architecture is usually required). When building your actual project, however, without setting up a proper architecture from the beginning, you are heading toward a world of utter mess.

When we say architecture, it doesn't mean that you need to design everything (but it helps). You just need to ensure that you plan what you are going to build before you build it instead of thinking about stuff and checking Google for information on how to do it. Even if you are using some kind of an agile method, you should have a good framework and goal for each step. This will guide you on what should be done and when, not just designing the project on the fly.

# MonoDevelop

When you create a new script in Unity, you will create a new class. To create a new script, select **Create | C# Script**.

When you double-click on the script, **MonoDevelop** will open. MonoDevelop is the **Integrated Development Environment (IDE)** that comes with Unity:

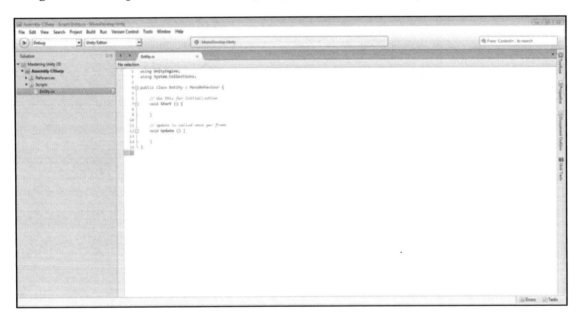

MonoDevelop an IDE

This means that all code will be open, edited, and ran from within MonoDevelop. You can use other editors, such as Microsoft Visual Studio, but we will use MonoDevelop exclusively in this text.

> If double-clicking on a script causes an editor other than MonoDevelop to open, you can change the default editor back to MonoDevelop by selecting **Edit** | **Preferences** | **External Tools** and making sure MonoDevelop is set as the **External Script Editor**:

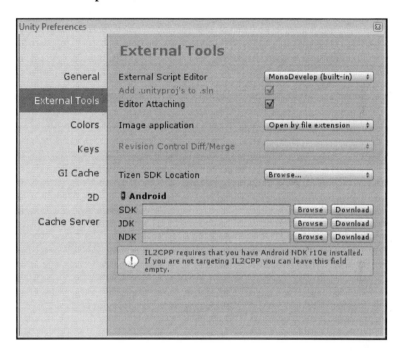

When a new script is created, its name must also match the class, as shown in the following screenshot:

```
                  Entity.cs                    x
No selection
    1    using UnityEngine;
    2    using System.Collections;
    3
    4 □ public class Entity : MonoBehaviour {
    5  |
    6  |      // Use this for initialization
    7 □     void Start () {
    8  |
    9  |      }
    10
    11 |      // Update is called once per frame
    12 □     void Update () {
    13 |
    14 |      }
    15 └ }
    16
```

# The object-orientated design

Unity is a fully **object-orientated** (**OO**) system with strict interfaces to ensure that the engine knows what to expect and when, so why shouldn't your game follow the same pattern? Unity is also component-based, which is something you should take into account while designing how your game will be put together.

At the core of any OO design, the focus is on reusability. If a set of attributes is repeatedly used across multiple objects, then they should be separated into one common *class* and shared. In addition to this, you should also reduce the amount of code that is doing the same job. This means that we can more easily make changes to this base set without having to re-edit all the classes that might need those attributes. The following diagram shows two approaches of using a base class to define common attributes over multiple code implementations:

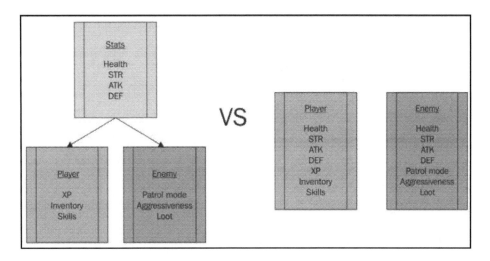

Another facet of OO design is to employ interfaces to govern exactly how a class should look if you have multiple objects of the same type. For example, if you have an Enemy class structure that defines how enemies in general should work, then, using that same structure, you specify all the enemy implementations. Interfaces can also define behaviors or methods on a class, so you can ensure that all the classes that implement that interface will always have the same common abilities, such as all the enemies will have patrol, Fight, and run away methods. This means that if you have an enemy object, it will always have those methods attached to them when you refer to them in the code.

The following diagram shows how you can plan for multiple inheritances, allowing you to add a common behavior pattern to each group of entities:

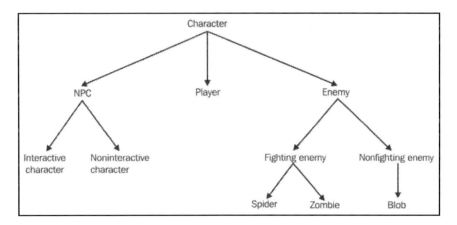

Knowing this helps us design our game effectively and ensures that we architect it correctly from the beginning.

We'll discuss these patterns in more detail when we implement them in the following sections.

# The game structure

To keep in line with the preceding architecture set, we'll design the layout of the class to support a flexible structure that will be easily extended in the future.

## The common game object

As almost every entity in our game will have statistics and some basic behaviors, we start with a generic object (Entity) to define the attributes that all the entities in our game will have. As there is only one entity type, we don't need to set up an interface for this object as all the other game objects will just use this one definition, as shown in the following diagram:

This shows that we have several common attributes for things such as health and strength.

Create a new class within your `Scripts` folder by selecting **Create | C# Script**. Name the script `Entity`.

Type the following code into your new `Entity` class:

```
using UnityEngine;
public class Entity : ScriptableObject {
    public string Name;
    public int Age;
    string Faction;
    public string Occupation;
    public int Level = 1;
    public int Health = 2;
    public int Strength = 1;
    public int Magic = 0;
    public int Defense = 0;
    public int Speed = 1;
    public int Damage = 1;
    public int Armor = 0;
    public int NoOfAttacks = 1;
    public string Weapon;
    public Vector2 Position;
}
```

An interesting feature of Unity involves its handling of `public` variables. Whenever a variable is set to public, its values can be easily accessed and adjusted from the GameObject's inspector, rather than actually adjusting it within the script.

## The player object

Basing the player's character on the `Entity` object makes the definition of the player a lot simpler. So, you only need to focus on what is specific to the player's character itself, that is, the differences between the player and all the other game entities:

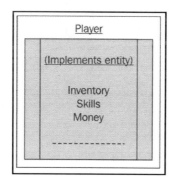

So, the player character we see here is the only one who has **Inventory**, **Money**, and **Skills** since they are specific to our hero's work in our game. Create another class within your `Scripts` folder. Name the script `Player`. In the following code, the player inherits all the properties from the `Entity` class:

```
using UnityEngine;
public class Player : Entity {
  public string[] inventory;
  public string[] skills;
  public int money;
}
```

Preferably, all the attributes of any class should be of the read-only type outside of the class itself (unless there is a very good reason for it). This is to ensure that you don't mistakenly change a class's value without knowing why. It might sound easier to just keep updating everything, but at some point, while you are debugging, you will want to know why things are changing. If any code updates these values, then you will literally spend hours trying to find why. If you need to change values, then you need to implement behaviors (see the following sections).

To show you how to build the architecture progressively in this project, we will add more classes to each section; we'll keep things simple and build the project with a strong foundation.

We already have our base entity in place from which all the game entities as well as our player are driven, so let's look at implementing them further.

# Planning behaviors

Behaviors are just a fancy way of saying *things or interactions that will happen in the game*. Breaking down these actions or reactions in this way helps to componentize how we think our game will work. Stopping and thinking about this from the very beginning means we won't get too many surprises later on. (There are always surprises after a good night's sleep.)

For example, behaviors can take the following forms:

- Attacking another entity
- Taking damage
- Collecting the loot, which could be money or items
- Teleporting to another land

Behaviors on classes should only affect the class that it is defined on. If you are going to affect another class's attributes, it should be through another behavior on that class.

# Behaviors for the common game object

As we have an existing class for common game objects (Entity), we can start to define some behaviors that are common to all the characters in our RPG game, namely the following objects:

- TakeDamage: This is an object where a character can be damaged. Keeping this object as common ensures that the calculation of damages is the same for all.
- Attack: This is an object where a character can attack another character; if successful, it deals with damage or, in rare occurrences, it makes characters hurt themselves. Again, having one way to calculate this helps in battle games so that attacks are balanced.

So, if we add these behaviors to our Entity object, we get something that looks like the following screenshot:

The behaviors shown in the preceding screenshot would add the following to the `Entity` class code:

```
public void TakeDamage(int Amount) {
    health=health-Mathf.Clamp((Amount-armor),0,int.MaxValue);
}

public void Attack(Entity Entity){
    Entity.TakeDamage(strength);
}
```

Make sure the preceding code is within the `Entity` class braces.

We'll not implement these actual behaviors in the code just yet as we will cover them in more detail when we visit the battle system. For now, we are just setting the ground work for what we expect to use in the game.

For now, we won't add any further behaviors to the player; we will simply evolve it as we require it.

# Coding with components

`Components` in Unity are the building blocks of any game; almost everything you will use or apply will end up as a `Component` on a `GameObject` in a scene. When a `GameObject` is selected, you can view each of its `Components` from its Inspector.

You will find that you need to access these various components with script. Next we will discuss the various ways on which you can do this.

# Accessing components

To reference the components of a GameObject from within your code, you need to use the GetComponent function. The following shows you examples of how this is achieved:

```
Rigidbody myScriptRigidBody;
void Awake()
{
  var renderer = this.GetComponent<Renderer>();
  var collider = renderer.GetComponent<Collider>();
  myScriptRigidBody = collider.GetComponent<Rigidbody>();
}
void Update()
{
  myScriptRigidBody.angularDrag = 0.2f * Time.deltaTime;
}
```

This way, the Rigidbody object that we want to affect can simply be discovered once (when the scripts awakes); then, we can just update the reference each time a value needs to be changed instead of discovering it every time.

# Referencing a component

Now, it has been pointed out (by those who like to test such things) that even the GetComponent call isn't as fast as it should be because it uses C# generics to determine what type of component you are asking for (it's a two-step process: first, you determine the type, and then get the component).

However, there is another overload of the GetComponent function in which, instead of using generics, you just need to supply the type (therefore removing the need to discover it). To do this, we will simply use the following code instead of the preceding GetComponent<>:

```
myScriptRigidBody =(Rigidbody2D)GetComponent    (typeof(Rigidbody2D));
```

The preceding code is slightly longer and arguably only gives you a marginal increase, but if you need to use every byte of the processing power, it is worth keeping in mind.

# Controlling the hero

A sprite that only stands on the screen isn't going to make much of a game, so we'll add a script to allow the player to move the hero to the left or right. Before we can do that, we need to add a few more components to the character. More specifically, we need to add the `Rigidbody2D` component and the `BoxCollider2D` component.

The `Rigidbody2D` component will allow our character to be manipulated by physics. This will give us the ability to give her a velocity (or speed) value. The `BoxCollider2D` component gives us the ability to check to see if she is touching other objects.

Let's add the two components to our character:

1.  Select the player from either the Hierarchy list or by selecting the sprite in your scene.
2.  Add a `Rigidbody2D` component by navigating to **Add Component | Physics 2D | Rigidbody 2D** in the player's `GameObject` inspector.
3.  Set the **Gravity Scale** parameter to 0 (as we are not using gravity) and check the **Freeze Rotation Z** checkbox.
4.  Next, add a `BoxCollider2D` component by navigating to **Add Component | Physics2D | Box Collider 2D**.
5.  Select **Is Trigger**. This lets Unity know that we will be using the `BoxCollider2D` to check if the character is touching object rather than stopping it from passing through objects.

This should give you the following view in the inspector:

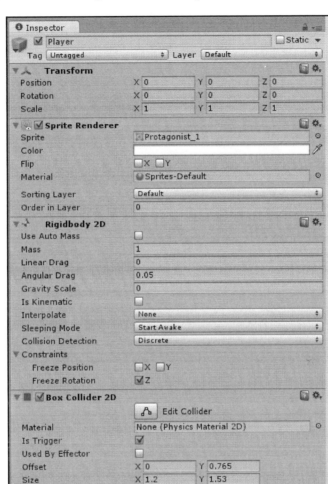

If we were making a game that used gravity, the Rigidbody2D component would allow our character to be affected by gravity. We would also give our character two BoxCollider2D components. One component to check to see if the character touched other objects (**Is Trigger** selected) and another to keep our character from passing through other objects (**Is Trigger** not selected).

To finish off this chapter, add a new C# script and save it as `Assets\Scripts\CharacterMovement.cs`. Open the script in the editor and replace its contents with the following script:

```
using UnityEngine;
using System.Collections;

public class CharacterMovement : MonoBehaviour{
  // RigidBody component instance for the player
  private Rigidbody2D playerRigidBody2D;


 //Variable to track how much movement is needed from input
  private float movePlayerHorizontal;
  private float movePlayerVertical;
  private Vector2 movement;

  // Speed modifier for player movement
  public float speed = 4.0f;

  //Initialize any component references
  void Awake(){
        playerRigidBody2D = (Rigidbody2D)GetComponent(typeof(Rigidbody2D));

  }

  // Update is called once per frame
  void Update () {
        movePlayerHorizontal = Input.GetAxis("Horizontal");
        movePlayerVertical = Input.GetAxis("Vertical");
        movement
          = new Vector2(movePlayerHorizontal,movePlayerVertical);

        playerRigidBody2D.velocity=movement*speed;

  }
}
```

The preceding script is fairly basic; it simply has some parameters to control the speed and its movement direction. We will adjust the character's sprite later when we learn to animate her. The update method checks if the player is controlling the game using the default horizontal keys (left and right) and vertical keys (up and down) and then applies force to move the hero accordingly.

To finish off, add the script to the player's game object by either dragging it to the object in the Hierarchy or navigating to **Add Component** | **Scripts** | **Character Movement**.

 You should note that this very simple controller code only uses a keyboard input. We will later discuss how to implement this for touchscreen devices.

If you run the project now by pressing the play button at the top of the screen, you should see our hero on the screen, and using arrows on the keyboard, the character will move around the screen.

# Going further

If you are of the adventurous sort, try to expand your project by adding the following:

- Add a few more characters from the pack and set up their sprite import settings correctly.
- Play with some of the other assets and tackle automatic and grid-based splicing.

# Summary

We have certainly covered a lot in this chapter simply because you were setting up the main structure of the game and covering the basics of importing sprites. We will use both of these features extensively throughout the text.

Until now, we have covered the following topics:

- The basics of game design and structure
- Creating new projects and scenes
- An overview of all the main sprite components (Sprite/Sprite Renderer)
- Importing new sprites
- Carving up individual sprites from Sprite Sheets
- Adding sprites to your game
- Basic character movement with arrow keys

Now that we have our character in our game, we can make her movement much more natural by adding animation and adjusting her code accordingly. We will add her animation in the next chapter.

# 3
# Getting Animated

Unity has a powerful built-in animation system. In this chapter, we will discuss animating using a sprite sheet to create the walk cycle for our main character.

The following topics will be covered in this chapter:

- Overview of animation features
- Sprite sheet animation
- Animation Controllers
- Access animators from scripts

## Fundamentals of sprite animation

In this section, we will discuss, in general, the features included in Unity that can be used to create a sprite sheet animation. There are three main features that will be used to create a fully animated sprite character: **Animation clips**, **Animation Controllers**, and **Animator components**.

# Animation clips

Animation clips are the heart of the animation system within Unity. All animations are saved with the `.anim` file extension. The animation **Dope Sheet** system (as shown in the following screenshot) is very advanced; in fact, it tracks almost every change in the Inspector for sprites, allowing you to animate just about everything. You can even control which sprite from a **sprite sheet** is used for each frame of the animation:

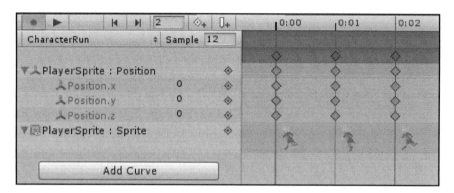

The preceding screenshot shows a three-frame sprite animation and a modified *x* position modifier for the middle image, giving a hopping effect to the sprite as it runs.

Sprites don't have to be picked from the same sprite sheet to be animated. They can come from individual textures or be picked from any sprite sheet you have imported.

Note that you are not limited to the whole character animation with the animation system; you can also construct characters from several sprites and animate them individually, as shown in Unity's own 2D platform sample, which is available at the Unity**Asset Store** (http://bit.ly/UnityPlatformer2D):

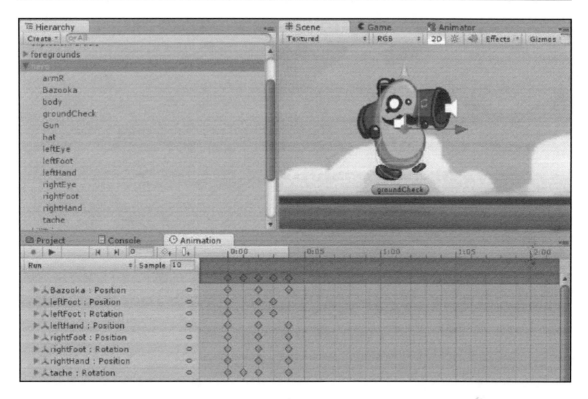

Character constructed from multiple Sprites

In the preceding screenshot, you can see all the parts of the hero in the **Hierarchy**, such as the body, mustache, feet, and bazooka as separate sprites; then, in the animation **Dope Sheet**, the **Run** animation alters the position of each of these sprites to emulate a fast walking effect. This feature can be used in a powerful way once you get your head around what is possible.

# Animation Dope Sheet

The animation **Dope Sheet** can be used to make simple or complex animations, as shown in the following screenshot:

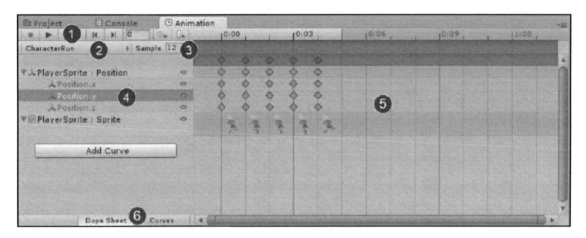

Animation Dope Sheet

Navigating around the **Animation** editor (as shown in the preceding screenshot), we have the following sections:

### The time/recording controls (1)

The time controls let you play or step through your recorded animation to see how it flows. This is especially useful when combined with the active play in the **Scene** and **Game** views.

The record button determines whether the changes in the **Scene** or **Inspector** panes will affect the **Animation** properties and will add new ones if a property has not been touched yet.

There are also the buttons to add new **KeyFrames** (specific points on the timeline at the currently selected time) or **Animation Events** (script launching points based on time).

### Animation drop-down selection (2)

This is a simple list of all the clips in the current animation set/controller. It also has the facility to add more clips directly from this drop-down menu.

## The sample rate (frames per second) (3)

The sample rate sets the number of frames per second available in the timeline. It controls the number of key frame points possible between time intervals. It defaults to 60fps.

Be sure to be aware of what frame rate your sprite sheets where made in. Many 2D animation systems run at 24fps, and you will likely need to adjust this for your animation to perform as expected.

## Animation properties (4)

Animation properties list all the different**Inspector** properties that are being controlled by this animation clip. If a property is touched in the editor while the record mode is active, it will create a new property in the animator or alter the existing property in real time.

While in the record mode, *any* change in the editor will be captured. This includes any child GameObject properties that you change. This becomes very useful if your animated objects comprise multiple sprites in the child GameObjects.

## Timeline (5)

The timeline window shows all the key frames being animated over the lifetime of the animation. Setting the sample rate higher and lower will control how many key points/frames will be available between time units.

You can also use the following keyboard shortcuts to navigate between the frames on the timeline:

- Press comma (,) to go to the previous frame
- Press period (.) to go to the next frame
- Press *Alt* + Comma (,) to go to the previous key frame
- Press *Alt* + Period (.) to go to the next key frame

## Curve view (6)

The timeline view has an alternate view mode to add finer control and curves between the key frame animations, as shown in the following screenshot:

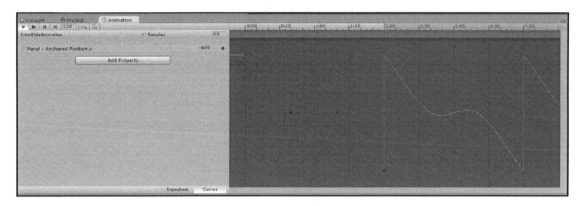

Curve view in Animation window

Editing the curves takes a little finesse but makes for a better looking transition than the default `Boolean` (on/off) effect.

You can further control the curves by setting the inbound and outbound tangents of the curve, setting either a smooth (linear), sharp (constant), or free-form curve. Simply play with these settings until you have the kind of curve you want.

We'll cover curves in `Chapter 9`, *Getting Ready to Fight*, where we'll learn a few of the slightly more complex curves and animations.

# The Animation Controllers

Animation Controllers are simply state machines, systems that store states and the transitions between them, that are used to control when an animation should be played and what conditions control the transition between each state. Animation Controllers are saved with the file extension `.controller`. An animation cannot play without a controller and a controller can contain many animations.

Lets look at the following screenshot:

Animation state machine

In the preceding screenshot, the gray rectangles represent animation states and the orange rectangle represents the default animation state. The states do not have to be animations, but instead can be a game state. The arrows represent transitions between animation states. **Entry** and **Exit** nodes were added to the **State Machine Transitions** in Unity 5 and they tell the state machine what it should do when it starts and when it should exit. You can have various layers of animation. We will discuss the use of this system to handle game states, rather than just animations, and describe state machines in further detail in Chapter 8, *Encountering Enemies and Running Away*.

A parameter is essentially a variable that we will be able to access later from our character controller script. Within our script, we can tell our parameters to take on values, thus making the animations transition when we want them to.

# The Animator component

To use an animation prepared in a controller, you need to apply it to a GameObject in the scene. This is done through the **Animator** component, as shown in the following screenshot:

Animator component

The only property we actually care about in 2D is the **Controller** property. In it, you specify which controller is to be attached to the GameObject.

 Other properties only apply to the 3D humanoid models, so we can ignore them for 2D.

# Animating the main character

Right now, our hero can move around the screen, but she is always facing toward the camera and she isn't animated. Her sprite sheet came with her walk cycle from three angles, so let's put that into action to liven up her movement.

We will accomplish this movement by creating some Animation clips and linking them up in an Animation controller. As described earlier, in order to get the animation running, we will need the following prerequisites:

- An **Animator component** on our GameObject
- An **Animator Controller** to manage our animation that is bound to the animator
- At least one **Animation clip** to play in the controller

When you create a new animation clip for a GameObject, the other items are automatically created for you.

Before you get started with animation, you want to make sure you can view the **Animation** and **Animator** windows. If you do not already have the two windows open, click **Window | Animation** from the menu bar and then **Window | Animator**.

You may want to rearrange your windows at this point. I recommend docking the **Animation** and **Animator** windows next to the **Game** window so you can see the `Project` folder while creating animations, as shown in the following screenshot:

This is easily done by dragging the tabs for the windows to the desired point. When it gets near a point in the editor where it can dock, it will do so automatically.

# Adding your first Animation Clip

The animation we will create first will be that of our character walking downward. To create your first animation clip, select the **Player** from the **Hierarchy** (or from the **Scene** view) and then open the **Animation** tab. You should see the following:

Prompt to create Animator and Animation Clip

Select **Create** and then save the animation as `PlayerWalkDown.anim` within your `Assets/Animation/Clips` folder, as shown in the following screenshot:

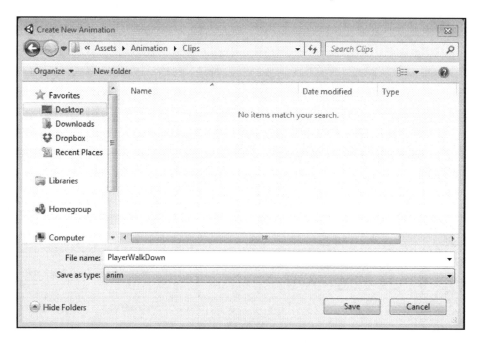

Animation file save menu

By selecting **Create**, Unity will automatically create an Animator for your **Player** and will automatically assign it within an Animator component on the Player. However, it has saved the new Animator in the `Clips` folder, as shown in the following screenshot:

Notice that the generated Animator Controller is called `Player.controller`. Any Animator that is automatically created in the way will always be named after the GameObject that was selected when it was created.

Go ahead and drag and drop that Animator into the `Assets/Animation/Controllers` folder so that we maintain the integrity of the folder structure we created.

Within the **Animation** window, you should now see **PlayerWalkDown** within the drop-down menu, as shown in the following screenshot:

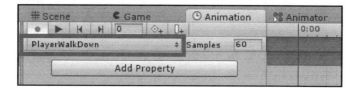

Within the **Project** view, navigate to the `Assets/Sprites/Characters` folder to find the character's sprite sheet and click on the arrow on the right of the sprite sheet to view all of the character's walk cycle sprites. The first three images represent the character's downward walk cycle:

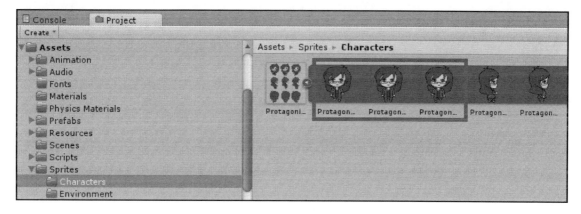

Character sprite sheet for downward walk cycle

Select all three of these images by clicking on the first image, holding down *Shift*, and then clicking on the third image. Now drag and drop these three images into the **Animation** window's **Dope Sheet**. You should now see the following:

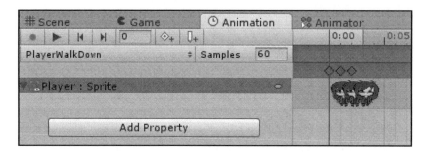

Currently, this animation is way too fast. Clicking on the play button to play the game will demonstrate this. We will slow this character's animation by reducing the frame rate to 6 fps, by changing **Samples** from **60** to **6**, as shown in the following screenshot:

You can slow an animation in two ways: by adjusting the frame rate or by spacing the images further apart along the timeline. To move the images further apart, simply click and drag them to the frame you wish to place them.

Remember that 1:00 represents 1 second, not 1 minute.

Press **Play** to play the game. You will now see that the animation is running much more naturally.

You can view the animation without running the game by pressing the play button within the Animation Window. However, to see this animation run, you will need to have both the animation and **Scene** windows open, and the window tab configuration we discussed earlier does not allow that. You can adjust the location of your various windows so that you can have both the animation and scene window present. I recommend experimenting with moving the various tabs around to see where they can be placed.

While the animation has a better speed, it is not complete. Even though only three frames are given for her downward walk cycle, you actually have to use the center image twice to make the walk animation loop perfectly. The following figure demonstrates the logic behind a three-frame walk cycle:

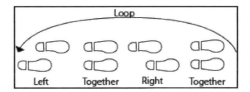

To make her animation complete, you must also have the second frame repeated at the end of the animation. So, place the `Protagonist_1` sprite as the fourth frame in the animation, as shown in the following screenshot:

Your animation should now appear as follows:

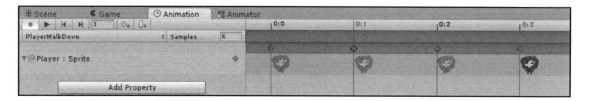

# Setting up the Animator and default state

Remember, when we created the `PlayerWalkDown.anim` animation, an Animator Controller named `Playercontroller` was automatically made for us. We moved it into the `Assets/Animation/Controllers` folder. It was also automatically assigned to an Animator component in the Player's **Inspector**, as shown in the following screenshot:

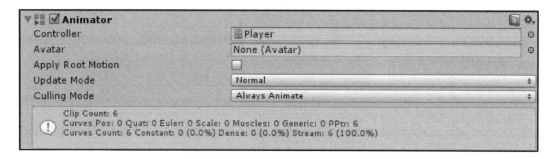

Animator component in Player's Inspector

We are going the leave all of the default settings in the Animator component, but we will rename the Animator to make it easier to recognize later on. Let's rename our Animator as `PlayerWalking.controller` (note that you do not have to type the `.controller` extension). You can accomplish this by clicking on it twice slowly or pressing *F2* on a keyboard:

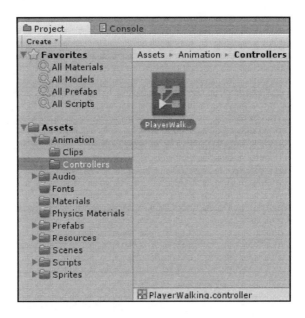

Renaming Animator component

You will see that this name has been updated in the Player's **Inspector**, as shown in the following screenshot:

When you open the Animator window, you should see the following:

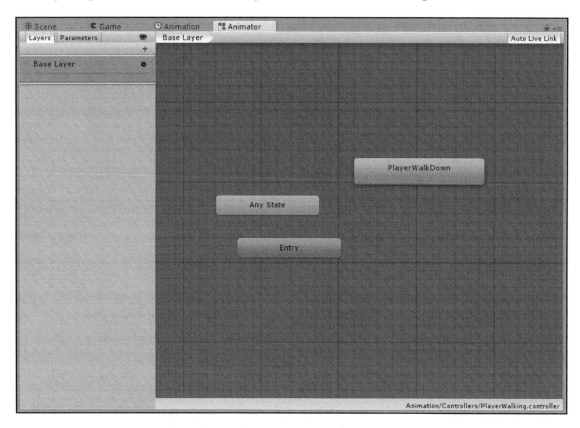

 Depending on how large your Animator window is, you may also see the red **Exit** state. Do not worry about that state at this time, as we will not be using it. Sometimes, when you have more than one animation controller, it can be difficult to tell which animator you are working on. Notice that it tells you that name of the controller you are working with at the bottom right-hand side of the Animator window.

The PlayerWalkDown.anim animation has already been added to the Animator, and since it was the first animation we created, it has been designated the default state (as demonstrated by the fact that the animation is colored orange). When we begin our game, our character automatically starts walking downward, even when she is standing still. However, we want her to just face downward until we make her start walking. The reason she is animating initially is her default state is set to PlayerWalkDown.anim.

Let's fix this by creating an empty default state. Right-click anywhere within the Animator Window and select **Create State | Empty,** as shown in the following screenshot:

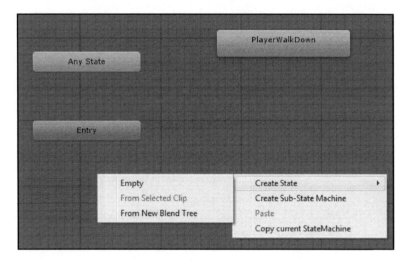

Rename this from New State to PlayerStandDown. Then right-click on it and select **Set as Layer Default State** to make this Empty State be the new default state, as shown in the following screenshot:

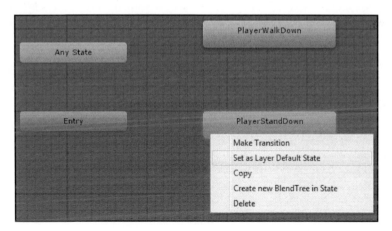

You should now have an Animator that looks something like the following:

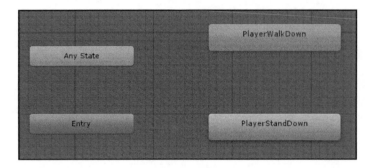

Animator window

Run your game and you will see that the player now no longer automatically animates. In fact, she no longer animates at all! To get her to animate only when she's walking, we're going to have to tell the controller how and when her animation needs to run. Before we do that, however, let's set up the other animations the character will need.

## Adding the other Animation Clips

The character's sprite sheet had two other animations within it that we will need to set up to let our character convincingly walk around the screen: walking to the right and walking upward.

 If you're wondering why we do not have a left walking animation, we will use the walking to the right frames to animate our character going both left and right.

Navigate back to the Animation window for the player. Now we will select **Create New Clip** from the animation selection drop-down menu, as shown in the following screenshot:

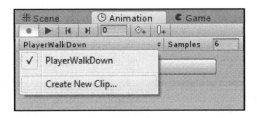

Name the new clip `PlayerWalkUp.anim` and make sure you save it in the correct folder. Create this animation, as you did the downward walking one, by dragging the three appropriate images into the **Dope Sheet**. Change the frame rate to 6, as done previously. You should see the following:

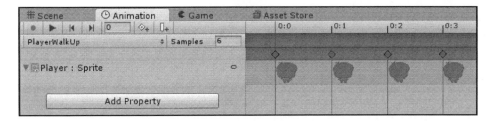

Dope Sheet in Animator window

Do the same thing for the right walking images. Name this animation `PlayerWalkHorizontal.anim`, as shown in the following screenshot:

# Planning the animation transitions

Before we begin linking up the animations, let's discuss how we plan the character to move so that the logic we use will flow naturally when we start working with the animator and start programming her movement.

The character can currently move all around the screen in an up, down, left, right, or even diagonally. The first decision that needs to be made is which animation should be used when she is walking diagonally. Do we use the side view animation or the upward and downward facing animations? I personally like the second option, as demonstrated with the following figure:

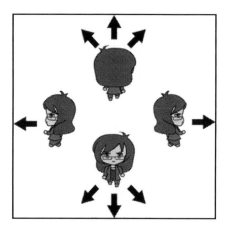

So, using the preceding image and the code we wrote in `Chapter 2`, *Building your Project and Character* look at what is happening to make her move in these ways as well as what needs to happen, as shown in the following screenshot:

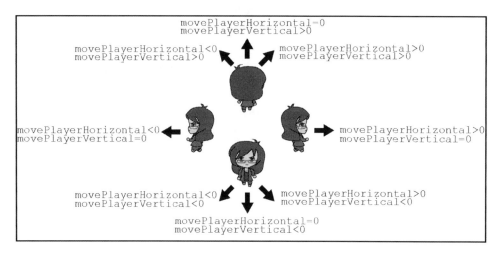

Character transition

The important facts to garner from the diagram are as follows:

- Only when `movePlayerVertical` is equal to 0, will the `PlayerWalkHorizontal` play
- If `movePlayerHorizontal` is less than 0, the `PlayerWalkHorizontal` animation must be flipped along the `x-axis`
- If `movePlayerVertical` is greater than 0, `PlayerWalkUp` will play
- If `movePlayerVertical` is less than 0, `PlayerWalkDown` will play

Also, when the character stops moving, she will need to stand still, with legs together facing the same direction she was moving previously. So, now that we have a general idea of how we want her to behave based on the code, we can start working on setting up the animation.

# Connecting the animation states

At the moment, our two states are not connected. So when we run the project, the hero is always standing still and facing downward; let's change that.

To tell the controller to move between the two states, we need the following prerequisites:

- A transition link between the two states
- A parameter or event to activate the transition
- Something to change the value of that parameter, usually in a script

Since we last viewed our Animator, we added two new walking animations. Return to your **Animator** window and adjust the position of your animations so that they look something like the following:

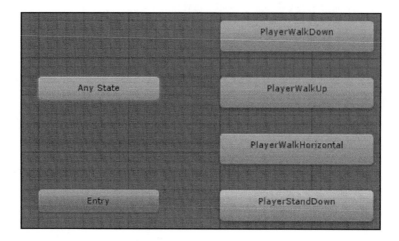

To allow our character to move between the animations, we need to set up **Transitions** between animations. She will be able to walk downward, upward, or horizontally, regardless of what her last animation was. So, this means that we want to transition from **Any State** to these three animations.

So, first, we create the transition between the **Any State** and the downward walking state by right-clicking on **Any State** and selecting **Make Transition**. This will change the mouse cursor to an arrow. Then, click on the state we want to transition to, which in this case is the **PlayerWalkDown** state. Do this from **Any State** to **PlayerWalkUp** and **Any State** to **PlayerWalkHorizontal** as well. When you are done, you should have something that looks like the following:

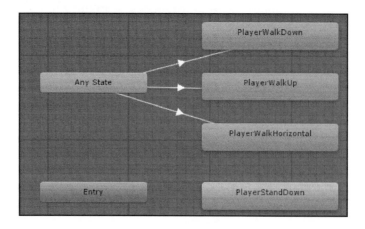

State machine for character transition

Setting up the transitions in this way tells the Animator that the character can be standing in the default state, and can go to any of the three animations and then from those animations can transition to any other animation.

Now that we have told the Animator what states can transition to these animations, we need to tell it when these transitions will occur. We will do this by setting up Parameters and Transition Conditions.

Clicking on the transition between **Any State** and **PlayerWalkDown** shows you the properties of that transition in the Inspector, as shown in the following screenshot:

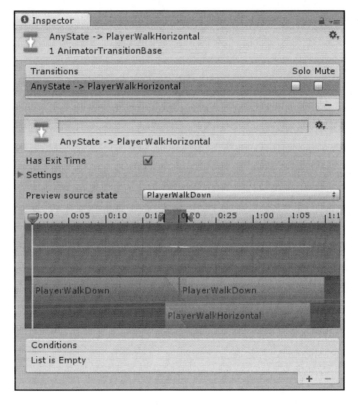

PlayerWalkDown transition properties

Clicking on the arrow next to **Settings** will show further information, as shown in the following screenshot:

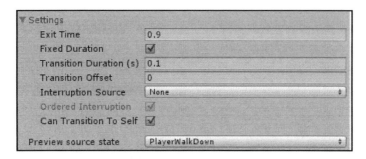

More PlayerWalkDown transition properties

As shown in the **Inspector** pane, by default, the new transitions are controlled by a single parameter called **Exit Time**, which simply means that when the first animation ends, it will transition to the second. We don't want that here as we want a specific event to control when the **PlayerWalkDown** animation is activated.

Change the **Settings** so that they appear as follows:

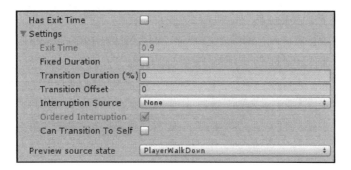

Changed settings for PlayerWalkDown

Change the settings for the transition between **Any State** and **PlayerWalkUp** and the transition between **Any State** and **PlayerWalkHorizontal** in the same way.

When you deselect **Exit Time**, you will see the following warning stating that a transition needs at least one condition:

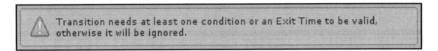

Transition needs at least one condition or an Exit Time to be valid, otherwise it will be ignored.

Deselect Exit Time warning

We will give it a condition by creating a **transition parameter**. To add a new parameter, select the **Parameters** tab, click on the + symbol in the parameter section, and then select **Int**, as shown in the following screenshot:

Name this parameter yMove, as shown in the following screenshot:

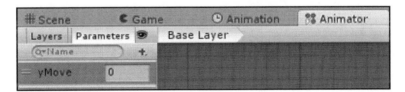

We will use this yMove parameter to tell the animator when to transition to the **PlayerWalkDown** and **PlayerWalkUp** animations, as shown in the following figure:

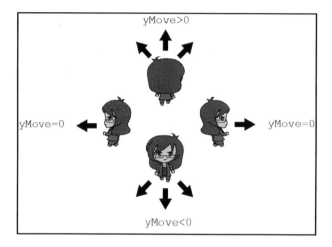

Select the transition between **Any State** and **PlayerWalkDown**. Select the + symbol in the **Conditions** section. Since yMove is our only parameter, it will automatically be placed as the condition parameter. Select **Less** from the drop-down menu, as shown in the following screenshot:

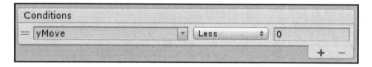

Selecting Less in Condition parameter

It is now stating that whenever the yMove parameter is less than 0, the Player will run her **PlayerWalkDown** animation.

We will do the same thing for the transition between **Any State** and **PlayerWalkUp**, but we will leave **Greater** in the drop-down menu, as shown in the following screenshot:

Selecting Greater in Condition parameter

Now we can set up a parameter for the transition between **Any State** and **PlayerWalkHorizontal**. For this, we will create a Boolean parameter by selecting Bool from the new parameter menu and naming it xMove, as shown in the following screenshot:

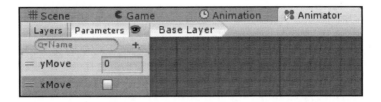

We will use this xMove parameter to tell the animator when to transition to the **PlayerWalkHorizontal** animation, as shown in the following figure:

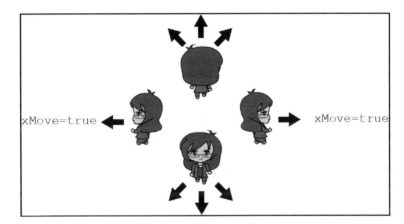

Now select the transition between **Any State** and **PlayerWalkHorizontal**. Change the **Condition** to xMove to true, as shown in the following screenshot:

Selecting true in condition parameter

If you run the game at this point, the character still doesn't walk when she moves. We've told the Animator when the transitions need to occur, but we haven't actually done anything to make these parameter values change. For this, we need to update our CharacterMovement script.

# Accessing controllers from a script

Now that we have an animator attached to our Player GameObject, we can adjust its parameters using scripts. To do so, we are going to update our `CharacterMovement.cs` script with the following two things:

1. Create a variable for the Animator so that we can reference it in the script.
2. Use `GetComponent` to find the Animator component attached to the Player.

Let's first create a variable for the Animator. Add the following code to your variable declarations:

```
// Animator component for the player
private Animator playerAnim;
```

Now let's reference the animator component and assign it to the new variable `playerAnim`. Add the following code to your `Awake()` function:

```
playerAnim=(Animator)GetComponent(typeof(Animator));
```

Now we can reference the player's animator within our script.

We also need to be able to access the player's sprite renderer from within the script. The `SpriteRender` now has the ability to easily flip a sprite in the *x* or *y* direction, and we will use this property to make the character face left when walking left. We will access the sprite rendered in the same way we accessed the animator, that is, by declaring a variable and then referencing it.

Let's first create a variable for the sprite renderer. Add the following code to your variable declarations:

```
//Sprite renderer for the player
private SpriteRenderer playerSpriteImage;
```

Now let's reference the sprite renderer component and assign it to the new `playerSpriteImage` variable. Add the following code to your `Awake()` function:

```
playerSpriteImage =(SpriteRenderer)GetComponent(typeof(SpriteRenderer));
```

Now we can reference the player's animator within our script.

Recall the values the parameters need to hold for the transitions to occur, as shown in the following screenshot:

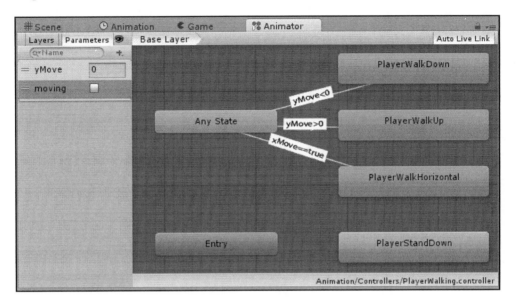

Parameter values for state transition

And recall the conditions that will make the parameters change, as shown in the following figure:

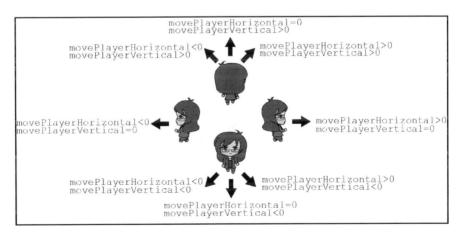

To reflect these conditions in the code, add the following lines of code to your `Update()` function:

```
if(movePlayerVertical!=0){
    playerAnim.SetBool("xMove",false);
    playerSpriteImage.flipX=false;

    if(movePlayerVertical>0){
        playerAnim.SetInteger("yMove",1);

    }else if(movePlayerVertical<0){
            playerAnim.SetInteger("yMove",-1);

    }
}else {
    playerAnim.SetInteger("yMove",0);

    if(movePlayerHorizontal>0){
        playerAnim.SetBool("xMove",true);
            playerSpriteImage.flipX=false;
    }else if(movePlayerHorizontal<0){
            playerAnim.SetBool("xMove",true);
            playerSpriteImage.flipX=true;

    }else{
            playerAnim.SetBool("xMove",false);
    }
}
```

Your character should now walk around the screen in all the appropriate directions. However, she won't stop walking when she stops moving! We're going to have to create a few more animations and another transition parameter to make this work appropriately.

# Making her stop animating and face the correct direction

We are almost done with our character's animation. We only need to do a little more so that she will stop animating when she stops moving. To accomplish this, we will first make three idle animations, one for each of her directions. The easiest way to do this is to duplicate her walking animations and then edit them appropriately.

Select the `PlayerWalkDown.anim` animation from the **Project** view and type *Ctrl + D* to duplicate the animation. Rename the new animation as `PlayerIdleDown.anim`, as shown in the following screenshot:

Drag and drop the new **PlayerIdleDown** animation to the Player's Animator, as shown in the following screenshot:

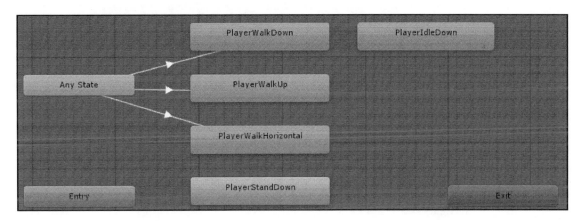

PlayerIdleDown animation

Open the Animation window and select the new **PlayerIdleDown** animation from the drop-down menu. The animation will only show up in this drop-down menu if you have already added it to the animator, as shown in the following screenshot:

Delete the first, third, and fourth images and then drag the remaining image so that it is in the 0:0 position. You should now have an animation with only a single image, the image in which the character is standing still and facing downward, as shown in the following screenshot:

Repeat this process to create PlayerIdleUp and PlayerIdleHorizontal animations. The following screenshot shows PlayerIdleUp:

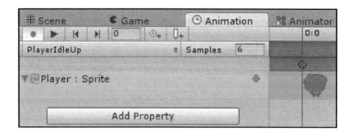

The following screenshot shows `PlayerIdleHorizontal`:

Now we need to set up our transitions in the **Animator**. Set up transitions from your walking animations to idle animations, as shown in the following screenshot:

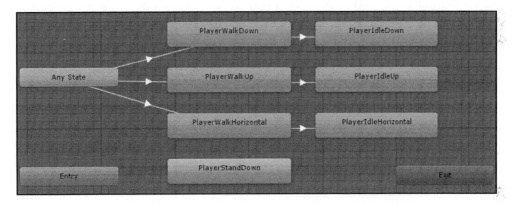

Change the settings on each of these transitions to the following:

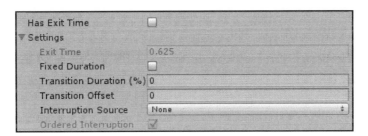

Now we will use a Boolean parameter to transition to these idle animations. Create a **Bool** parameter called moving, as shown in the following screenshot:

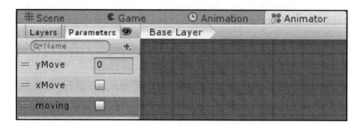

Now, set the conditions of each of the new transitions so that they run when moving is **false**, as shown in the following screenshot:

The only thing we have to do now is adjust the code to tell moving to change from true to false. This is actually simpler than the preceding animation code and can be accomplished by adding the following code to the Update() function:

```
if(movePlayerVertical==0 && movePlayerHorizontal==0){
        playerAnim.SetBool("moving",false);
}else{
        playerAnim.SetBool("moving",true);
}
```

Add the preceding code to the Update() function before the if statement that triggered the animations and after the statement that assigns the player's velocity.

Now your character should be able to walk around and stand around while facing the correct direction!

# Going further

If you are of an adventurous sort, try expanding your project to add the following features:

- Instead of quickly changing direction, have her slowly transition and turn.
- Expand the animation and curves for the hero. Try playing with some of the other options that were described in the overview.

# Summary

The **Animation** system provides so many features that nearly any animation you can envision can be created with it. I've not covered everything as that would deserve another book entirely, so feel free to experiment further. The state machine system isn't just for animation either, and we will return to this later on.

We covered an overview of all the main sprite animation components (**Animator, Controller, Clips, Keyframes**, and **Curves**), importing new sprites, animating sprites, and controlling states.

In the next chapter, we will build an environment for our character to walk around and allow our camera to follow her.

# 4
# The Town View

With our main character in hand, let's give her a home and a place to walk around. In this chapter, we will cover the basics of creating immersive areas where players can walk around and interact, as well as some of the techniques used to manage those areas.

The following topics will be covered in this chapter:

- Working with environments
- Looking at sprite layers
- Creating a script to move the camera with the player
- Handling multiple resolutions

## Backgrounds and layers

Now that we have our hero in play, it would be nice to give her a place to live and walk around, so let's set up the home town and decorate it.

First, we are going to need some more assets. So, from the asset pack you downloaded earlier, grab the following assets from the `Environments` pack and place them in the `Assets\Sprites\Environment` folder:

- `background.png`
- `skyline.png`
- `buildingsAndRoads.png`
- `townObjects.png`

# To slice or not to slice

As we progress through this book, you will notice that some assets are single textures, whereas others contain multiple images, and you may wonder which method is best to create your assets and why it is best.

The answer (as it is in a lot of these situations) depends on the needs of your title.

It is always better to pack many of the same types of images on to a single asset/atlas and then use the **Sprite Editor** to define the regions on that texture for each sprite, as long as all the Sprites on that sheet are going to get used in the same scene. The reason for this is when Unity tries to draw the Sprite to the screen, it needs to send the images to draw to the graphics card; if there are many images to send, this can take some time. If, however, it is just one image, it is a lot simpler and more performant with only one file to send.

There needs to be a balance; too large an image and the upload to the graphics card can take up too many resources; too many individual images and you have the same problem.

The basic rules of thumb are as follows:

- If the background is a full-screen background or a large image, then keep it separate.
- If you have many images and all are for the same scene, then put them into a single sprite sheet/atlas.
- If you have many images but all are for different scenes, then group them as best you can; common items on one sheet and scene-specific items on different sheets. You'll have several sprite sheets to use.

You basically want to keep as much stuff together as makes sense and not send unnecessary images that won't get used to the graphics card. Find your balance.

# The town background

First, let's add a background for the town using the `Assets\Sprites\Environment\background.png` texture, as shown in the following screenshot:

With the background asset, we don't need to do anything to the import settings other than ensure it has been imported as a **Sprite (2D and UI)** (in case your project is in 3D mode), as shown in the following screenshot:

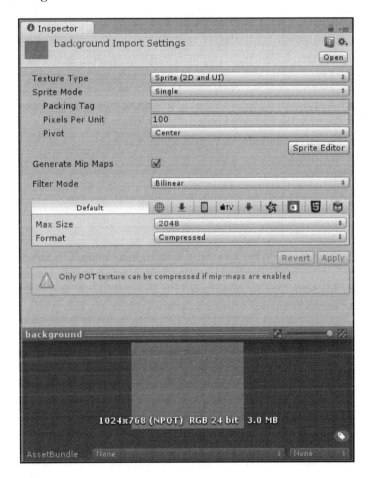

Background Import settings menu

There are two other Sprites that will be incorporated into the background and they are in the `Assets\Sprites\Environment\skyline.png` image file. The `skyline.png` image contains two rows of white skyscraper silhouettes. The following screenshot shows the image with its transparencies:

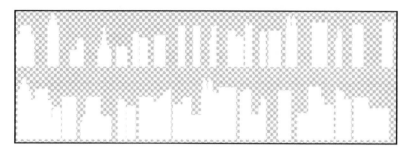

To have these Sprites display appropriately, we will have to manually slice the image into two Sprites using the **Sprite Editor**. We start editing this sprite sheet in the same way we edited the sprite sheet of the character in `Chapter 2`, *Building Your Project and Character*. Change the **Sprite Mode** to `Multiple` and load up the **Sprite Editor** using the **Sprite Editor** button, as shown in the following screenshot:

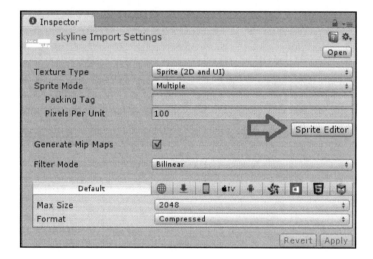

Loading the Sprite Editor

Hit **Apply**, when prompted:

If you try to use the automatic slicing technique that we used for the character, each of the *islands* of buildings will be selected as separate Sprites. We do not want this. We want all the buildings in the top row to be a single Sprite and all the buildings in the bottom row to be a second Sprite. We will begin slicing this by using the **Grid By Cell Count** slice **Type**. Change the **Column & Row** setting to 1 and 2 as shown in the following screenshot, and then hit **Slice**:

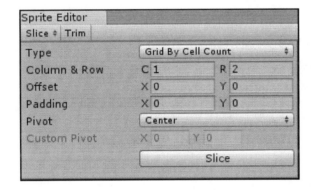

You should now see the following:

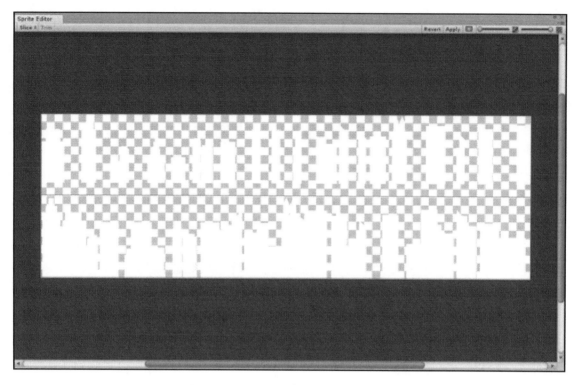

Second Sprite Sheet

This is almost what we want, except there is too much space at the bottom of the top sprite. When you select the top sprite, you will be able to adjust the Sprite's bounding box by dragging the edges to their desired location. Drag the bottom edge so that it at the very bottom of the buildings as shown in the following screenshot:

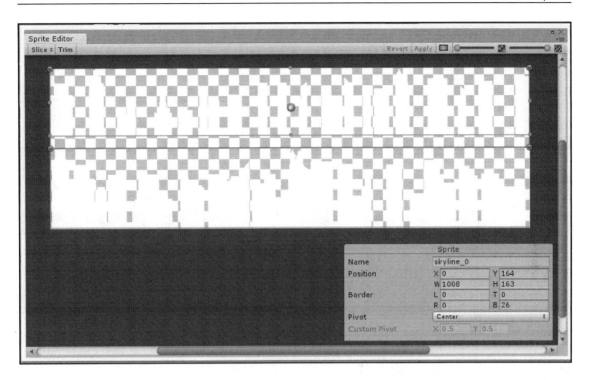

If you are having trouble seeing the buildings, you can select the **Alpha/Color** button at the top of the **Sprite Editor**, as shown in the following screenshot:

Doing so will make the opaque regions stand out from the transparent regions much more drastically, as shown in the following screenshot:

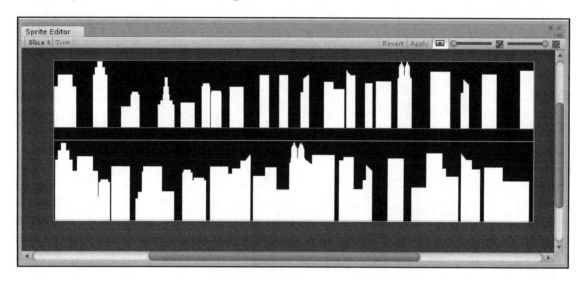

Once you have both rows of buildings boxed in, select **Apply** at the top of the **Sprite Editor** and then close the **Sprite Editor**.

Don't worry if you don't perfectly box in the two skylines. A little room on the top or bottom won't be the end of the world.

## The town buildings and roads

Next we will add the town's buildings and roads from the `Assets\Sprites\Environment\buildingsAndRoads.png` file, as shown in the following screenshot:

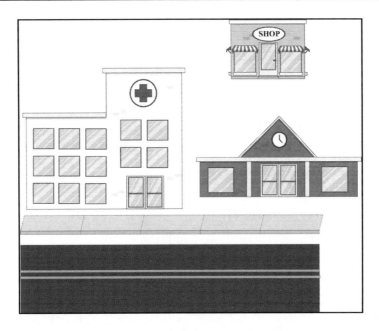

These images can be separated quite well with the automatic slice setting. Follow the steps provided in Chapter 2, *Building Your Project and Character*, to automatically slice the image. When you have finished, you should have four images, as shown in the following screenshot:

# The extra scenery

Now let's add some extra assets to the scene. If we look at the image containing all of the scene objects (`Assets\Sprites\Environment\townObjects`), we will see the following:

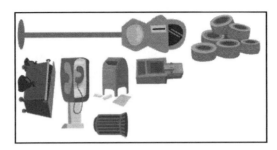

As with the other images, change its **Sprite Mode** to **Multiple** and run the **Sprite Editor**. Now perform **Slice** | **Automatic** on it. You should see the following:

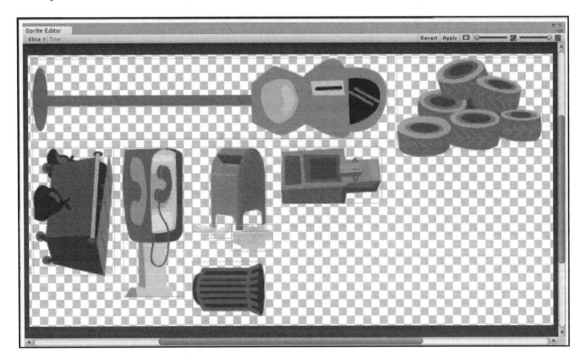

Notice that one of the sprites, the mailbox, does not get detected very well; altering the automatic split settings in this case doesn't help, so we need to do some manual manipulation. Click on the two bounding regions around the scattered mail and delete them by pressing Delete with the two regions selected, the two regions that are highlighted in the following screenshot for clarification:

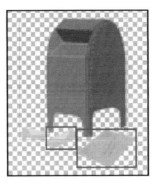

Manually change the size of the region that is around the mailbox so that it also includes the scattered mail, as shown in the following screenshot:

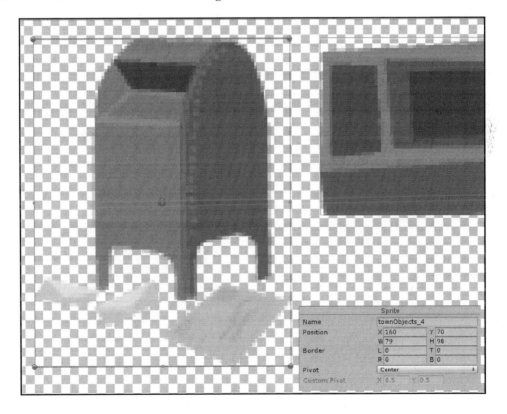

This gives us some nice additional assets to scatter around our town and give it a more interesting look, as shown in the following screenshot:

# Building the scene

Now that we have some assets to build with, we can start building our first town, by placing images within the scene.

## Adding the town background

Returning to the scene view, you should see the following:

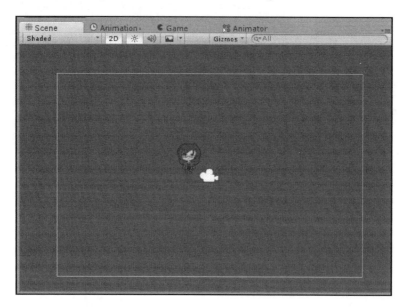

If, however, we add our town background texture to the scene by dragging it to either the project Hierarchy or the scene view, you will end up with the following:

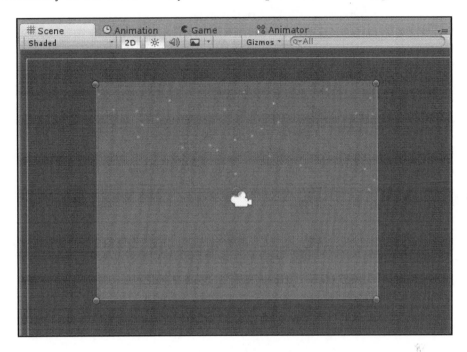

*Our player has vanished!* The reason for this is simple: Unity's sprite system has an ordering system that comes in two parts.

# Sprite sorting layers

**Sorting Layers (Edit | Project Settings | Tags and Layers)** are a collection of Sprites, which are bulked together to form a single group. Layers can be configured to be drawn in a specific order on the screen, as shown in the following screenshot:

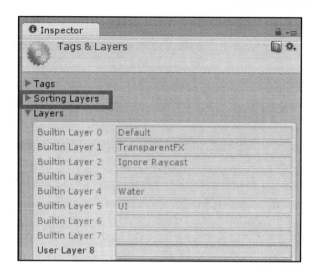

# Sprite Sorting Order

Sprites within an individual layer can be sorted, allowing you to control the draw order of sprites within that layer. The sprite **Inspector** is used for this purpose, as shown in the following screenshot:

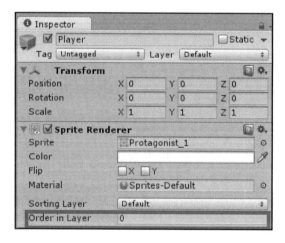

Sprite's **Sorting Layers** should not be confused with Unity's rendering layers. Layers are a separate functionality used to control whether groups of GameObjects are drawn or managed together, whereas **Sorting Layers** control the draw order of Sprites in a scene.

The reason our player is no longer visible is she is behind the background. As the two sprites are in the same layer and have the same sort order, they are simply drawn in the order that they are in the project Hierarchy.

# Updating the scene sorting layers

To resolve the update of the scene's sorting layers, let's organize our Sprite rendering by adding some Sprite sorting layers. Open up the **Tags and Layers** Inspector pane, as shown in the following screenshot (by navigating to **Edit** | **Project Settings** | **Tags and Layers**) and expand the **Sorting Layers** menu:

You can add new sorting layers by selecting the plus sign. Add the following **Sorting Layers**:

- **Background**
- **Middleground**
- **Foreground**

These layers need to be listed in the ordered they are bulleted. Images in the sorting layer on the top of the list will appear to be the furthest back and images in the sorting layer on the bottom of the list will appear to be the closest. You should see the following:

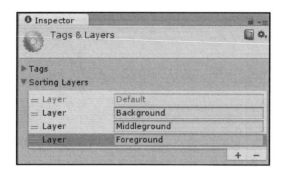

You can reorder the layers underneath the default anytime by selecting a row and dragging it up and down the sprite's **Sorting Layers** list.

With the layers set up, we can now configure our GameObjects accordingly. Select the background to view its **Inspector**. In the **Sprite Renderer** component, **Background** will now be available in the drop-down menu for **Sorting Layer**, as shown in the following screenshot:

Now, set the **Sorting Layer** on our **background** Sprite to the **Background** layer, as shown in the following screenshot:

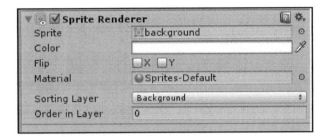

Now, select the player GameObject and set its **Sorting Layer** to **Middleground**. You should now see the player in front of the background, as follows:

# Building out the scene

Before we add more objects to the scene, let's add a few more background images to expand the size of the scene. First, set the background's **Transform** position to (0,0,0). Now, duplicate the background twice by selecting the image and pressing *Ctrl + D* two times. Using the move controls (or by adjusting the transform x position) move `background (1)` to the right of `background` and `background (2)` to the left of `background`. Make sure you do not see spaces between the background images. You should now have the following:

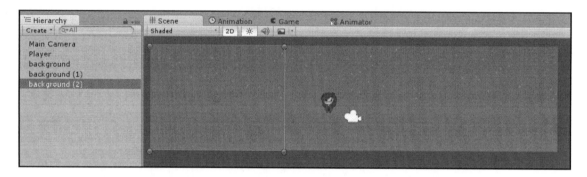

It can be rather cumbersome to have a bunch of objects in your hierarchy. Also, sometimes you want objects to be grouped together so that you can move them as a single object. You can create empty objects in your scene and use them in a similar fashion as folders to group objects together.

From the **Create** drop-down menu, select **Create Empty**, as shown in the following screenshot:

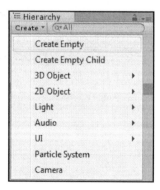

Rename the new GameObject **Backgrounds** and set its **Transform** position to (0,0,0). Now, select the three background images and drag them until you are hovering over the

**Backgrounds** GameObject in the Hierarchy. This will make the background images children of the **Backgrounds** GameObject. Now, you can move all of the background images at once. You can also minimize the arrow next to **Backgrounds** to declutter your Hierarchy, as shown in the following screenshot:

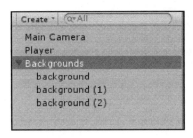

Now add the sidewalk and road sprites to the scene. When you do so, you will notice they appear behind the background. Change their GameObject names to `sidewalk` and `road`, respectively. For the `road`, change its **Sorting Layer** to `Background` and its **Order in Layer** to `1`, as shown in the following screenshot:

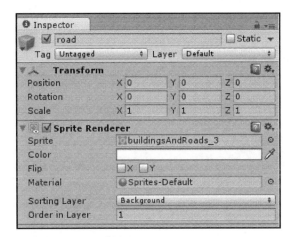

For the sidewalk, change its **Sorting Layer** to Background and its **Order in Layer** to 2, as shown in the following screenshot:

Duplicate each of them once. Create an empty GameObject named Roads and an empty GameObject named Sidewalks to contain the groups. Make sure you set each of these empty GameObjects' **Transform** position to (0,0,0) before making the Sprites children of the empty GameObjects. Move the sidewalks and roads into position so that your scene looks like the following:

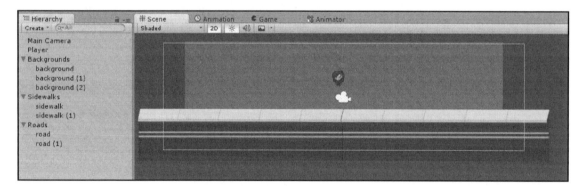

Right now our character is floating in the air and can walk places other than the road and sidewalk, but we will fix that shortly.

# Working with the camera

If you try and move the player left and right at the moment, our hero happily bobs along. However, you will quickly notice that we run into a problem: the hero soon disappears from the edge of the screen. To solve this, we need to make the camera follow the hero.

When creating new scripts to implement something, remember that just about every game that has been made with Unity has most likely implemented either the same thing or something similar. So, in most cases, we will have something to work from. Don't just start a script from scratch (unless it is a very small one to solve a tiny issue) if you can help it.

Once you become more experienced, it is better to just use these scripts as a reference and try to create your own and improve on them, unless they are from a maintained library.

Create a new script called `FollowCamera` in the `Assets\Scripts` folder, remove the `Start` and `Update` functions, and then add the following variable declarations:

```
using UnityEngine;
using System.Collections;

public class FollowCamera : MonoBehaviour {

    // Distance between player and camera in horizontal direction
    public float xOffset = 0f;
    // Distance between player and camera in vertical direction
    public float yOffset = 0f;
    // Reference to the player's transform.
    public Transform player;
}
```

The `xOffset` and `yOffset` variables are provided so that we can make the player not perfectly centered with the camera.

Before we go further, we will attach the `FollowCamera.cs` script to the **Main Camera**. Select the **Main Camera** from the Hierarchy and drag and drop the `FollowCamera.cs` script into the **Inspector** of the **Main Camera** below the **Add Component** button. The **Inspector** should now look like the following:

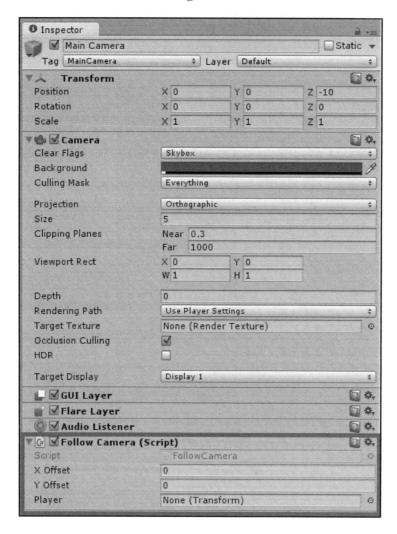

Because we initialized all of the variables as `public`, they can all be adjusted from within the Inspector without having to open the `FollowCamera.cs` script by simply changing the numbers in the slots next to the variables.

Notice that the `player` variable was declared as a `public Transform`, and there is a slot next to **Player** that says `None (Transform)`. This means that we can drag and drop any transform into the **Player** slot. However, we don't want to put just any **Transform** in the slot, we want our player character's GameObject to appear in that slot. Because the GameObject **Player** has a **Transform** component attached to it, we can place it in this spot.

Drag and drop the **Player** GameObject from the Hierarchy into this slot. You should now see the following:

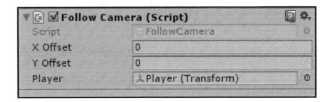

Rather than dragging and dropping the `Player` into the **Player** slot, you could have also included the following code in an awake function:

```
void Awake(){
// check the player reference.
player = GameObject.Find("Player").transform;
    if (player == null){
        Debug.LogError("Player object not found");
    }
}
```

It is really a matter of preference. I personally prefer the drag and drop method as I feel that functionality is a big benefit of Unity's interface.

To finish our script, we need to write code that will make the camera follow the player. Before we can do that, let's discuss the differences between the `Update()`, `FixedUpdate()`, and `LateUpdate()` functions.

# Comparing Update, FixedUpdate, and LateUpdate

There is usually a lot of debate about which update method should be used within a Unity game. To put it simply, the `FixedUpdate` method is called on a regular basis throughout the lifetime of the game and is generally used for physics and time-sensitive code. The `Update` method, however, is only called after the end of each frame that is drawn to the screen, as the time taken to draw the screen can vary (due to the number of objects to be drawn and so on). So, the `Update` call ends up being fairly irregular. `LateUpdate` is the last of the update functions to be called. It is called after all other update functions have been called.

General rules of thumb are as follows:

- `Update()`: This is used for most things that you want to have continually checked or run.
- `FixedUpdate()`: This is the best update function to be used with physics.
- `LateUpdate()`: This is best for camera movement or other items you want to update after everything else has been updated.

While the preceding are general rules of thumb, they are not set in stone, and it really depends on the game and what you are trying to accomplish.

# Moving our camera with the player

We want the camera to follow the player left and right, but not up and down. As stated earlier, generally, the best update function to use with a camera is the `LateUpdate`, so we will use the following code to make the camera follow the player:

```
void LateUpdate() {
    this.transform.position = new Vector3(player.transform.position.x +
        xOffset, this.transform.position.y + yOffset, -10);
}
```

The preceding code sets the camera's x position with that of the player plus some padding. It also fixes the camera's y and z positions.

# The perils of resolution

When dealing with cameras, there is always one thing that will trip us up as soon as we try to build for another platform-resolution.

By default, the Unity player in the editor runs in the **Free Aspect** mode, as shown in the following screenshot:

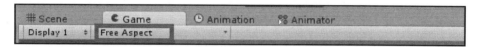

The **Aspect** mode (from the **Aspect** drop-down) can be changed to represent the resolutions supported by each platform you can target.

 You can also make your own resolutions by clicking the plus sign at the bottom of the drop-down menu and providing your own values.

To change the build target, go into your project's **Build Settings** by navigating to **File | Build Settings** or by pressing *Ctrl + Shift + B*, select a platform, and click on the **Switch Platform** button, as shown in the following screenshot:

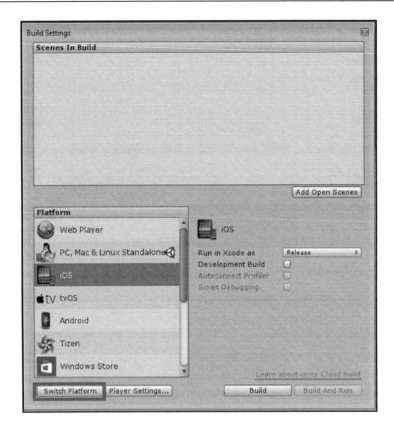

When you change the **Aspect** drop-down menu to view in one of these resolutions, you will notice how the aspect ratio for what is drawn to the screen changes by either stretching or compressing the visible area. If you run the editor player in full screen by clicking on the **Maximize on Play** button and then clicking on the play icon, you will see this change more clearly. Alternatively, you can run your project on a target device to see the proper perspective output.

The reason I bring this up here is that if you used fixed bounds settings for your camera or GameObjects, then these values may not work for every resolution, thereby putting your settings out of range or (in most cases) too undersized.

# Setting our aspect ratio and camera parameters

For now, we will leave our target build as **PC, Mac, & Linux Standalone**. Change the aspect ratio to 4 : 3 in the **Game** view. Also, change the size variable to 5, as shown in the following screenshot:

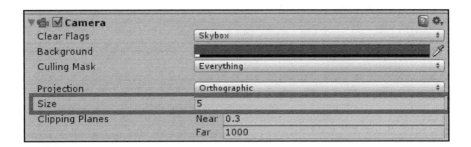

You should now see the following in the **Game** view:

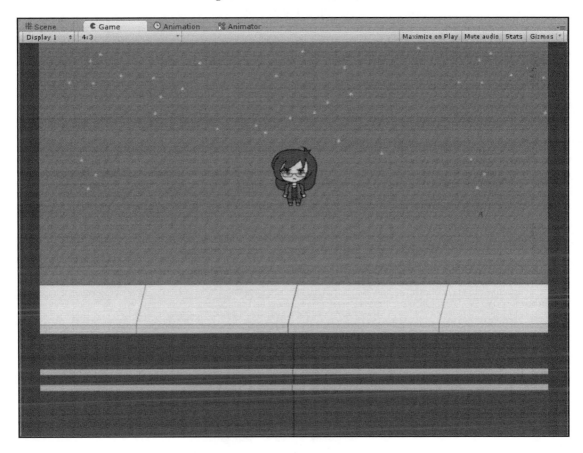

# Transitioning and bounds

Our camera follows our player, but our hero can still walk off the screen and keep going forever, so let's stop that from happening.

# Towns with borders

As you saw in the preceding section, you can use Unity's camera logic to figure out where things are on the screen. You can also do more complex ray testing to check where things are, but I find these are overly complex unless you depend on that level of interaction.

The simpler answer is just to use the native **Box2D** physics system to keep things in the scene. This might seem like overkill, but the 2D physics system is very fast and fluid, and it is simple to use.

We already added the physics components, `Rigidbody 2D` (to apply physics) and a `Box Collider 2D` (to detect collisions), to the player in `Chapter 2`, *Building your Project and Character*. Now we can make use of these components by adding some additional collision objects to stop the player from running off.

To accomplish this and to keep things organized, we will add three empty GameObjects (either by navigating to **Create | Create Empty** or by pressing *Ctrl + Shift + N*) to the scene (one parent and two children) to manage these collision points. We will initially place each of them at position (0,0,0). I've named them **WorldBounds** (parent), and **LeftBorder** and **RightBorder** (children), as the shown in the following screenshot:

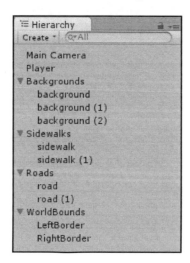

To make these objects slightly easier to see, we will change their icons. Select the **LeftBorder**, and in the **Inspector**, expand the icon selection drop-down menu. Select the blue oval. Do the same for the **RightBorder**, shown in the following screenshot:

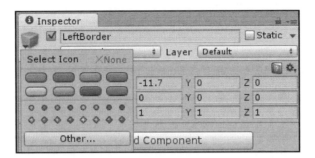

Next, we will position each of the child GameObjects to the left and right-hand sides of the screen, as shown in the following screenshot:

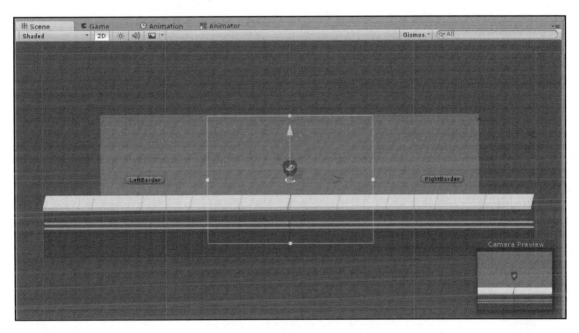

Next, we will add a **Box Collider 2D** to each border game object and increase its height just to ensure that it works for the entire height of the scene. I've set the **Y** value to 15 for effect, as shown in the following screenshot:

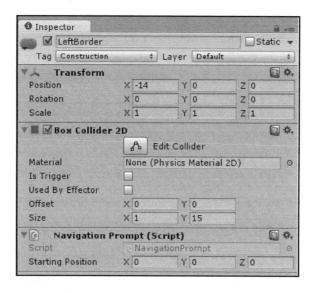

Move the **LeftBorder** and **RightBorder** so that their x positions are −14 and 14, respectively. The end result should look like the following screenshot with the two new colliders highlighted in green:

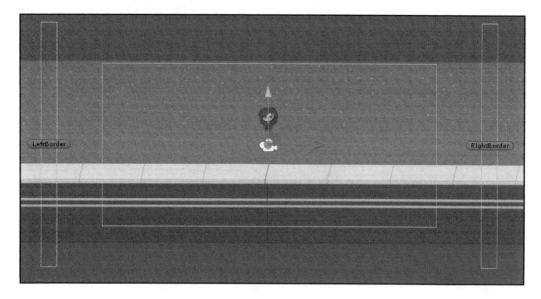

Alternatively, you could have just created one of the children, added the **Box Collider**, duplicated it (by navigating to **Edit** | **Duplicate** or by pressing *Ctrl + D*), and moved it. If you have to create multiples of the same thing, this is a handy tip to remember.

If we run the project, our character can still walk past the borders!! That is because the character only has a **Box Collider** with a **Trigger** Component. That will check if she collides with things, but won't stop her from passing through things. Let's give her a collider that will stop her from passing through things.

Select the options drop-down on her **Box Collider 2D** component (represented by the little cog on the right side of the component). Then select **Copy Component**, as shown in the following screenshot:

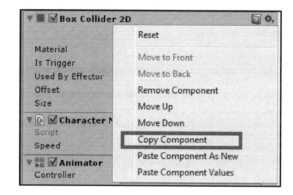

Now select the options drop-down again and select **Paste Component As New**, as shown in the following screenshot:

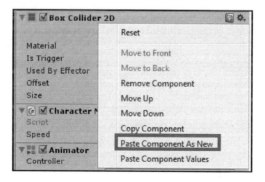

You should now see a second **Box Collider 2D** component at the bottom of the **Inspector** list. For the new **Box Collider 2D**, deselect **Is Trigger**, as shown in the following screenshot:

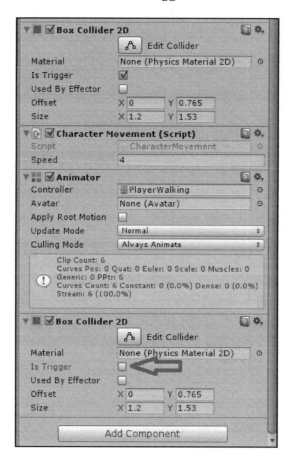

If you run the project now, you will see that our hero can no longer escape this town, but we can see the edge of the background, as shown in the following screenshot:

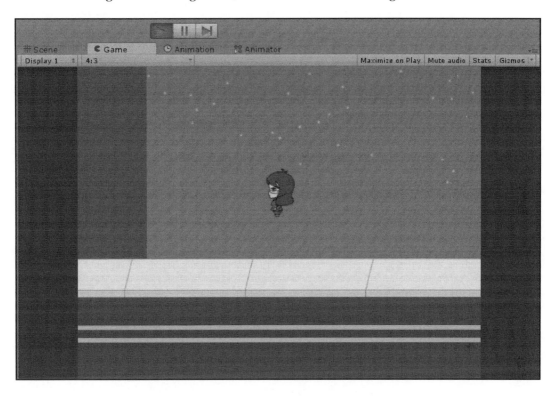

Add two more background images to deal with this issue:

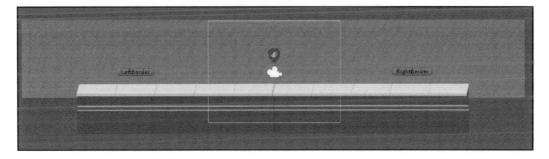

Right now, she can walk in the sky. We can fix this is the same way we stopped her from walking too far left or right. Create two more empty GameObjects and make them children of the WorldBounds. Name them Upperbound and Lowerbound. Give them red oval icons. Add the **Box Collider 2D** component to each with an X size of 30. Move the player on to the road and position the upper and lower bounds, as shown in the following:

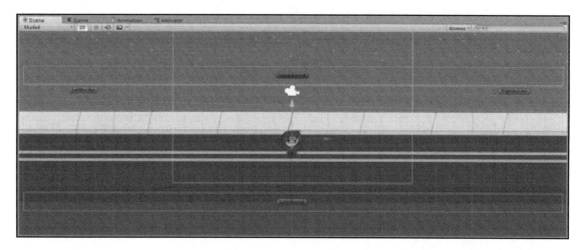

Now she walks where she should! However, as we want to let her leave, we can add a script to the new Boundary GameObject so that when the hero reaches the end of the town, she can leave.

# Journeying onward

Now that we have collision zones on our town's borders, we can hook into this by using a script to activate when the hero approaches.

Before we can do that, let's give our left and right borders a tag to make them easily accessible through script. Select **LeftBorder** and expand the **Tag** drop-down menu. Then select **Add Tag...**, as shown in the following screenshot:

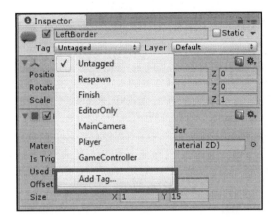

Select the + sign on the empty list:

And create a tag called **Borders**:

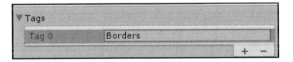

Reselect **LeftBorder**, and now **Borders** will be available from the **Tag** drop-down menu. Select it to give the **LeftBorder the Borders tag**:

Tag the **RightBorder** with the **Borders** tag as well. Now that our borders are tagged, we can create a script that will trigger an event when the player reaches the borders.

Since we don't have anything set up to happen when she reaches the edges, we will just have a message displayed in the Console.

Create a new C# script called `NavigationPrompt`, clear its contents, and populate it with the following code:

```
using UnityEngine;
using System.Collections;

public class NavigationPrompt : MonoBehaviour {

    void OnCollisionEnter2D(Collision2D col){
        if(col.gameObject.CompareTag("Borders")){
            Debug.Log("leave town");
        }
    }

}
```

Attach the `NavigationPrompt` script to the player character to view the Console prompt "leave town" when she collides with a border. It's not terribly interesting right now, but we will update the script to make something actually happen when the character hits the border in chapter 6, *NPCs and Interactions*.

# Going further

If you are the adventurous sort, try expanding your project to add the following:

- Add some buildings to the town
- Add the skyscraper skylines to the scene and give each a different Sprite renderer **Color** property, maybe even add a script to randomly set the color
- Research parallaxing backgrounds and parallax the skyscraper skylines
- Add objects to the `foreground` layer that always render in front of the player
- Add more objects to the `middleground` layer to create a more interesting scene

# Summary

This certainly has been a very long chapter just to add a background to our scene, but working out how each scene will work is a crucial design element for the entire game; you have to pick a pattern that works for you and your end result once, as changing it can be very detrimental (and a lot of work) in the future.

In this chapter, we covered the following:

- Some more practice with the Sprite editor and sprite slicer including some tips and tricks when it doesn't work automatically (or you prefer to slice it yourself)
- Some camera tips, tricks, and scripts
- An overview of Sprite Layers and Sprite Sorting
- Defining boundaries in scenes

In the next chapter, we will cover the basics of the UI system that was implemented in Unity 4.6.

**5**

# Working with Unitys UI System

The next few chapters are going to require us to create a **User Interface (UI)**. However, before we begin with that, I want to discuss the various features of the Unity UI system. This chapter will provide an overview of each of the elements available with the UI system and we will utilize them in the future chapters.

The UI system was implemented in **Unity 4.6** and has made the incorporation of a UI system significantly easier than it was in the past. This UI system has essentially made any of the old GUI functions a thing of the past. These functions are still useful for procedurally generating a UI, but, for the most part, if you see a reference to GUI functions, it was written prior to version 4.6 and is handling UI in a much harder way than necessary.

The following topics will be covered in this chapter:

- UI Canvas
- UI Text and Images
- UI Layout and Rect Transform
- UI Buttons

# UI Canvas

The **UI Canvas** is essentially the object that holds all of your UI elements. You can manually add a UI Canvas or it will be automatically added to your scene when you add any other UI element. All UI elements, including the UI Canvas, can be added by the **Create** menu in the **Hierarchy**. All of your UI elements will be children of your canvas. When you add a Canvas to the scene, the **EventSystem** object will also be added to the **Hierarchy**. This object allows you to use buttons and the other UI components in an interactive way, as shown in the following screenshot:

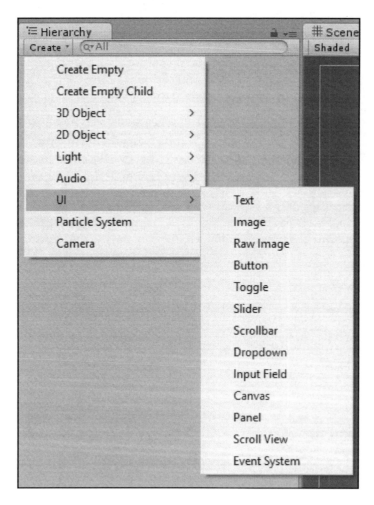

When you first start using Canvases, you may become a little confused by the location of your Canvas and the objects that are actually in your scene. When you first create a Canvas, you should see a large rectangle appear in your scene, as shown in the following screenshot:

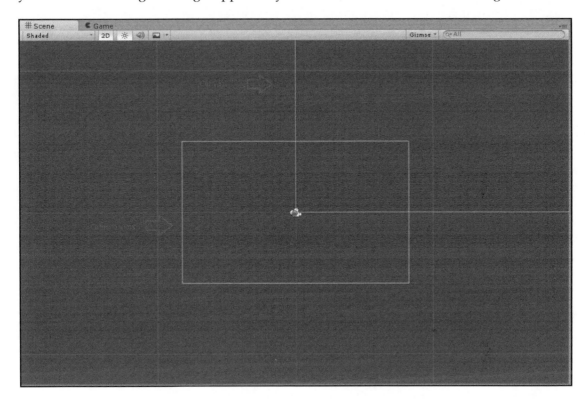

Double-click on the canvas in the **Hierarchy** to zoom out your scene view to see the full canvas, as shown in the following screenshot:

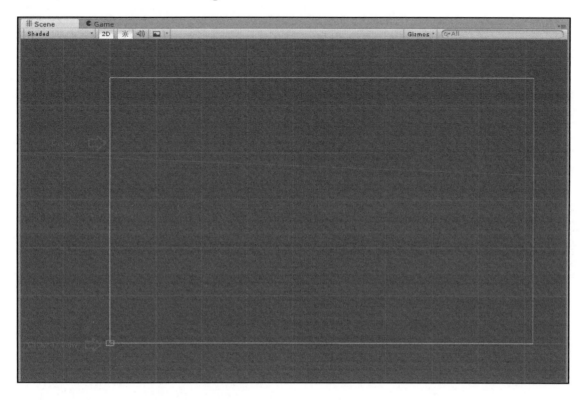

This large size of the canvas lets you easily see all the elements that will be in your UI without the objects in your actual scene cluttering your view.

# EventSystem

As stated previously, when you create a Canvas, a GameObject called **EventSystem** will be added to the **Hierarchy**. This is an empty GameObject that will hold a few scripts, as shown in the following screenshot:

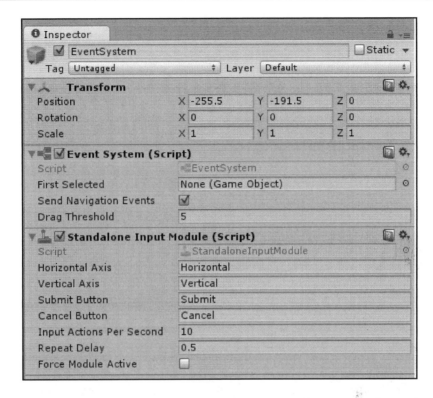

The EventSystem is a built-in functionality that lets you send events to objects based on some type of input. When using UI, you need this so that your mouse inputs will work on the respective UI element. For example, this functionality allows you to use the OnClick() functionality of a button (described in the UI Buttons section).

# Canvas Render Mode

One of the most important aspects of Canvases, in my opinion, is the ability to change the **Render Modes**. These modes essentially determine how or if the various objects in your Canvas will scale and position when the camera size changes. Setting this property correctly will make the process of publishing to multiple platforms significantly easier, as shown in the following screenshot:

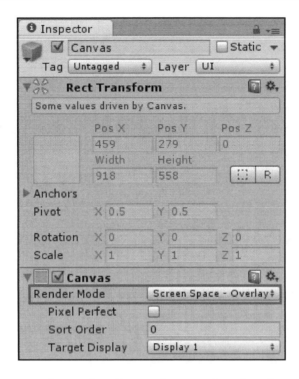

There are three different render modes: **Screen Space – Overlay**, **Screen Space – Camera**, and **World Space**.

# Screen Space – Overlay

**Screen Space – Overlay** rendering mode will make the objects in your UI automatically scale based on the resolution of the game. It does not consider the camera. The following screenshot shows the properties you can edit when using the **Screen Space-Overlay** rendering mode:

Every object in the UI will render in front of all objects within the world, as shown in the following screenshot:

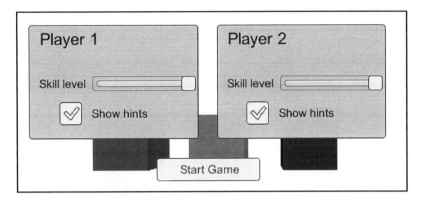

Screen Space-Overlay Canvas Render Mode example provided by Unity's Manual

# Screen Space – Camera

**Screen Space – Camera** mode is similar to that of **Screen Space – Overlay**, but instead of being completely independent of the camera, it renders all UI objects as if they are a specific distance away from the camera. The following screenshot shows the properties you can edit when using the **Screen Space – Camera** rendering mode:

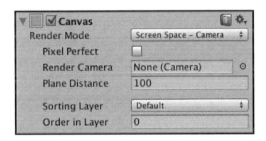

You can see in the preceding screenshot that for this rendering mode to work correctly, you have to specify which camera will be used to determine how the objects render, as shown in the following screenshot:

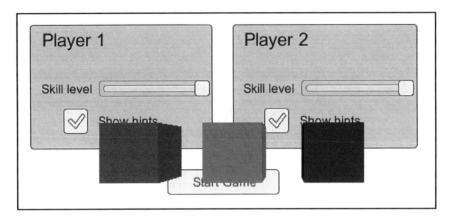

Screen Space-Camera Canvas Render Mode example provided by Unity's Manual

This mode is particularly helpful if you want to have a background image in your 2D game that will automatically scale with the camera.

# World Space

**World Space** rendering mode allows you to render the UI elements as if they are on a plane positioned within the 3D space of the scene. The position and rotation of these elements can be set through the Canvas's **Rect Transform**. They will scale based on their location relative to the camera. The following screenshot shows the properties you can edit when using the **World Space** rendering mode:

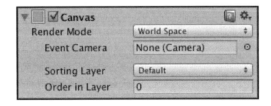

This rendering mode is great for UI elements that appear in a 3D game view, such as health bars that float over characters' heads and damage or health text that pop up in the scene, as shown in the following screenshot:

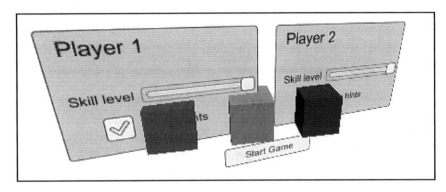

World Space Canvas Render Mode example provided by Unity's Manual

# Using multiple Canvases

You are not restricted to using a single canvas. You can have as many Canvases as you like and each can have their own render mode. This can be very helpful if you need different UI items to render in different modes. For example, you may want to put **Heads-Up-Display (HUD)** UI elements in a canvas with a **Screen Space – Overlay** rendering mode and a background image in a Canvas with a **Screen Space – Camera** rendering mode. You can even place Canvases as children of other Canvases, if you want to get fancy!

In general, if you have multiple Canvases with the same rendering mode and you haven't fiddled with their sorting order, Canvases will appear so that the one positioned lowest in the **Hierarchy's** list will render in front.

# UI Text and Images

The most basic components of the UI are the Text and Image objects. While you can add interaction to them, for the most part, these will be static objects in your UI that display information to the player.

# UI Text

The UI Text object allows you to place blocks of text on the Canvas. From the Text component, which is automatically attached to any UI Text object you create, you can control all of the properties of the text, as shown in the following screenshot:

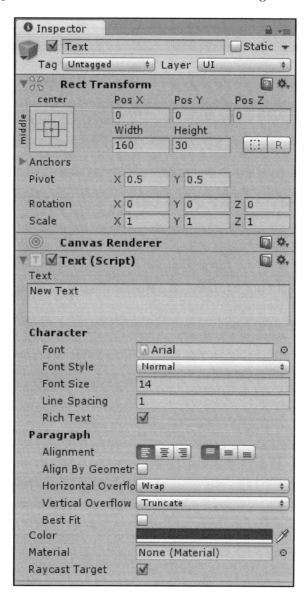

You can also adjust these individual properties through code by accessing the **Text** component. The default font for all text is **Arial**, but if you want to use any other font, you will have to import the font into your project.

# UI Image

When you create a UI Image, an object with the image component on it will be automatically added to your Canvas. It will initially appear as a white square until you replace the source image. The source image must have its **Texture Type** in its import settings set to **Sprite (2D and UI)** to be used as a UI Image. You can control all of the properties of the image, as shown in the following screenshot:

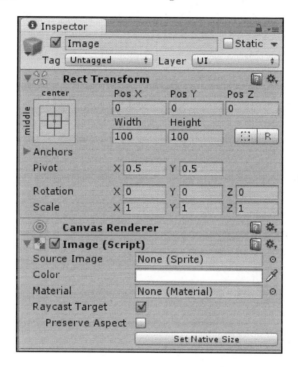

 Remember, if you are working in 2D mode, all images you bring into your project will automatically be set to **Sprite (2D and UI)** texture type.

The **Color** property will work essentially like a color overlay if you change the color from white to a different color the image will be tinted based on the color you select. From the **Color** property, you can also adjust the image's transparency.

If for some reason you want to use an image in the UI that does not have its import **Texture Type** set to **Sprite (2D and UI)**, but instead want to use an image that was imported as a **Texture**, you can use a **Raw Image** UI object. However, the image UI object should be used in most cases. The following screenshot shows the properties of the **Raw Image** UI element:

# UI Layout and Rect Transform

As you may have noticed in the three preceding images, all UI objects are automatically given a **Rect Transform** component when they are created, as shown in the following screenshot:

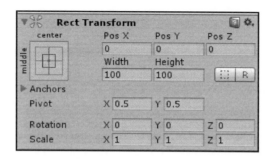

The **Rect Transform** component works similarly to the **Transform** component, in that it allows you to position the object. However, unlike **Transform**, it also has the properties of **Width**, **Height**, **Pivot**, and **Anchors**.

> Remember that UI objects have the **Rect Transform** component, whereas other objects have the **Transform** component. It's important to realize the difference, especially if you try to access these components in code.

You can manually enter values for its position, rotation, and scale, or you can use the Move, Size, Rotate, and Rect tool, as shown in the following screenshot:

One thing to keep in mind when working with UI objects is that all of the coordinates are relative to the Canvas, not the actual world (unless you have your canvas render mode set to **World Space**).

# Rect Tool

The Rect Tool can be used to change the size, position, or rotation of UI objects, just as it can with other non-UI elements within your scene; but it works slightly differently on UI elements. One thing you will notice about resizing a UI object with a **Rect Transform** component is that when you change its size with the **Rect Tool**, it will change its **Width** and **Height**, but not affect the scale value.

# Pivot

The **Pivot** of your UI object determines where its location will register, the point at which the object will rotate around, and the point at which the object will scale from. Adjusting the X values of the pivot will move it left and right from the position you selected with the anchor preset (described in the following section). Adjusting the Y values of the pivot will move it up and down from the position you selected with the **Anchor Preset**. If you have yet selected an **Anchor Preset**, the pivot will be positioned in the center by default.

# Anchors

The **Anchors** property determines where the object will be attached or anchored to its parent. Anchoring also allows the UI object to resize relative to its parent object. Each **Rect Transform** will have an **Anchor Preset** button in the top-left corner, as shown in the following screenshot:

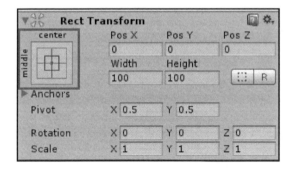

Clicking on it will reveal the **Anchor Presets**, as shown in the following screenshot:

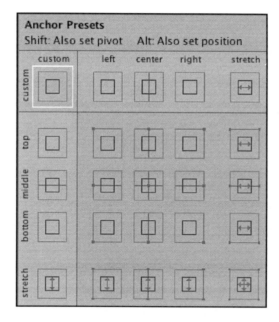

Anchor Presets

Holding down *Shift* while clicking on one of the **Anchor Presets** will set the pivot, holding down *Alt* will set the anchor position, and holding down *Shift + Alt* will set both the pivot and anchor position. Once you select a preset, the **Anchor Preset** button's image will show the preset you selected.

# UI Buttons

UI Buttons are objects that are meant to be clicked, but they can also respond to other actions, for example, when the mouse hovers over them; the following screenshot shows the **Button** component:

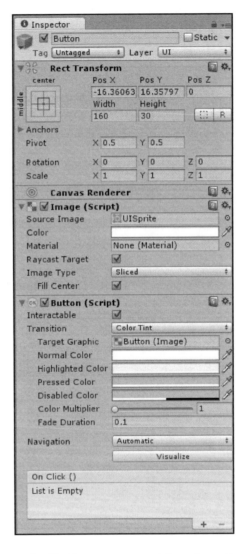

When you create a UI button, the **Button** component is automatically added to it, but an **Image** component is also automatically added to it. This determines what the **Button** will look like in its normal state.

# Transition types

By selecting from the **Transition** drop-down menu, you can determine how the button reacts to being pressed, when it is hovered over, or when it is disabled. The three **Transition** options are **Color Tint**, **Sprite Swap**, and **Animation**, as shown in the following screenshot:

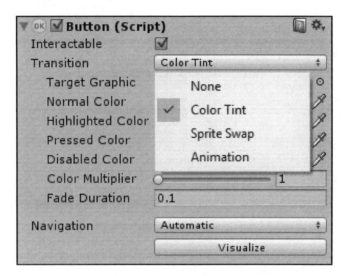

# Text child

When a UI Button is created, a **Text** child is automatically added to the **Button**, as shown in the following screenshot:

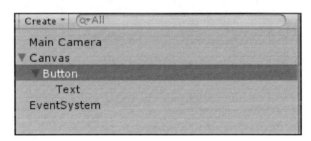

This child gives the button a **Text** label. If you don't want it, you can simply delete the child. In the following screenshot, the **Button** object's **Text** child is selected and its **Inspector** is shown:

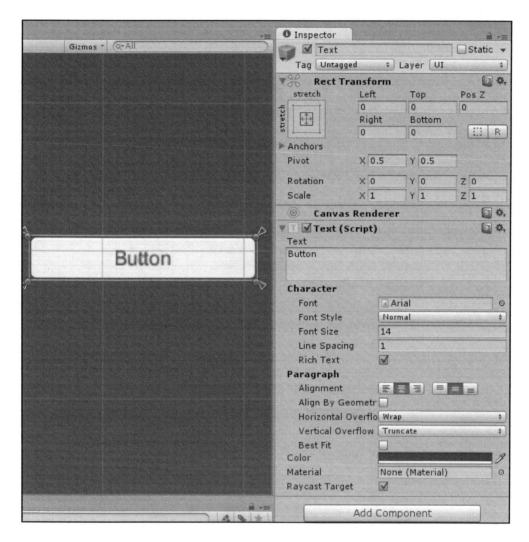

# On Click ()

The most basic functionality of a button is to click it. So, the **On Click ()** event is already available in a button's Inspector when it is created, as shown in the following screenshot:

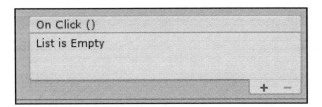

To tell the button what to do when clicked, simply click the *plus* sign at the bottom of the **On Click ()** event:

To tell the button what to do, you first select whether you want the event to run during **Runtime Only** or **During Editor and Runtime**. Then you have to tell it what function is to run when the button is clicked. You do this by first dragging the object that has the script you want to access attached to it in the object slot. Once you do that, the drop-down menu that states **No Function** will list all the scripts attached to the object. Once you select the script, you can then select the specific function.

You can have more than one action performed when the button is clicked by simply adding more **On Click ()** events to the list.

Buttons have the **On Click ()** event by default, which states what will happen when the button is clicked; however, you can add different events by adding the **Event Trigger (Script)** component:

The **Event Trigger** component allows you to add many different types of events, as shown in the following screenshot:

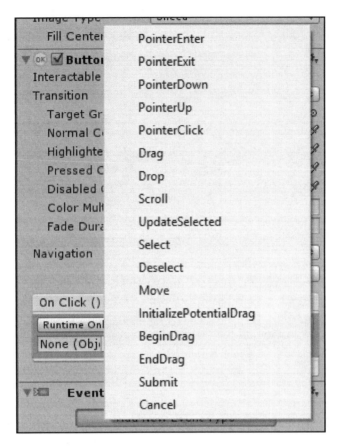

Once you select the event, hooking the event up is done in the same way in which you assigned a function to the **On Click ()** event.

# Going further

If you are the adventurous sort, try expanding your project to add the following:

- Put two images on the canvas and adjust their anchor and pivot points. Then see what happens when the resolution of the game window is changed significantly.
- Place a few buttons in a canvas and experiment with the different transitions to see how they work.

# Summary

In this chapter, we covered a basic overview of the main elements of the UI system. It's a lot of information to digest at once; therefore, this chapter is really meant to be more of a reference chapter. We will be doing a lot with each of these types of UI element in nearly every subsequent chapter, so don't worry, you'll get a lot of practice!

In this chapter, we covered the following topics:

- Canvases
- UI Text and Images
- UI Layout and Rect Transform
- UI Buttons

In the next chapter, we will build a conversation system. Be prepared for some heavy scripting!

# 6
# NPCs and Interactions

Interacting with other characters is a key feature of RPGs. So, in this chapter, we'll look to add some more characters and give them something to say.

This chapter will discuss, in general, advanced programming techniques. Some of the techniques may not be implemented in our game, but they are still good to know about. Each technique will be accompanied by an example.

After we discuss the advanced programming techniques, we will implement some of these techniques in our game to create a dialog system.

 This is a heavy scripting chapter. All the techniques explained are not used in this chapter but are important to know, and what's more important is to know the difference between them and when to use them.

The lists of topics that will be covered in this chapter are as follows:

- Advanced coding, delegates, events, and messaging
- Coroutines
- Scriptable objects and custom importers
- Building a conversation system

## Considering an RPG

When making an RPG, there is a lot to consider. So far, we have just modeled our player using some standard statistics, but this could be done for any type of game. The thing that sets RPGs apart is their sheer depth and interaction with the living world.

If you are building an RPG (or a game with RPG elements), you need to get some research under your belt and construct your world, the places you can visit (and why), and the characters you will be talking to or fighting with. Some games even go so far as to construct an elaborate backstory that has nothing to do with the actual game.

RPGs have a rich history as they have been around for a long time, and there is a wealth of information, examples, and resources to help you make a great game. One site that provides this is called **DriveThruRPG** (http://rpg.drivethrustuff.com/index.php), which even today has an ever-growing catalog of playbooks, magazines, and materials. As this site is constantly expanding, you have a perpetual resource to continue to build your game beyond the bounds of its first release. If you intend to make the best game out there, it'd be best to consider its long-term future and additional content to add in later.

A lot of content on DriveThruRPG is on a paid basis; however, there is also a lot of free resources to get you started, and a lot of the magazines are free. Just be sure to check the license of whatever you buy to either use it as is in your game or as a base for your own content.

*Always check the license of anything you use.*

Breaking it down, the main parts of an RPG that this chapter will focus on are as follows:

- Interactive NPCs
- Non-interactive NPCs
- Enemy characters
- Conversations
- Experience
- Maps and places
- Battles

Other things you should consider (but are not covered) are as follows:

- Missions
- Backstory
- Supporting characters (team)
- Cutscenes (not essential, but they really make the game stand out)

The list might seem endless. However, if you focus on these main elements, you can always expand later.

A common mistake that a lot of new developers make is to design everything for their game from the beginning. Through experience, though, you will learn that it is better to start small; first, you should build the main parts of your core game mechanics and then add more content or features over time. If you architect your game in the right way from the beginning, additional content can be added as expansions later on as extra revenue options.

# Advanced programming techniques

As part of this chapter, we will start to go in depth with some advanced programming techniques. These enable us to structure our code better and add management to our game project, instead of just adding GameObjects to the scene.

 Some of the scripts created in the following sections will only be for example purposes and will not be implemented in our game. However, it is recommended that you follow along. Any scripts that will be needed for our game will be readdressed in the *Adding NPCs and A Conversation System* section.

# Singletons and managers

Any project of a sufficient size and complexity is going to run into issues related to managing your GameObjects as and when they are added and removed from a scene. If you don't get your design right from the start, you are setting yourself up for a world of mess later. A common way to handle this is to use one of the three patterns—single instance managers, singletons, or a dependency—system to manage these controllers for you.

Singletons are scripts that are ubiquitous to your project. They are called singletons, because the scripts creates only a single instance of itself. There are two main ways through which you can implement the singleton pattern in Unity. The first way is to use a public static parameter within a class to maintain the runtime class. This also allows any other script to access it from anywhere in the game and is useful if you want other events to cause the manager to do something, for example, things related to conversation systems or traps. You can also use an empty GameObject in the scene and attach a singleton pattern script to it. However, you could cause conflicts if you add more than one pattern.

Managers, on the other hand, are just central scripts that are particular to an individual scene to control and maintain the flow of the scene for one or many items.

# The manager approach – using empty GameObjects

Whereas singletons are game wide, there is often a cause for just a scene-based manager. Implementing this using an empty GameObject is very easy. Simply use **Create Empty** from the **GameObject** menu or the keyboard shortcut, as shown in the following screenshot:

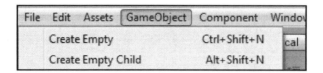

The placement of the new GameObject is up to you. If your controller's position is important (like with an enemy spawner), place it where you want the objects to spawn from. If not, it doesn't matter; it just needs to be in the scene somewhere. As it's an empty GameObject, it will not be visible within your scene.

Then, create your manager script, and simply attach your script to the new empty GameObject.

For example, if you wanted to spawn enemy objects from a collection according to a simple repeating interval, you could use the following code:

```
public class EnemySpawnManager : MonoBehaviour{
    public float spawnTime = 5f;
    //The amount of time between each spawn.
    public float spawnDelay = 3f;
    //The amount of time before spawning starts.
    public GameObject[] enemies;
    //Array of enemy prefabs.

    void Start (){
        //Start calling the Spawn function repeatedly after a delay.
        InvokeRepeating("Spawn", spawnDelay, spawnTime);
    }
    void Spawn (){
        //Instantiate a random enemy.
        int enemyIndex = Random.Range(0, enemies.Length);
        Instantiate(enemies[enemyIndex],
            transform.position, transform.rotation);
    }
}
```

Then, simply attach your script to the new empty GameObject. For it to function, you will need to assign the prefabs of the types of `enemies` you want to appear in the scene by attaching them to the **Enemies** property, as shown in the following screenshot:

The the preceding code, the **Enemies** property is an array. If you view the preceding screenshot you will see that the **Enemies** property has an arrow next to it. This indicates that the property can be expanded. When adding objects to an array in the Inspector, you simply drag the object over the name of the array. It will then be added as an object in the array. You will see technique implemented later in this chapter as well as in future chapters.

# The singleton approach – using the C# singleton pattern

The manager approach is fine in most cases, but you have to control each instance of the controller where it is placed. Moreover, you cannot interact with it or trigger it without more configurations added to the `Manager` class, and then either bind the manager to other objects or use the `Find` function.

If you need a true manager, a better approach is to employ the singleton pattern for `Manager` class; refer to the following example:

```
public class MySingletonManager : MonoBehaviour {

    //Static singleton property
    public static MySingletonManager Instance {
        get; private set;
    }

    //public property for manager
    public string MyTestProperty = "Hello World";

    void Awake(){
        //Save our current singleton instance
        Instance = this;
    }

    //public method for manager
    public void DoSomethingAwesome()
    { }
}
```

The preceding code is just a very basic singleton implementation, which you can attach to any GameObject in the scene.

Then, you can access the properties and functions within the singleton script by simply calling the following method from anywhere within your project:

```
//Set the public property of the singleton
MySingletonManager.Instance.MyTestProperty = "World Hello";

//Run the public method from the singleton
MySingletonManager.Instance.DoSomethingAwesome();
```

The class can run just as any other class with updates, fixed updates, and so on. It can also be expanded very quickly.

One of the other common uses of this pattern is the use of global variables for your project. However, if you intend to use your singleton class across the scenes, you will also need to ensure that it is not destroyed when the scene unloads with a simple update. This is done by calling `DontDestroyOnLoad` when you initialize the class, as shown in the following code:

```
public class MySingletonManager : MonoBehaviour {
        //static singleton property
        public static MySingletonManager Instance {
```

```
        get;
        private set;
    }
    //public property for manager
    public string MyTestProperty = "Hello World";
    void Awake(){
        //First we check if there are any other instances conflicting
        if (Instance != null && Instance != this)
        {
            //Destroy other instances if they are not the same
            Destroy(gameObject);
        }
        //Save our current singleton instance
        Instance = this;
        //Make sure that the instance is not destroyed
        //between scenes (this is optional)
        DontDestroyOnLoad(gameObject);
    }
    //public method for manager
    public void DoSomethingAwesome()
    {   }
}
```

There are more complicated setups for singletons. If you so wish, you can read them at
`http://wiki.unity3d.com/index.php/Singleton`.

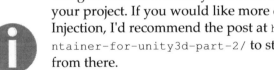

There is another pattern named **Dependency Injection**. A more robust way to handle the need of manager- or factory-type requirements in any project is to implement an **Inversion of Control (IoC)** pattern, such as Dependency Injection.

Dependency Injection is a large subject, so we won't cover it in this book. The goal here is to make you aware of all the options when architecting your project. If you would like more detailed information on Dependency Injection, I'd recommend the post at `http://blog.sebaslab.com/ioc-co ntainer-for-unity3d-part-2/` to start with, and then you can work up from there.

Dependency Injection is a very powerful tool when employed correctly and can make your project a lot easier, so it is worth looking at it if you are serious. However, care is needed in its use, and it should not be used everywhere; it should only be used where it solves a particular problem.

A good Unity-based IoC framework is **StrangeIOC**, which can be found at `http://strangeioc.github.io/strangeioc/TheBigStrangeHowTo.html`.

# Communicating between GameObjects

In any game, there are planned interactions between any components within the game. These could be as follows:

- Physics collision tests
- Reacting to being shot or shooting
- Opening and closing doors
- Triggers, switches, or traps
- Two or more characters talking

There are several ways in which you can achieve this, and each has its own particular traits. The selection of the implementations depends on what you need to achieve. The methods are as follows:

- Delegates
- Events
- Messaging

In this section, we will go through each method in detail and highlight the best uses of each.

# Delegates

We encounter delegates in our everyday lives. Sometimes they are managers, sometimes they are subordinates, and they could even be the barista at your local coffee shop. Effectively, delegates are methods that accept pieces of work to do on behalf of someone else.

 Another form of delegates is to use the C# generics and the `Action` or `Action<T>` methods, which is a shorthand version of the implementations mentioned in the next section. For more information about generics and `Action`, refer to
http://msdn.microsoft.com/en-us/library/018hxwa8(v=vs.110).aspx.

There are two main patterns in which delegates are used: the configurable method pattern and the delegation pattern.

# The configurable method pattern

The configurable method pattern is used when a piece of work or function is passed to another method to be used to complete a task. This pattern is usually used where different pieces of code can perform a common task in unique ways, such as walking, running, or patrolling. All these tasks can be the default behaviors of a character. Refer to the following figure:

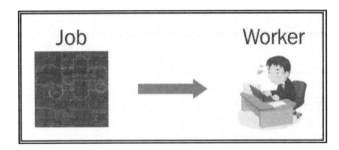

Here, you will have your code calling a Delegate method, but the contents of this method can be different depending on what you have set it to.

For instance, refer to the following code:

```
using System;
using UnityEngine; public class Delegates1{
    //Define delegate method signature
    delegate void RobotAction();
    //private property for delegate use
    RobotAction myRobotAction;
    void Start (){
        //Set the default method for the delegate
        myRobotAction = RobotWalk;
    }
    void Update(){
        //Run the selected delegate method on update
        myRobotAction();
    }
    //public method to tell the robot to walk
    public void DoRobotWalk(){
        //set the delegate method to the walk function
        myRobotAction = RobotWalk;
    }
    void RobotWalk(){
        Debug.Log("Robot walking");
    }
    //public method to tell the robot to run
```

```
public void DoRobotRun(){
    //set the delegate method to the run function
    myRobotAction = RobotRun;
}
void RobotRun(){
    Debug.Log("Robot running");
}
}
```

This means that when the DoRobotWalk method is called, it will set the delegate to the Walk method, and once updated, it will run the Walk behavior. If you call the DoRobotRun public method, it will change the delegate to the Run behavior, and once updated, it will run the Run behavior. This is a very simple kind of state machine with no conditions around.

# The delegation pattern

The delegation pattern is used where a method calls out to a helper library, and on completion of the required task, continues on back in the main function, as shown in the following figure:

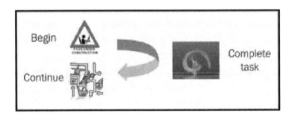

This is usually used with what you might download from the Web. When the download is finished, we do something with what we have downloaded.

For instance, refer to the following code:

```
using System;
using System.Collections.Generic;
public class Delegates2{
    public class Worker{
        List<string> WorkCompletedfor = new List<string>();
        public void DoSomething(string ManagerName,Action myDelegate){
            //Audits that work was done for which manager
            WorkCompletedfor.Add(ManagerName);
            //Begin work
            myDelegate();
        }
}
```

```
        }
    public class Manager{
        private Worker myWorker = new Worker();
        public void PieceOfWork1(){
            //A piece of very long tedious work
        }
        public void PieceOfWork2() {
            //You guessed it, yet more tedious work
        }
        public void DoWork() {
            //Send worker to do job 1
            myWorker.DoSomething("Manager1",PieceOfWork1);
            //Send worker to do job 2
            myWorker.DoSomething("Manager1", PieceOfWork2);
        }
    }
}
```

Alternatively, you could just express it using the C# lambdas, which simply means you don't need to declare separate functions:

```
public void DoWork2(){
    private Worker myWorker = new Worker();
    //Send worker to do job 1
    myWorker.DoSomething("Manager1", () =>
    {
        //A piece of very long tedious work
    });
    //Send worker to do job 2
      myWorker.DoSomething("Manager2", () =>
      {
            //You guessed it, yet more tedious work
      });
}
```

If your delegate also uses a string as a parameter, the preceding example could be used as a download pattern where a helper library does the entire download and just returns the XML asset. This asset can then be unpacked and used in the game in your main function.

# Compound delegates

Both the configurable method pattern and delegation pattern are very powerful techniques when used correctly.

Another feature of delegates is that they can be compounded, meaning you can assign multiple functions to a single delegate. Also, when a delegate is called, all the methods assigned to the delegate will run, as shown in the following code. This feature is very handy when you want to chain several common functions together instead of one:

```
using UnityEngine;
using System.Collections;
public class WorkerManager{
    void DoWork() {
        DoJob1();
        DoJob2();
        DoJob3();
    }
    private void DoJob1(){
        //Do some filing
    }
    private void DoJob2(){
        //Make coffee for the office
    }
    private void DoJob3(){
        //Stick it to the man
    }
}
```

You can achieve the same output but with more flexibility using the following code:

```
//A more intelligent WorkerManager
public class WorkerManager2{
    //WorkerManager delegate
    delegate void MyDelegateHook();
    MyDelegateHook ActionsToDo;
    public string WorkerType = "Peon";
    //On Startup, assign jobs to the worker; note this is
    //configurable instead of fixed
    void Start(){
        //Peons get lots of work to do
        if (WorkerType == "Peon"){
            ActionsToDo += DoJob1;
            ActionsToDo += DoJob2;
        }
        //Everyone else plays golf
        else{
            ActionsToDo += DoJob3;
```

```
        }
    }
    //With Update, do the actions set on ActionsToDo
    void Update(){
        ActionsToDo();
    }
    private void DoJob1(){
        //Do some filing
    }
    private void DoJob2(){
        //Make coffee for the office
    }
    private void DoJob3(){
        //Play Golf
    }
}
```

This also means it's dynamic and you can add additional functions to the delegate that will be called whenever the delegate is called.

Word to the wise: only use chained delegates when you absolutely need the flexibility to do so, as they are a more complex pattern to implement. They are also difficult to debug should something untoward happen.

# Events

We can describe events as *expected announcements*. Imagine you have a bat phone at your desk; when it rings, you know it's *Batman* on the other end, usually telling you some trouble has been averted. Events are similar to this pattern where there is a hook; this is where you can listen for something to happen and then do something with that event. When it occurs, additionally, through events, you can pass this information to provide yourself with additional informaon about what has occurred, as depicted in the following image:

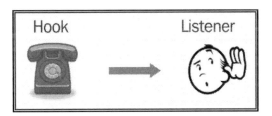

In the following code, events use delegates to describe how they are going to communicate. It defines the form that communication will take and what information will be passed when the event is fired:

```
//Delegate method definition
public delegate void ClickAction();

//Event hook using delegate method signature
public static event ClickAction OnClicked;
```

Now, when an event needs to be initiated in your class, all it needs to do to notify any other code that is listening to the event is call the event such as a method using delegate as the signature.

 However, what you must be careful about is if no one is listening to the event (no one has subscribed to it). To avoid this, you need to check that delegate is *not* null before you call it.

Refer to the following code:

```
void Update(){
   //If the space bar is pressed, this item has been clicked
   if (Input.GetKeyDown(KeyCode.Space)){
      //Trigger the event delegate if there is a subscriber
      if (OnClicked != null){

         OnClicked();
      }
   }
}
```

With the event exposed, any other class or GameObject that needs to be informed about the occurrence of the event just needs to subscribe to the event as follows, using the += syntax:

```
void Start(){

   //Hook on to the function's onClicked event and run the
   //Events_OnClicked method when it occurs
   OnClicked += Events_OnClicked;
}

   //Subordinate method
   void Events_OnClicked(){
      Debug.Log("The button was clicked");
   }
```

```
void OnDestroy(){
  //Unsubscribe from the event to clean up
  OnClicked -= Events_OnClicked;
}
```

 It's always a good idea to clean up after yourself and unsubscribe from the events when you no longer need them, as shown in the preceding code, using the -= syntax.

This is a very simple example, but you could imagine exposing an event for when an enemy is destroyed and hooking your score system into it so that the score is incremented every time an enemy dies.

A better way is to write a separate method to call when you need to trigger the event; refer to the following code. In this way, you don't have the preceding code repeated throughout:

```
//Safe method for calling the event
void Clicked(){
  //Trigger the event delegate if there is a subscriber
  if (OnClicked != null){
    OnClicked();
  }
}
```

Now, all you have to do whenever the event needs to be fired is call the Clicked method that is shown in the preceding code, which is always safe and won't crash if there are no subscribers.

As a help, this code is the template I always use when creating an event. To simplify its creation, all you have to do to use it each time is change the name, and if necessary, the delegate signature if you need additional parameters; the following code will tell you how to do this:

```
//Logging template to send a string/report every time something //happens
public delegate void LogMessage(string message);
public static event LogMessage Log;

void OnLog(string message){
  if (Log != null){
    Log(message);
  }
}
```

# Messaging

Communication is a key factor in any game. A lot of times, we just use colliders or physics to notify two components that there is something to be aware of. This is a very basic form of communication. Other times, we use referencing or (in the case of Unity) trawl through the project's Hierarchy to find another GameObject to communicate with or notify.

Unity has its own messaging-type functions, such as `SendMessage` and `BroadcastMessage`. Both functions actually implement event-style code (as in the preceding case) without actually declaring events, but they are very slow and shouldn't be used extensively.

The `SendMessage` function will call a named method on a GameObject (any method with the same name) with a *single* optional parameter as follows:

```
void OnCollisionEnter(Collision col)
{
  col.gameObject.SendMessage("IHitYou");
}
```

So, it will call the `IHitYou` method on whatever you will collide with. By default, this will not cause an error to be raised if whatever you collide with does not have the `IHitYou` method. However, if you wish, you can change this by adding `SendMessageOptions` when you call `SendMessage`, as follows:

```
void OnCollisionEnter(Collision col)
{
  col.gameObject.SendMessage("IHitYou",
SendMessageOptions.RequireReceiver);
}
```

If you want to send a value (there can only be one) with the call, just add it after the method name and before `SendMessageOptions` (if set).

The `BroadcastMessage` method works in a similar way but will attempt to run your selected method on the selected `gameObject` and *all* its children, as follows:

```
void OnCollisionEnter(Collision col)
{
  col.gameObject.BroadcastMessage("IHitYou");
}
```

Using either of the methods (as stated) is very slow. This is because it has to try and discover (under the hood) if the GameObject (and its children if using broadcast) has the method first; it will then attempt to run it. As Unity will not know until your game starts running and whether a GameObject will have that method, it has to perform this each and every time you try it.

# A better way

To break this dependency between the GameObjects and the need to keep references or the need to discover each other at the design or runtime stage, we need an intermediary that all objects know about, that is, a `Manager` class.

With this `Manager` class, it will manage the list of GameObjects that want to listen to the messages and provide an easy way to notify anyone who's listening.

To implement this, we will use the singleton behavior described earlier by creating three simple, reusable components as a test case.

 The `MessagingManager.cs`, `MessagingClientBroadcast.cs`, and `MessagingClientReceiver.cs` scripts created next will be used with our game.

First, we create the `Manager` class itself. So, create a `MessagingManager.cs` C# script and then replace its contents as follows:

```
using System;
using System.Collections.Generic;
using UnityEngine;

public class MessagingManager : MonoBehaviour
{
  //Static singleton property
  public static MessagingManager Instance { get; private set; }

  // public property for manager
  private List<Action> subscribers = new List<Action>();
}
```

The first property is the singleton instance for the `Manager` class, while the second is a list of delegates that will be used to keep track of who needs to be notified.

Next, we add the `Awake` function to initialize the singleton approach:

```
void Awake()
{
  Debug.Log("Messaging Manager Started");
  //First, we check if there are any other instances conflicting
  if (Instance != null && Instance != this)
  {
    //Destroy other instances if it's not the same
    Destroy(gameObject);
  }

  //Save our current singleton instance
  Instance = this;

  //Make sure that the instance is not destroyed between scenes
  //(this is optional)
  DontDestroyOnLoad(gameObject);
}
```

This is the same as before but with a little extra debug information, so you can see when it is initialized in the **Console** window.

Then, we add a method, so we can register recipients or subscribers to the messages (with the associated `UnSubscribe` and `ClearAllSubscribers` methods), as follows:

```
//The Subscribe method for manager
public void Subscribe(Action subscriber)
{
  Debug.Log("Subscriber registered");
  subscribers.Add(subscriber);
}

//The Unsubscribe method for manager
public void UnSubscribe(Action subscriber)
{
  Debug.Log("Subscriber registered");
  subscribers.Remove(subscriber);
}

//Clear subscribers method for manager
public void ClearAllSubscribers()
{
  subscribers.Clear();
}
```

This method just adds the delegate you passed to the `Manager` class to be added to the notification list.

Finally, we add a `Broadcast` method that tells the messaging system to let all the subscribers know that something has happened; the following code tells us how to do this:

```
public void Broadcast()
{
  Debug.Log("Broadcast requested, No of Subscribers = " +
subscribers.Count);
  foreach (var subscriber in subscribers)
  {
    subscriber();
  }
}
```

Here, we simply loop through all the subscribers and notify them using their delegates; very simple!

As you can see, this is just a very basic messenger that, when called, will tell anyone who is listening that something has happened; there will be no extra information, no details, just an event. This is like the fire alarm in your building; when it goes off, you just run, you don't (usually) ask, you don't question, you just know that when that alarm goes off, you need to get out of the building!

To finish this `Manager` class off, simply create an empty GameObject in your scene and add the script to it. There are ways to do this automatically, but I find this way to be cleaner so that you always know what the active agents in the scene are.

Putting this to use is simple. As mentioned before, we need three scripts; we have the `Manager` class, so now we need a client and a broadcast agent.

For the broadcast agent, create a C# script named `MessagingClientBroadcast` and replace its contents with the following code:

```
using UnityEngine;

public class MessagingClientBroadcast : MonoBehaviour {

  void OnCollisionEnter2D(Collision2D col)
  {
    MessagingManager.Instance.Broadcast();
  }
}
```

The preceding code is just a simple example so that when attached to an object with a 2D collider, it will trigger a broadcast. To test it, just add it to one or both of the border objects in our game scene. In this way, if the player tries to leave the scene, it will ring the alarm bells.

At the moment though, no one is listening, so let's add a listener/receiver. Create another C# script and name it `MessagingClientReceiver`. This script will register for events and log in to the **Console** window with some information about the object it's attached to (obviously, there will be no information from the broadcast event as it has none); the following code will tell you how to do this:

```
using UnityEngine;

public class MessagingClientReceiver : MonoBehaviour
{
  void Start()
  {
    MessagingManager.Instance.Subscribe(ThePlayerIsTryingToLeave);
  }

  void ThePlayerIsTryingToLeave()
  {
    Debug.Log("Oi Don't Leave me!! - " + tag.ToString());
  }
}
```

In simple words, when the GameObject script is attached to a startup, it will register itself with the `MessagingManager` script, telling the `Manager` class to run the second method in the script when the event occurs. As stated before, this just logs in to the **Console** window for now so that we have something to see.

Just for fun, also add this script to one or both of the borders in our scene; this is simply because we don't have anything else at the moment. You could add it to the player, making the event an alarm that goes off and changing the `ThePlayerIsTryingToLeave` method to cause the player to run in the opposite direction if you wish.

If you run the project now, you will get the following results:

- One message telling you that the `MessagingManager` script has started.
- One message per subscriber that has registered with the manager (although in the **Console** window, you may just see **2** next to the event because it is the same, if you have **Collapse** in the **Console** window selected).
- When the event is triggered, you will get one message per subscriber to tell you that they have received it. Note that each message from the client is particular to the GameObject you attached it to as the message is different.

Now, you could have just executed the preceding code using the `Send` or `Broadcast` Unity methods, and it would have been much simpler. However, you should note that since we are using a single `Manager` class, which is a static instance in the scene, at no point should any of the GameObjects involved need to know about each other. There is no need to search the Hierarchy or add components to each other at editing time; it just works.

# Background tasks and coroutines

Next up in the fabulous journey of scripting, we will cover the treacherous realm of background tasks. We use the background tasks to start something (in the background) so that it runs independently of the normal game update and draw cycle.

The following diagram shows that we can have a second process that runs alongside our main game:

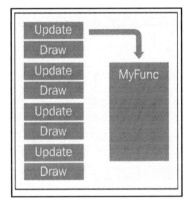

This is usually used for systems that are continually running and not for the main events on the screen, such as AI, a background trading system, or even a continual webservice gathering data for the game.

Unity also has the ability to synchronize these background threads with a simple function that pauses the operation (or returns the control back to Unity) until the next frame of the game is drawn (`WaitForEndOfFrame` or `WaitForFixedUpdate`), which gives you a pattern similar the following diagram:

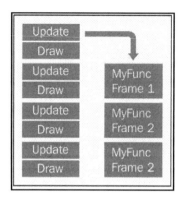

The benefit of this is that you can wait for the last update or draw cycle to finish before running your process. You might do this if you want to render what is drawn on the screen to an image, and either save it to a disk or upload it to a web service or website.

 The Unity documents provide a good example of using this behavior; you can find them at `https://docs.unity3d.com/Documentation/ScriptReference/WaitForEndOfFrame.html`.

# Enter coroutines

The proper way to implement long-running tasks in Unity is through the use of a feature called **coroutines**. In simple words, coroutines are Unity's way of launching code in the background, but they do have a few caveats and features around them, though.

 Coroutines, by default, run on the same thread as the normal game loop. If you are not careful, they can stop your game from running.

For more information on coroutines and the default execution order of methods, refer to the article in the Unity docs at `https://docs.unity3d.com/Documentation/Manual/ExecutionOrder.html`.

Coroutines are also helpful for creating functions that you want to trigger after a set amount of seconds.

# IEnumerator

At their core, coroutines are just normal methods, but they are implemented using a particular generic interface named IEnumerator as their return type. This enables Unity to track the method's state through several iterations (runs).

Don't confuse IEnumerator with IEnumerable when defining your coroutines; otherwise, you will find that they won't work.

To create a basic coroutine, you simply need to set up the method shown in the following code:

```
IEnumerator MyCoroutine()
{
  //Do something
  //Then return
  yield return null;

}
```

This creates a simple single-use coroutine that performs a single function, and when it's finished, it will die and go away.

A more common pattern is to have a loop of some kind within the function that will not finish until some condition is met; this is done by either using a while or for loop as follows:

```
IEnumerator MyCoroutine (){
  bool complete = false;
  while (!complete)
  {
    //Do some repetitive task
    //When done set complete to true

    //Then return control after each step
    yield return null;
  }
}
```

The preceding code will simply run in the background until the condition is met; for example, a timer that is counting down should stop when it reaches 0.

# Yielding

The `yield` operator suspends the current method on the current instruction line until the operation is complete; however, it also allows the CPU to continue between each result that is returned by the called method or the instruction. The following example will pause the loop for 2 seconds between the iterations while returning the control back to the process.

Here's an example; say we have a function to print 10 lines:

```
IEnumerator Print10Lines()
{
  for (int i = 0; i < 10; i++)
  {
    print("Line" + i.ToString());
    yield return new WaitForSeconds(2);
  }
}
```

When the preceding code runs, it will simply loop 10 times, and each time it will print out the line number. However, before continuing, it will wait for 2 seconds.

> Do not confuse `IEnumerator` with `IEnumerable`. coroutines and the `yield` keyword only work in a method that returns an `IEnumerator` feature. This is an easy mistake that can leave you scratching your head for hours.

# Starting coroutines

There are actually two types of coroutine (it is best to think of them in that way, even though they are actually the same thing): those that are just launched (`fire` and `forget`) and those that can be managed. The difference is just in the way they are called. The `fire` and `forget` coroutine functions are simply called using the following code:

```
StartCoroutine(MyCoroutine()); //or
StartCoroutine(MyCoroutine(MyParameter)); //to use parameters
```

In the preceding code, the `MyCoroutine` function is started using the `delegate` method. Once started, it will not finish until either the function ends or `StopAllCoroutines()` is called. Now, start the coroutine using the following code:

```
StartCoroutine("MyCoroutine"); //or
StartCoroutine("MyCoroutine", myParameter); //to use parameters
```

In the preceding code, you specify the name of your coroutine function and the method's name using a string. This enables you to stop the coroutine from running any time (and from anywhere) using the following code:

```
StopCoroutine("MyCoroutine");
```

The invocation path is something to be kept in mind. You might ask why not just use the second method all the time. The answer is simple. Unity has to use slower methods to discover the method it needs to track when you provide the coroutine's name as a string; just passing the method's name is quicker and smoother. The best advice would be to use each type according to its strengths. Only use the string launch method when you need to manage a background task and use the method names when it is a short-lived function that is solely aimed at accomplishing a single task. For everything else, just weigh up the pros and cons of each approach as you implement it.

Coroutines can be powerful additions to the arsenal of your game's framework, but they need to be implemented wisely; too many additions to your game (obviously) will just grind it to a halt. If you only ever use the `fire` and `forget` coroutines, you won't be able to stop them without shutting down all the rest as well (including those you started by naming them as a string).

# Closing the gap

So now that we understand how we call coroutines, to make the `Print10Lines` method described earlier, we will call it as follows:

```
void Example1()
{
  StartCoroutine(Print10Lines());
  print("I started printing lines");
}
```

As explained, the preceding code will kick off the `Print10Lines` function and then continue forward while the routing to print the lines continues simultaneously. On the other hand, the following code will print 10 lines, and only after it is finished will it continue and notify you that printing has finished:

```
IEnumerator Example2()
{
  yield return StartCoroutine(Print10Lines());
  print("I have finished printing lines");
}
```

Any method that has a return type of IEnumerator has to be called using one of the StartCoroutine methods; just calling any method with IEnumerator on its own will do nothing. So, keep this in mind if you are wondering why something is not being called.

# Serialization and scripting

To finish with our theory for this chapter, we need to cover serialization in Unity. Now, Unity already serializes just about everything from the editor to your scene automatically (with a few exceptions) when it saves and loads the scene.

There are a few fringe cases where Unity will not serialize some data. These cases have to do with the current limitations of the Mono 2 framework that Unity uses under the hood. A full explanation of what doesn't work can be found in the following article; note that it is very technical and includes a link to the error report in Unity where it is recorded:

http://www.codingjargames.com/blog/2012/11/30/advanced-unity-serialization/

However, what if we want to actually use this serialization to our advantage within our game to save and load levels. We need bits of raw game data (or as we will continue with this later, saving conversations for our NPCs). To accomplish this, the best way is to use a Unity-inherited object named ScriptableObject.

The ScriptableObject entity allows you to save the data within the class that uses it for an .asset file in your project.

# Saving and managing asset data

To achieve this, we simply need to create a script (named ScriptingObjects) with some properties we want to serialize; then, we change its class inheritance from MonoBehaviour to ScriptableObject as follows:

```
using UnityEngine;
public class ScriptingObjects : ScriptableObject {
  public Vector2[] MyPositions;
}
```

Great! So we have some serializable data. However, to use it in the editor, we need to create an option in the editor to create and save these assets for us. Create a new folder called `Editor` under `Assets\Scripts`.

Create a new script named `PositionManager` in the `Assets\Scripts\Editor` folder, and replace its contents with the following code:

```
using UnityEngine;
using UnityEditor;

public class PositionManager : MonoBehaviour
{
  //Define a menu option in the editor to create the new asset
  [MenuItem("Assets/Create/PositionManager")]
  public static void CreateAsset()
  {
    //Create a new instance of our scriptable object
    ScriptingObjects positionManager =
      ScriptableObject.CreateInstance<ScriptingObjects>();

    //Create a .asset file for our new object and save it
    AssetDatabase.CreateAsset(positionManager,
      "Assets/newPositionManager.asset");
    AssetDatabase.SaveAssets();

    //Now switch the inspector to our new object
    EditorUtility.FocusProjectWindow();
    Selection.activeObject = positionManager;
  }
}
```

 Any script that uses the `UnityEditor` namespace has to be placed in a special `Editor` folder. This ensures that it is only packaged with the editor solution and not used in the deployed game. Game projects are not deployed with the editor.

There is a lot to explain about the preceding code, but it is all commented very well. In short, the code works as follows:

- We define a menu option from where we will call our creation code
- We set up a new object that we want to serialize and create the file where it is to be stored
- We change the view of the editor to focus the inspector on the new object

If you create custom classes to be used in serialization, you must tag those classes with the `[System.Serializable]` attribute. Otherwise, Unity will not know that they are for serialization. We will cover more on this later in the implemented example.

If you return to Unity now and right-click on the `Asset` folder (or click on the **Create** menu option in the **Project** view), you will see the new menu option you just created, as shown in the following screenshot:

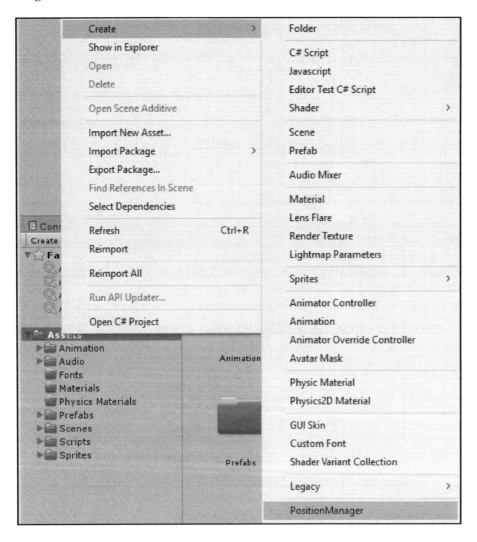

After clicking on it, you will see your new asset in the **Project** view (in the location you saved it to, in this case, the root of the `Asset` folder) and the **Inspector** view for your item, as shown in the following screenshot:

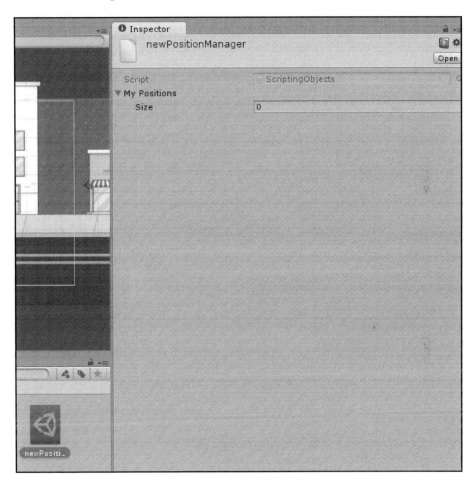

If we rename our new serialized object, give it some values, and save the scene or project, we will see the following screenshot:

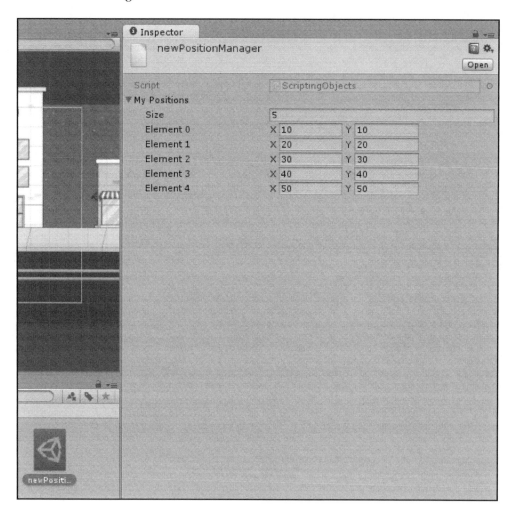

We go from the preceding screenshot to the following code stored in the `.asset` file (when opened from the `.asset` file generated in Unity from **File Explorer**):

```
%YAML 1.1
%TAG !u! tag:unity3d.com,2011:
--- !u!114 &11400000
MonoBehaviour:
  m_ObjectHideFlags: 0
  m_PrefabParentObject: {fileID: 0}
  m_PrefabInternal: {fileID: 0}
  m_GameObject: {fileID: 0}
  m_Enabled: 1
  m_EditorHideFlags: 0
  m_Script: {fileID: 11500000, guid: fa9c23f7a21df484a96802b68617f3b6,
type: 3}
  m_Name: MyPositions1
  m_EditorClassIdentifier:
  MyPositions:
  - {x: 10, y: 10}
  - {x: 20, y: 20}
  - {x: 30, y: 30}
  - {x: 30, y: 30}
  - {x: 40, y: 40}
```

There is a fair amount of Unity information in the preceding code, but what is important is our serialized data at the bottom. So, if we wish, we can edit this file outside of the editor and it will be reimported next time you open Unity.

# Using the serialized files in the editor

Using the files in the editor is a very simple task. Simply create a property in any script using the type of your serialized asset and then assign a project asset in the editor.

For example, edit the `MessagingManager` script and add the following property:

```
public ScriptingObjects MyWaypoints;
```

Then, the script will be exposed in the **Inspector** pane and you can assign it normally, as shown in the following screenshot:

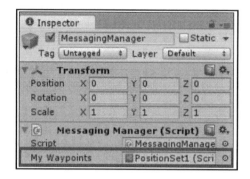

You will also be able to access the contents of the serialized object from that script as well.

 You cannot edit the contents of the serialized file in the assigned property by default. This is only achievable using a custom property inspector. However, it is still editable in the editor by opening the Asset folder.

# Accessing the .asset files in the code

Now, if you don't want to assign the asset through the editor, there is a way to just load the .asset file directly from the project.

Firstly, to do this, you will need to store your .asset files in a special folder named Resources in your Asset folder. You can read them there directly using Unity's own resource functions once.

As an example, open the PositionManager script and add the following function:

```
public static PositionManager ReadPositionsFromAsset(string Name)
{
  string path = "/";

  object o = Resources.Load(path + Name);
  PositionManager retrievedPositions = (PositionManager)o;
  return retrievedPositions;
}
```

This function, which is available from anywhere as it is static, will perform the following tasks:

- Using the `Name` parameter, it will read the `.asset` file from the root of the `Resources` folder
- It will convert the retrieved file to the correct object type
- It will return the deserialized object to the calling function

Now you can call up the data contained within your `.asset` file anywhere in your game project.

The same kind of pattern can also be used to download the `.asset` files from the Web for your project to add DLC or expand the levels of your game. A word to the wise, though; if you do go down this route, be sure to compress and encrypt your assets that are meant for downloading to protect your IP.

Also, if you have any dependent files, such as images, be sure to download them separately.

However, to use the downloaded files as assets in your scene, you will require them to be packaged as asset bundles.

# Adding NPCs and a conversation system to our game

Right, after all of that *brain input*, let's start applying it to our game. In this chapter, we are aiming to add an NPC to our scene that will interact with the player.

Before moving forward, we should also do with a little tidying up of our `Scripts` folder, since we are generating a lot more content now. To do this, perform the following steps:

- Under `Assets\Scripts`, create three new folders: `Classes`, `Messaging`, and `Navigation`.
- Copy the `Entity` and `Player` scripts to the new `Classes` folder or create them if you haven't already.

- You may delete all of the files created in this chapter (or place them in an `Examples` folder) except `MessagingManager.cs`, `MessagingClientBroadcast.cs`, and `MessagingClientReceiver.cs` as we will use those shortly.

- If you created the `Messaging` scripts, move the `Messaging` to the `Messaging` folder, and likewise, the `Navigation` scripts to the `Navigation` folder.

In `Chapter 4`, *The Town View*, we added the street, sidewalk, and sky to the scene. Included in the `buildingsAndRoads.png` sprite sheet were some buildings as well. If you have not already done so, import the hospital, the shop, and the town hall in to the scene. When you do so, make sure you set their Sorting Layer to Background so that they will display properly.

You can place the hospital and shop wherever you want; just makes sure you place their entrances between your **LeftBorder** and **RightBorder**. I scaled the hospital down a bit to place it in my scene. In `Chapter 11`, *Shopping for Items*, we will allow the character to enter the shop so that she can go shopping for inventory items. Place the town hall toward the **LeftBorder** so that the Mayor, when standing in front of the building, can act as a gatekeeper for that **exit**.

The following screenshot demonstrates the way I laid out my town's buildings:

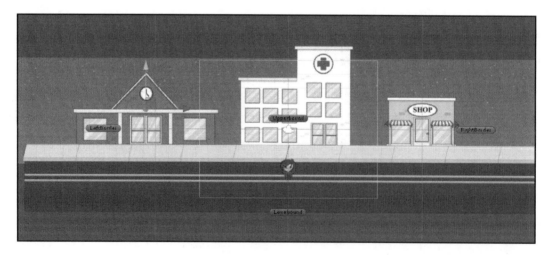

The sprite sheets for three NPCs are included with the book files: `Doctor.png`, `Mayor.png`, and `Shopkeep.png`:

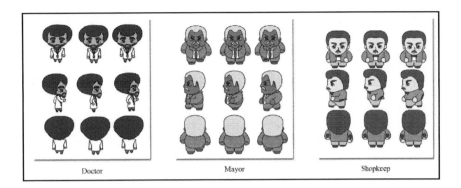

You can import all three of these sprite sheets into the project, set their sprite mode to **Multiple**, and **Automatically Slice** each with the pivot set to Bottom now, but we will only use the Mayor character in this chapter. We will use the Shopkeep NPC in `Chapter 11`, *Shopping for Items*, when we start discussing inventory.

 By now, you should be a pro at slicing sprite sheets, but if not, refer to the steps presented in `Chapter 2`, *Building Your Project and Character*, that we used to import the player character.

Also, since the player and the Mayor will be conversing, import the `MayorFace.png` images and `PlayerFace.png` as single sprite images:

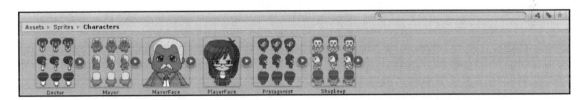

We need to add some personality to our NPCs as well as our hero. In `Chapter 2`, *Building Your Character and Project*, we outlined some classes to describe and manage the entities in the game, so let's bring them in now.

Add the Mayor to the left-hand side of the scene, next to the LeftBorder and in front of the town hall door. We are placing him here because in the next section, he is going to stop our hero from going further in this direction, as it is just too dangerous for such an impetuous youth.

To do this (using the lessons you have learned already), perform the following steps:

1. If you haven't done so already, import the Mayor.png character sprite sheet and use **Sprite Editor** to slice it up.
2. Drag the sprite labeled Mayor_1 (the one of the Major facing forward) in to the scene in front of the town hall.
3. Rename the new GameObject created Mayor.
4. In the **Sprite Renderer** component, set the Sorting Layer to **Middleground**.
5. Finally, add a **Box Collider 2D** component with the settings shown in the following screenshot. This is so that the collider is of the same width as that of the Mayor but with a larger height so that the player will collide with it whenever she walks in front of him. Also, set the **Is Trigger** property to true/checked.

The final result will look something like the following screenshot:

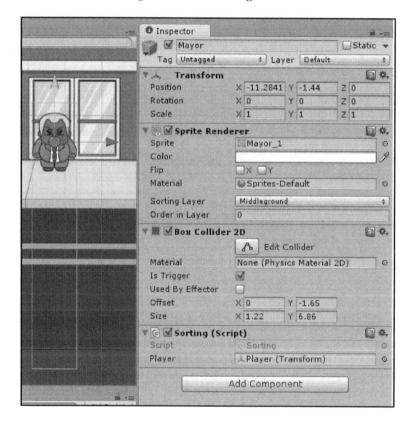

# Let the player walk around the NPC

Currently, when the player walks behind the Mayor, she appears behind him, but when she walks in front of him, she also appears behind him!

Set the Mayer's **Order in Layer** under the **Sprite Renderer** component to –1. This will make the player (whose sorting order is set to 0) always appear to be in front of the Mayor:

But this still doesn't work! Now, when she walks behind the Mayor, she still appears in front of him!, as shown in the following screenshot:

To fix this, we will have to use (you guessed it!) code.

Create a new C# script in your Assets/Scripts folder, and call it Sorting.cs:

```
using UnityEngine;
using System.Collections;
public class Sorting : MonoBehaviour {
    public Transform player;
    // Update is called once per frame
    void Update () {
        if(transform.position.y>=player.transform.position.y){
            Debug.Log("behind player");
            GetComponent<SpriteRenderer>().sortingOrder =
                (player.GetComponent<SpriteRenderer>().sortingOrder)-1;
        }
        if(transform.position.y<player.transform.position.y){
            Debug.Log("in front of player");
            GetComponent<SpriteRenderer>().sortingOrder =
                (player.GetComponent<SpriteRenderer>().sortingOrder)+1;
        }
    }
}
```

The preceding code will continually check the position of the player versus the position of the object on which this code is attached. It will then move the object in front of or behind the Player through the sorting order.

For this code to work properly your player and Mayor must both have their pivot points (determined when you sliced their sprite sheets) set to bottom. So, if the code does not work correctly for you, check their pivot points.

Attach the script to the Mayor and then drag the Player to the `Player` slot, as shown in the following image:

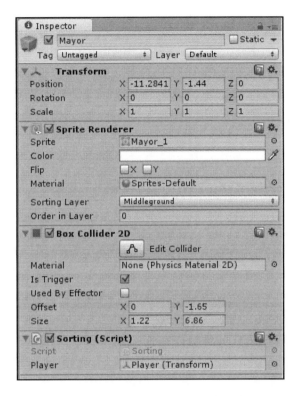

In the preceding screenshot, I reset the Mayor's **Order in Layer** to 0, but it really does not matter what it is set to, as the `Sorting.cs` script will override the value.

You can use this Sorting.cs script on other objects you want the player to walk around. But, be warned, if you have objects in the scene in the Middleground layer that only appear appropriately with specific sorting orders, the script will remove those sorting orders.

# Stopping the player from walking through the NPC

So, the player can walk circles around the Mayor (no pun intended), but she can also walk straight through him. To stop this, we are going to use a `Box Collider 2D` componet.

Currently, we have a `Box Collider 2D` component attached to the Mayor, but it has **Is Trigger** set to true. The box collider will be used to trigger a dialog box, but it does not actually stop her from passing through it.

The thing that makes this difficult, is we cannot actually use one Box Collider 2D to stop her from passing through the character, if we want her to still be able to walk around him. To demonstrate what I mean, add a standard box collider to the Mayor that encompasses his whole sprite:

This is going to cause the player to stop before she even really appears to get close to him and it is going to stop all of the fancy stuff we did in the previous section with sorting order from even being apparent.

So, to fix this, we are actually going to add two new `Box Collider 2D` components to the Mayor and we are going to turn them on and off depending on where the player is in relation to the Mayor, similar to the way we handled the sorting order.

Add the two Box Collider 2D Components with the following properties:

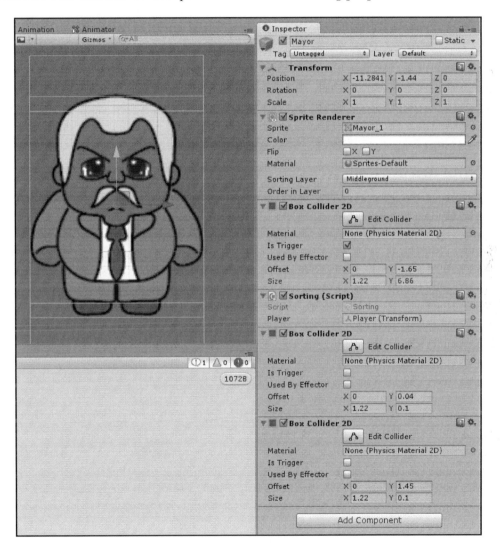

I hid the town hall and the sidewalk in the previous screenshot so that you could more easily see the colliders in the image.

Now, we are going to update our Sorting.cs script so that it turns these Box Collider 2D components on and off based on the player's position.

Adjust your Sorting.cs script so that it reads as follows:

```
if(transform.position.y>=player.transform.position.y){
    Debug.Log("behind player");
    GetComponent<SpriteRenderer>().sortingOrder =
        (player.GetComponent<SpriteRenderer>().sortingOrder)-1;
    GetComponents<BoxCollider2D>()[1].enabled=false;
    GetComponents<BoxCollider2D>()[2].enabled=true;
}
if(transform.position.y<player.transform.position.y){
    Debug.Log("in front of player");
    GetComponent<SpriteRenderer>().sortingOrder =
        (player.GetComponent<SpriteRenderer>().sortingOrder)+1;
    GetComponents<BoxCollider2D>()[1].enabled=true;
    GetComponents<BoxCollider2D>()[2].enabled=false;
}
```

Let's look more closely at the code that reads GetComponents<BoxCollider2D>()[1] and GetComponents<BoxCollider2D>()[2].

Since we had more than one **Box Collider 2D** component attached to the Mayor, to enable and disable the specific ones we wanted, we had to use GetCompoents. The brackets after the parentheses state which BoxCollider2D we wanted to access. This is because GetComponents returns an array and the first one (in order from top to bottom) in the Inspector is at **index 0** of the array, the second at **index 1** of the array, and so on. The following screenshot demonstrates this point:

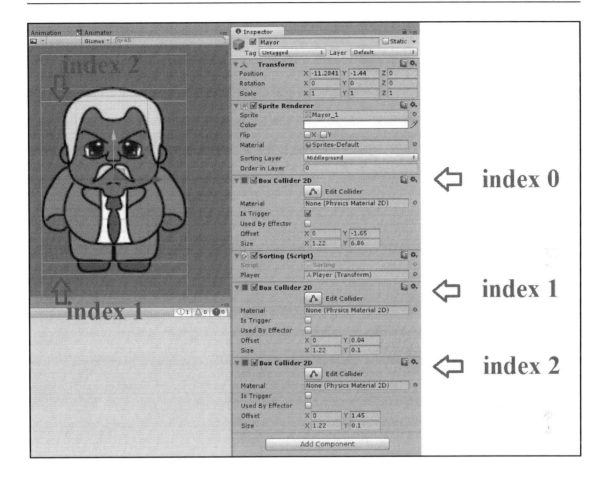

# Getting the NPCs talking

So far in this chapter, we have our town populated with characters and buildings. Now, let's give our hero something to talk about.

While building a conversation system for any game, there are many factors to consider, which are as follows:

- How long a conversation is going to be (we don't want the player to get bored with miles of text)?
- How many parties are likely to be involved in any discussion?
- Is this a flat one-sided conversation (such as a cutscene), or will the player be allowed to make decisions?

- Are there going to be branches in the conversation so that the conversation will change based on the player's response?
- How much content do you expect to be used in conversations ( text, video, cutscenes, animation, and so on)? All of this content will decide just how extensible your system needs to be.
- Will the conversation need to support any outbound triggers or states? Will the conclusion of a conversation unlock a door or grant the player some experience or items?

There are lots of other factors that will affect both the design and implementation of a robust conversation for your game, so think about it carefully before touching the code.

 For this book, we are going to build a basic conversation system that is enough to meet the goals of the project at hand. However, I am explaining each part along the way, so if you want to expand on it, you can.

## The conversation object

When we want to start talking in the game, we first need to decide what you want to include in the conversation. You can include the following things:

- The name of the character who is speaking
- The text of the conversation
- An image of the character talking
- Choices
- The position of the chat

The more you look at it, the more you can dream about what you want to include. You just need to remember the **KISS** principle (**Keep it simple, stupid**), that is, start small and then build on it.

So, create a new C# script, name it `ConversationEntry` in `Assets\Scripts\Classes`, and populate it with the following code:

```csharp
using UnityEngine;

[System.Serializable]
public class ConversationEntry {
    public string SpeakingCharacterName;
    public string ConversationText;
    public Sprite DisplayPic;
```

```
}
```

This gives us just the basics for our conversation system with regards to who's speaking—an optional picture that can be displayed in the conversation and most importantly, the conversation text to be displayed.

We also tag this class with the `System.Serializable` code attribute so that the Unity serializer knows what to do with it.

## Saving and serializing the object for later

With our core conversation entry object generated, we can start to store the conversations in the `.asset` files for use in our game and also make it possible to create the conversations outside of Unity if you wish.

As a conversation is (usually) more than just an opening line, we need a management object that will support several lines/entries of the conversation and a couple of switches to denote whether the conversation has already been played. This way, if you have multiple conversations configured for a character, it will simply play the next conversation and not repeat itself. You could just track this on the object that you attach the conversations to, but this is cleaner.

> As a rule of thumb, you should always keep flags, settings, or properties for a thing with another thing. If you start having variables to track the state of a thing elsewhere, it can get very messy. The only time this is not true is when a thing is meant to be shared across multiple objects.

> Also note that the `ScriptableObject` entities are a fickle beast. They let us attach them to the GameObjects, and they can be automatically serialized and saved as part of the project. However, they are fixed assets that should only be edited in the editor. If you need to alter them as part of the game, you will need to save and store that change of state separately.

> This is just a simple note to remember when architecting such things.

So, create another C# class in `Scripts\Classes` named `Conversation` and populate it with the following code:

```
using UnityEngine;

public class Conversation : ScriptableObject {

    public ConversationEntry[] ConversationLines;
```

```
}
```

Now, the first thing you will note is that this class is derived from a scriptable object class. As described earlier, this is what enables us to use Unity's serialization methods and store them as an `.asset` file.

We are not done yet as we need that final hook to enable us to create these (at least initially) in the editor.

Earlier, I showed you all of the code needed to create the asset for serialization, but this is rather a lot of code to be generated all the time. So, it's better to place that logic in a separate helper class that we can reuse rather than repeat ourselves all the time.

Earlier, with the `PositionManager` example, we created assets in the editor and reused them. You can reuse this code if you wish, but to simplify things, I added a little helper script to the example project in `Assets\Scripts\Editor` called `CustomAssetUtility.cs`.

The `CustomAssetUtility` class does all the work that the preceding code does. It also uses the C# generics so that it can be reused for any type of `SerializableObject` you want to throw at it. You don't have to use the class I provided; you can just use the code earlier instead if you wish; just replace the code where the helper function is used.

If you have not done so already, create a new folder in `Assets\Scripts` named `Editor`, get the `CustomAssetUtility` class, and place it in the `Assets\Scripts\Editor` folder.

 C# generics is a fairly advanced C# topic, which we won't go into in this book. If you want to know more, check out `http://msdn.microsoft.com/en-us/library/ms379564(v=vs.80).aspx`; alternatively, it will be better to try *The C# Programming Yellow Book, Rob Miles, Department of Computer Science, The University of Hull*, which is a fantastic C# primer book available at `http://www.robmiles.com/c-yellow-book/`.

To show how we use this, let's create our editor script, which will create the conversation assets for us. Create a new script named `ConversationAssetCreator` in the `Editor` folder under `Assets\Scripts` and then replace its contents with the following code:

```
using UnityEditor;
using UnityEngine;

public class ConversationAssetCreator : MonoBehaviour {

    [MenuItem("Assets/Create/Conversation")]
```

```
public static void CreateAsset()
{
  CustomAssetUtility.CreateAsset<Conversation>();
}
}
```

 Remember, any script that uses the `UnityEditor` namespace has to be placed in a special `Editor` folder. This ensures that it is only packaged with the editor solution and not used in the deployed game. Game projects are not deployed with the editor.

So, by using the helper function, instead of all the tangle of code to first generate our asset and then save it, we simply call our utility, tell it the type of asset we want to create (in angle brackets), and away it goes. I have crated the utility as well, so it can also take a string parameter if you want to force the folder you want to create the asset in; otherwise, it will take whatever is currently selected in the editor.

To test this out, create a new folder in the `Asset` folder named `Resources` (so, we can call assets directly from the code if we so wish) and then create another folder in `Resources` named `Conversations`:

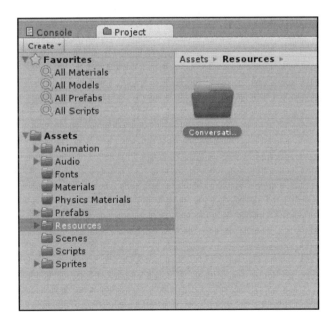

This just keeps all our conversations in one place and doesn't clutter up the hierarchy. If you wish, you could create further subfolders to identify characters, places, or whatever else you fancy. It won't have an impact on the running of the game; it will just keep it tidy.

With the `Conversation` folder under `Assets\Resources\` selected, click on **Create** in the **Project** menu. You will see a new option named **Conversation** (as you can see in the script earlier, this is what we named it):

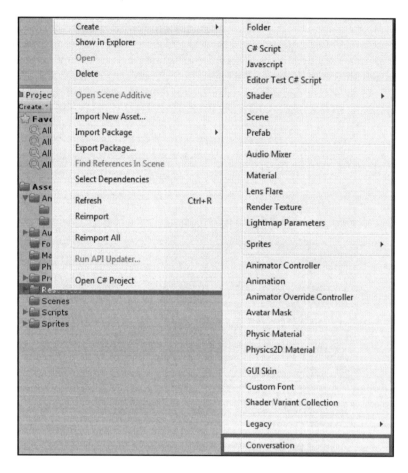

When you click on it, a new **Conversation** asset will appear, as shown in the following screenshot, which is ready for you to start configuring:

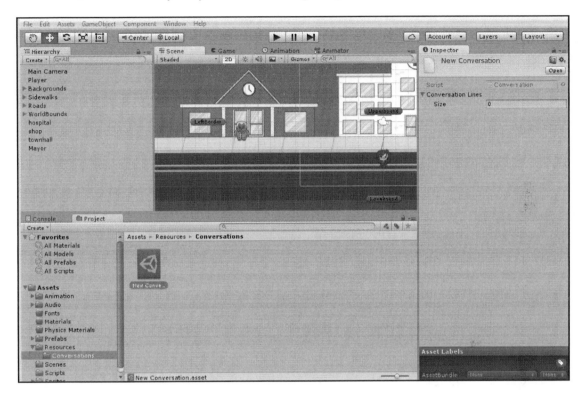

Name the conversation`MayorWarning` and give it the lines and images shown in the following screenshot:

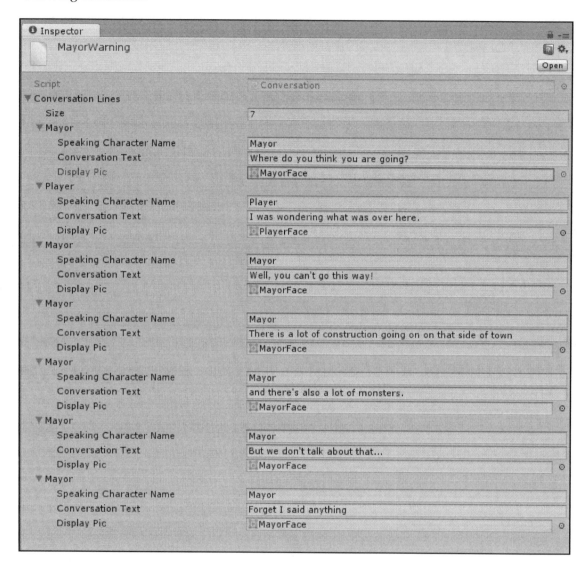

# The conversation component

The last thing we need is a simple component that enables us to attach conversations to a character or other GameObject.

So, create a new class in the `Assets\Scripts\Classes` folder named `ConversationComponent` and replace its contents with the following code:

```
using UnityEngine;
public class ConversationComponent : MonoBehaviour {
    public Conversation[] Conversations;
}
```

Nothing's complicated for now; the preceding code just holds an array of the possible conversations that the GameObject can have. Ideally, you would want to expand on this for a fuller conversation system, such as a pointer to the next conversation, or a way to track how many conversations have taken place, and so on.

# Building a basic conversation system

In order for our conversation assets to be of any use, we need a mechanism to play these conversations on the screen and have the user interact with them (if that's how your game rolls). For this, we need another manager that will take in conversations from characters and display them on the screen. If we had any logic, branching, or decisions in our conversations, it would handle those too.

Now, there are two basic approaches that we could take with the conversation system: one being reactive (where we use a messaging system to notify the manager that a conversation needs to take place) and one being just a utility (where scripts can request for a conversation to take place). Both are valid approaches, and it really comes down to personal preference as to which one you want to implement. To keep things simple, let's create the basic utility first and then point out where it can be enhanced.

## The manager

If we create our conversation manager as we did before with the messaging manager, we start with the simple singleton framework. However, we will lean on one of the great examples from **Unity Wiki** as our base.

In the sample project under the `Assets\Scripts\Classes folder,` you will find a
`Singleton` class that was sourced from `http://wiki.unity3d.com/index.php/Singleton.`
This simply saves us time and code while creating singleton objects for use in our games
and ensures they always have the same consistency. Get this script and place it in your
`Assets\Scripts\Classes` folder.

> Make sure you get the `Singleton.cs` script and put it in your project or
> the following `CoversationManager.cs` script will not work.

With this in place, we can define our `Conversation` manager quite simply. Create a new
C# script in `Assets\Scripts` named `ConversationManager` and replace its contents with
the following code:

```
using System.Collections;
using UnityEngine;

public class ConversationManager : Singleton<ConversationManager>
{
  //Guarantee this will always be a singleton only -
  //can't use the constructor!
  protected ConversationManager () {}

}
```

Now that we have our manager, we can start adding functionality to it.

## Starting a conversation

We want our manager to take one of our conversation items and do something with it
because we have a manager. So, create a new function as follows:

```
public void StartConversation(Conversation conversation)
{}
```

This enables us to start a new conversation anywhere in the code using the following code:

```
ConversationManager.Instance.StartConversation(conversation);
```

# Preparing the UI

The manager is in place and we have a method to start a conversation, but it's not doing much right now. We will use the built in UI functionality discussed in Chapter 5, *Working with Unity's UI System.*

When the player walks in front of the Mayor, we are going to have a pop-up window display the conversation that ensues. To achieve this, we will create a panel that holds the text and image from the conversation we just set up.

To begin, create a Canvas, by navigating to **Create** I **UI** I **Canvas**:

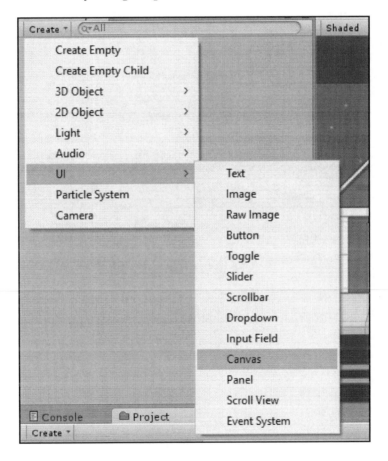

When you create the Canvas, the Event System is also automatically created. To keep my hierarchy nice and tidy, I prefer to drag this on to the canvas so that it becomes a child of the canvas, as shown in the following screenshot:

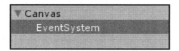

Now, we are going to use a panel to serve as the window in which the dialog appears.

Right-click on the canvas, and select **UI | Panel**. To view the panel and the Canvas, double-click on the panel in the hierarchy.

You will see something like this:

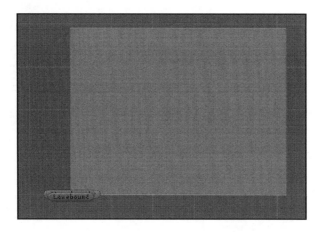

When initially created, the panel appears as a semi-translucent rectangle that fills the entire area of the Canvas. Rename the panel **Dialog Box**.

Now, let's make it a bit smaller. Start by setting the **Anchor** and **Pivot Point** to center-middle, by holding down *Alt + Shift* and selecting the middle-most **Anchor Presets**.

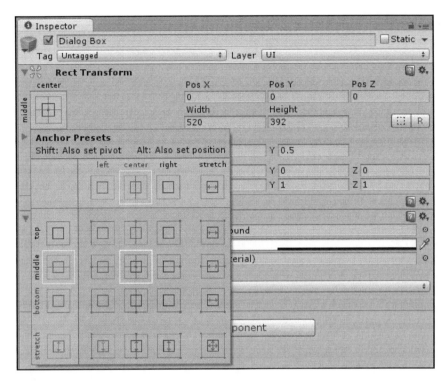

Now, change the width and height of the **Rect Transform** component to 300 and 100, respectively:

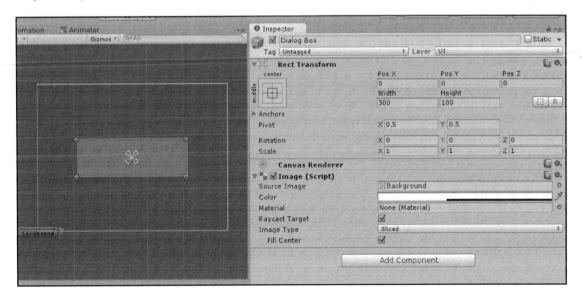

If you press play, you should now see a greyed box permanently in the center of the screen. Don't worry, we will make it go away shortly.

Now, let's add a place for the image and text to appear. Right-click on the panel, and select **UI | Image**. Then right-click on the panel, and select **UI | Text.** You will see the following:

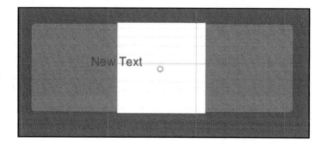

We are going to now make the image appear on the left side of the dialog box and the text on the right. We also want them to stretch to the height of the box.

Let's start with the image. Rename it **Speaker Image**. Change the **Rect Transform** settings of the image so that they appear as shown in the following screenshot. Also, in the **Image** component, select **Preserve Aspect Ratio**:

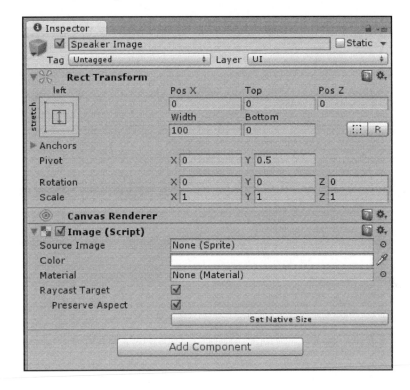

Now, rename the text **Dialog Text**. Also, change the **Rect Transform** settings and the **Text** component settings so that they appear, as shown in the following screenshot:

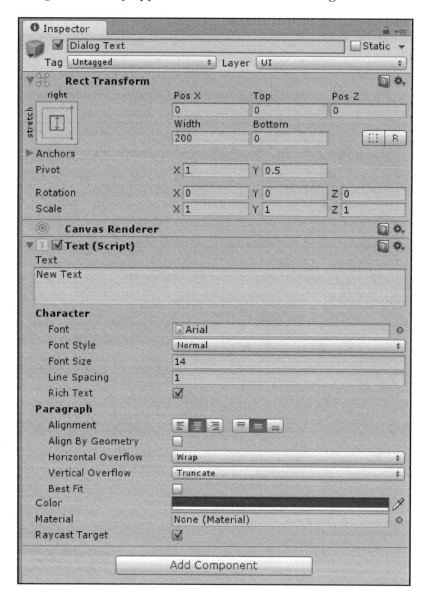

Your panel will now appear as follows:

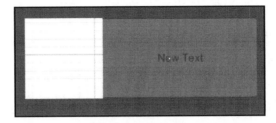

Let's also change the image settings of the dialog box so that it is slightly more opaque as, right now, it is a little difficult to see. Select the white box next to the **Color** property on the **Image** component of the dialog box. Increase the **A** (alpha) value to around **230**, so the box will still be slightly transparent:

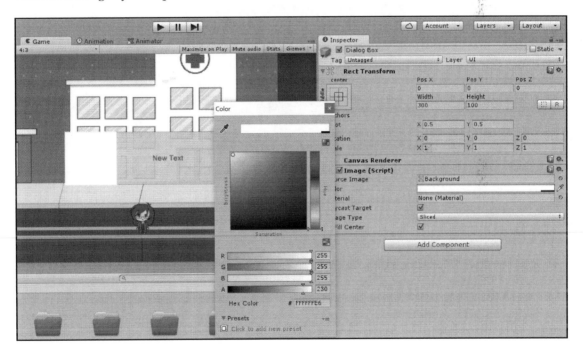

We are now done setting up our panel so that it can hold the image and text. Now, all we need to do is make it not appear permanently on the screen. To do this, we will add a new component to the panel, the **Canvas Group** component. In the **Dialog Box**'s Inspector, select **Add Component** | **Layout** | **Canvas Group**.

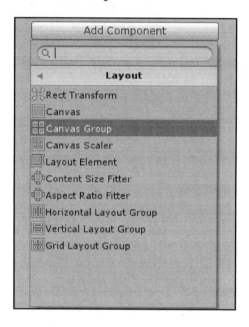

The Canvas Group will allow us to affect the alpha, intractability, and blocks raycast settings of the panel. Change the settings of the Canvas Group so that they appear as follows:

Now, you should no longer see the **Dialog Box** in the scene, since we set its alpha to 0.

For now, we are done working with the UI and will do everything else via code. Don't worry, though, you will get more practice with the UI systems, as we will use the UI system more in nearly every chapter from here on out.

# Displaying the conversation

Now, let's add some simple logic to display the text of the conversation on the screen.

Starting things off, we need some new properties in ConversationManager to control what needs to be displayed. So, open up the ConversationManager script and add the following properties to it:

```
//Is there a converastion going on
bool talking = false;

//The current line of text being displayed
ConversationEntry currentConversationLine;

//the Canvas Group for the dialog box
public CanvasGroup dialogBox;

//the image holder
public Image imageHolder;

//the text holder
public Text textHolder;
```

Each property explains its use, but everything will become clear as we add the rest of the functionality.

To use the UI properties, we must add the following line at the top of the script:

```
using UnityEngine.UI;
```

Next, we'll add a coroutine that will take a Conversation object and loop through all the lines to be displayed. Add the following function to the ConversationManager script:

```
IEnumerator DisplayConversation(Conversation conversation)
{
    talking = true;
    foreach (var conversationLine in conversation.ConversationLines)
    {
        currentConversationLine = conversationLine;
        textHolder.text = currentConversationLine.ConversationText;
        imageHolder.sprite = currentConversationLine.DisplayPic;
        yield return new WaitForSeconds(3);
    }
    talking = false;
}
```

This simple coroutine takes the conversation passed to it and loops through each of the individual lines of the conversation's text. Before we start, we set the `talking` flag to denote that a conversation is in progress; then, for each conversation line, we perform the following tasks:

- Set a pointer to the current conversation item in the list with the `currentConversationLine` property
- Add the text and image to the text and image holders
- Wait for three seconds before moving on to the next conversation item
- When we run out of conversation lines, we set the `talking` flag to `false` to show that we have finished

So, we have a coroutine looping through the text. The next thing to do is to use this information to display it on the screen. For this, we need an `OnGUI` method in our scripts as follows:

```
void OnGUI()
{
    if (talking)
    {
        dialogBox.alpha = 1;
        dialogBox.blocksRaycasts = true;
    }
    else{
        dialogBox.alpha = 0;
        dialogBox.blocksRaycasts = false;
    }
}
```

Remember when we set up the dialog box, we set its alpha to 0 and made it so that it would not block raycasts. Now, we will turn the alpha and ability to block raycast back on when `talking` is true and back off if `talking` is false.

So, when the `talking` flag is set, Unity will know that it has to display our conversation GUI on the screen.

To finish this off, we need to call the coroutine from our `public` method, which other scripts can use to start a conversation and find the information for the dialog box and its subobjects:

```
public void StartConversation(Conversation conversation)
{
    dialogBox = GameObject.Find("Dialog Box").GetComponent<CanvasGroup>();
    imageHolder = GameObject.Find("Speaker Image").GetComponent<Image>();
```

```
textHolder = GameObject.Find("Dialog Text").GetComponent<Text>();
//Start displying the supplied conversation
if (!talking)
{
    StartCoroutine(DisplayConversation(conversation));
}
}
```

# Connecting the dots

So now that we have something to talk about, we just need to be able to attach it to the characters and then start displaying it on the screen for the player to interact with.

First, we need an empty class for our NPCs. So, create a new C# script named `Npc` in the `Classes` folder under `Assets\Scripts` and replace its contents with the following code:

```
using UnityEngine;
public class Npc : MonoBehaviour
{
  public string Name;
  public int Age;
  public string Faction;
  public string Occupation;
  public int Level;
}
```

As NPCs are things we generate and place into the scene, we actually need to break the convention to inherit from the `Entity` class. This is actually a limitation in Unity, because only scripts that derive from `MonoBehaviour` can be attached to GameObjects in a scene. If you try to attach a class that uses or derives from `ScriptableObject`, the editor will throw an error. So, as we are adding NPCs in our scene in the editor, we need to use a separate script.

If you were generating the towns procedurally or loading them from a pre-built save file, then you could still use classes based on `ScriptableObject`.

With that created, add the `Npc.cs` script to the Mayor in our scene (don't forget to name your character in the **Inspector** pane as well).

Next, add the **Conversation** component to the Mayor's **NPC script** and then drag the conversation we just built to that character in the **Conversations** array. Do this by dragging it over the word **Conversations**.

The **Inspector** pane will now look like the following screenshot:

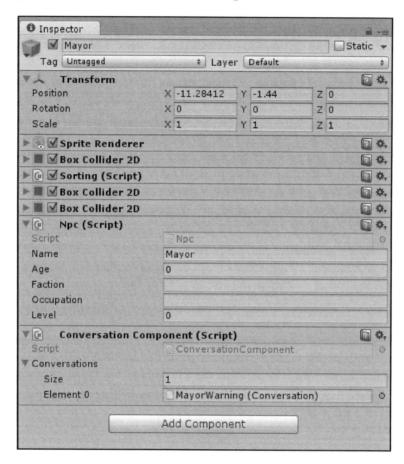

So now that our character has a script and we have the `ConversationManager` set up, we just need to trigger the conversation when the hero tries to exit the left side of the screen.

To broadcast the message when the player touches the long Box Collider attached to the Mayor, we need to add the `MessagingClientBroadCast` script to the Mayor. Since the Box Collider 2D attached to the Mayor we want to interact with is set as trigger, we need to update our `MessagingClientBroadCast` script to include the following:

```
void OnTriggerEnter2D(Collider2D col)
{       MessagingManager.Instance.Broadcast(); }
```

So, now when the player walks in front of the Mayor, the message will be broadcasted.

To finish off, we just need to get the Mayor NPC to listen for the message the player will leave and then start his conversation. So, remove the `MessagingClientReceiver` script (that was created in the *Messaging* section) from the left border that you set up earlier and add it to the Mayor NPC GameObject.

The Mayor's inspector will now appear as follows:

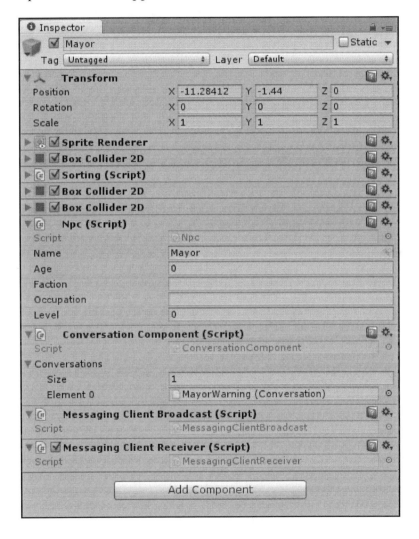

Now, the Mayor is subscribing to and receiving the messages for the player leaving. Next, update the `MessagingClientReceiver` script (in the `Messaging` folder under `Assets\Scripts`) and update the `ThePlayerIsTryingToLeave` method with the following code:

```
void ThePlayerIsTryingToLeave()
{
  var dialog = GetComponent<ConversationComponent>();
  if (dialog != null)
  {
    if (dialog.Conversations != null && dialog.Conversations.Length > 0)
    {
      var conversation = dialog.Conversations[0];
      if (conversation != null)
      {
        ConversationManager.Instance.StartConversation(conversation);
      }
    }
  }
}
```

Here, we look to see if a `ConversationComponent` script is on the GameObject it is attached to. If it is, we see if there are any conversations defined for this NPC; if yes, we call the `ConversationManager` script and ask it to start the first conversation.

Granted, this is a simple example and should be extended in a full system to track conversations that are played or conditions that need to be met for a conversation to be played.

At the moment, the conversation system will keep on going even after you have left the vicinity of the character that you are talking with.

Lastly, if you did not do so earlier in the *Messaging* section, create an empty GameObject in the scene, name it Messaging Manager, and attach the `MessagingManager` script to it. Open the `MessagingManager` script and remove the following code, if you added it earlier, as this is not going to be used in the game:

```
public ScriptingObjects MyWaypoints;
```

Now, if you run the project and try to exit on the left side, the Mayor will harass you, as shown in the following screenshot:

# Going further

If you are of the adventurous sort, try to expand your project to add the following features:

- Add other objects to the scene and have their sorting order update appropriately compared to the player. The Sorting.cs script is a very basic sorting script. You may need to create a much more complex version if there are multiple objects in the scene that need specific sorting orders.
- Create an idle animation for the Mayor using the forward facing sprites, so it appears that the Mayor is fidgeting; then, add it to a new **Animator** component attached to the Mayor's GameObject.
- Apply the scriptable object technique to other areas of the level.
- Extend the Conversation manager to step the text letter by letter in the conversation text with another coroutine.
- Expand the event's messenger to support different types of event, passing text, or an object.
- Have another conversation start if the player returns to the Mayor after their initial conversation.
- Add some conversation logic to terminate the conversation if the player gets too far from the source.

# Summary

What a marathon! This certainly has been the heaviest chapter so far, but there were a lot of advanced techniques to cover, and to do them justice, they needed a lot of explanation. Building a conversation system for any game needs a lot of planning to ensure you get the features you need for your game.

The lessons you learned in this chapter will set you in good stead for the future features.

We covered the ways to communicate between the GameObjects using events, delegates, and messaging solutions. We also covered working with background tasks and coroutines, serialization and scriptable objects, and constructing our own conversation system.

In the next chapter, we will set up a world map that will allow the player to go places other than the town in which she starts out.

# 7
# The World Map

As we start considering the wider bounds of our RPG world, we need to look at alternate views for the game. It's important to keep players engaged and make them feel that they are entering a vast arena with lots of places to explore, especially when you initially release your game and you only have a few towns to visit.

Another thing to consider is whether you want fixed maps in your game or you want to venture down the rabbit hole of procedural generation. Both are valid routes and there's nothing to say that you only have to use one. In this chapter, we'll cover all the options and then implement a nice and simple system to walk through the basics.

The following topics will be covered in this chapter:

- Resources to build a map
- Structuring and adding points of interest
- Working with prefabs
- Transitioning between scenes

## The larger view

Our budding hero is now ready to pack her bags and leave the shelter of her hometown for the wider world. So, we need to widen the scope of what the player can see and build a large map with places of interest to visit.

This usually opens the floodgates for just how big your game will be. Planning can decide whether your game will be a hit or feel just too short.

Maps in RPGs certainly aren't mandatory; several hit games just go from place to place with maybe an animation or cut scene to show movement. However, in the best cases, a map just opens up the scope of the game and gives the player an understanding of the world they are traveling in.

# Types of map

When looking at what kind of map or world you are going to choose to connect the dots between places to visit or secret hideaways, there are a few paths you can take. Generally, there are two options, which are as follows:

- **Fixed**: In this option, images are usually drawn by an artist and have extensive detail of the world surrounding the player or are blank, exposing places as the player travels to or discovers them
- **Generated**: In this option, each run of the game completely randomizes the places to go or events that will take place, with the focus being on unpredictability

Both the preceding options are perfectly valid and there's nothing to say you need to focus on just one or the other-mix it up if you wish. Generally, the greater the variety, the better the chances of the player being engaged in your game—it will entice them to explore and play more.

Another keen element is that it should support repeatability and replayability—let players return to existing locations and discover new things, and reuse what you have to the fullest.

# Fixed maps

There are many resources to get maps for your title if you don't have a dedicated artist and, in some ways, these also provide insight or creative juice for how you want your maps to look.

The first site to mention, primarily because it is also completely free, is `http://freefantasymaps.org/`. Another useful site is the **Cartographers' Guild** at `http://www.cartographersguild.com/`. This is a veritable map paradise with lots of content available for use in most projects. Unlike the preceding site, all works are protected and you will need to purchase them or gain rights to use them. However, they are of a very high quality.

When browsing maps and art, *always* be sure to check the license and usage policies of the images you download. This should be done whenever you acquire art, even from Google. Be safe, check, and get permission.

The same can be said for code and any other kind of asset. If in doubt, check the license and even if it's free, just check with the author whether they feel it's okay to use in your project.

Always check the license on anything you download and use.

# Generated maps

There are also many other resources out there to get maps for your game. Another method is to use an online map generation system. Now, to be fair, most are aimed at tabletop gamers and most are of a low quality, but there are a few gems to be found. For example, `http://donjon.bin.sh/fantasy/world/` provides fairly high-resolution generated images and includes world features and places.

DonJon's site also offers a vast array of other generators to build maps and other RPG elements. There are even name and game dialog generators, so it really does meet most RPG needs.

## In-game generated maps

Now, if you want more control over what the player sees or will have in their game, you can go all the way and start building maps and more through either Unity's asset pipeline or in code within the game.

External tools such as **Tiled** (`http://www.mapeditor.org/`), which is shown in the following image, can be used to build and design maps. It has many interesting features and can even output several layers. You can use either top-down, 2D side scrolling, or even isometric maps.

A great Unity example of this is a project called `uTiled` (`https://bitbucket.org/vinull/utiled`), which provides a Unity asset that can read maps from Tiled.

Alternatively, you could use procedural techniques (see the *Going procedural* section of this chapter) to build the map while the game is running by using the framework to knit individual segments of your map together. We will discuss this more later.

# Going procedural

If you are the bold or adventurous sort, another route to flesh out your world is to procedurally generate it. What you usually see when you look for procedural generation in Unity are dungeon generators. In fact, some of the best examples I've seen out there involve randomly generated dungeons where every run of the game is different from the last. Other examples are usually found in endless running games where a style of procedural selection is done to choose the next running area or to put random scene items in.

When we try to apply this to RPG games, we want to balance the fixed part of the world/story we are looking to convey with a more random placement of towns/villages or places of interest. This will make the world we see different for every player but still convey the background of the theme.

Now, the whole subject of procedural generation is far too large to go into for this book, but I can give you a few points for where to look.

The best place to start is the **Procedural Content Generation Wiki** available at `http://pcg.wikidot.com/`; it's the go-to place to start learning the following general techniques:

- **Iterated function systems**: These are fractals to create land masses or structured areas.
- **L-systems**: These are used for road or path generation
- **Diamond-square and midpoint displacement algorithms**: These are used to create random height terrain
- **Perlin and simplex noise system**s: These are used to add further randomness to the generation

### A word to the wise

Procedural generation is not for the faint of heart. There is a lot of math involved and a lot of trial and error. However, if you can master small parts, you can achieve a truly wondrous game with lots of replayability.

Procedural generation is too large a subject for this book. Hopefully, I've given you a few tips and tidbits to get you going so you know what to look for should you want to venture down this road.

# Creating our game's map

Moving on from theory, we need to look at something to put on our map of the world, such as somewhere for our player to travel to and explore.

We not only need to provide graphical support in the game to open up areas on the map or just show the journey between two points, but we also need to connect these points with scenes in our game.

# Adding the world map

Start off by copying the following `map` image into your project in the `Assets\Sprites\Environment` folder:

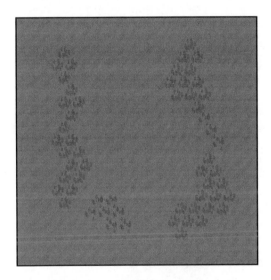

I created the preceding map image very quickly using the **Hexagon Pack** provided by Kenny on opengameart.org found at `http://opengameart.org/content/hexagon-pack-3` `1x`. You can find the full set in the code bundle that accompanies the book. I thought these tiles were incredibly well made and, dare I say, adorable. You can easily combine these assets in some photo-editing software to create a map of your choice.

If you are interested in a free photo-editing program to help with game art creation, check out the program called GIMP found at http://www.gimp.org /.

I highly suggest you check out the other art provided by this artist at http://opengameart.org/users/kenney. He has provided many free high-quality art assets that can assist you in making 2D games of various genres.

With that imported into your project, open the scene named Overworld that you created in Chapter 2, *Building Your Project and Character*. Drag your map image to the scene. Increase the size of the MainCamera to 6 and position the map sprite so that you you scene appears as shown in the following screenshot:

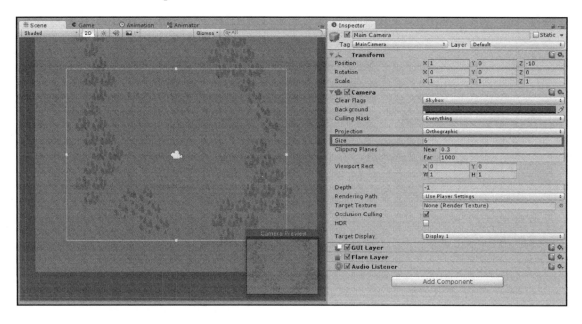

Remember that the size of the camera simply determines the size of the rectangular area the camera will display.

# Adding a player prefab to the overworld

Let's add the player to the scene. Instead of creating the player sprite and adding all of the appropriate components, let's create a prefab for the player to save ourselves some time. Navigate back to your Town scene.

Select **Player** from the Hierarchy and drag it to the Assets/Prefabs/Characters folder. Upon doing so, you should now see the following in your Project view:

Also, **Player** should now be represented by blue text instead of black in the Hierarchy. Select the prefab and set its **Transform** coordinates to 0.

It's a good practice to reset the position transform for prefabs to 0; this makes reusing them a whole lot easier.

When you create a prefab, you essentially create an object that you can reuse that contains all of the same properties. This is really helpful when you have an object in one scene that you want to duplicate to another.

> When you create a prefab and use it in your scene, any changes to the prefab will be automatically updated on all the objects you created with that prefab. However, changes to those objects do not update the prefab or any other copies. All changes are one way from the prefab.
>
> If you want to update the prefab, select the **Prefab** option in the editor and change it. Alternatively, select an instance in the scene, change the required properties, and then click on **Apply** to save the changes back to the prefab, as shown in the following screenshot:

> This will only affect existing components and properties that were already on the prefab. To add new components or scripts to the prefab, you must edit the prefab itself.

Now that we have a Player prefab, navigate back to your Overworld scene. Drag the Player prefab into your scene, as shown in the following screenshot:

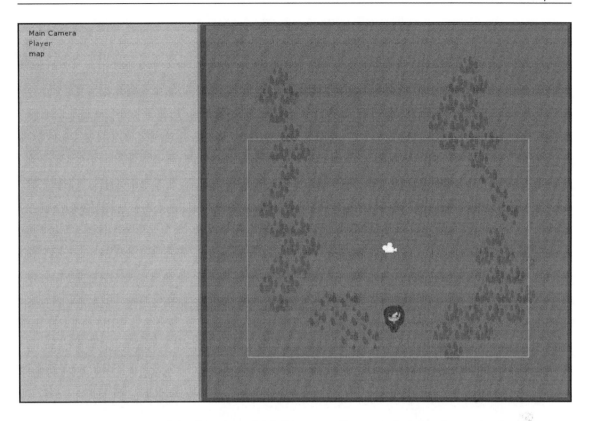

Because we used the prefab, the player's ability to walk around and animate is already included!

# Adding places of interest

Now that we have a general map in place, let's add some places for the player to go. We will start by adding a sprite to represent the town that we have been working with in the last few chapters. I chose the `hexagon-pack/PNG/Tiles/Modern/modern_oldBuilding.png` sprite from the Hexagon Pack to represent my town (the following figure), since it looks similar to the town hall in the `Town` scene. Feel free to peruse the other premade tiles provided or make your own tiles with the images in the `hexagon-pack/PNG/Tiles/Terrain` and `hexagon-pack/PNG/Objects` folders.

Import the image into your project by placing it in the `Assets\Sprites\Environment` folder. Then place it in your scene wherever you want your town to be located. Place the character near the town so that, when the scene starts, it looks as if she had just exited the town, as shown in the following screenshot:

Rename the object `MapPoint` and add a `Box Collider 2D` component to it. Set the **Box Collider 2D** to `Is Trigger`. Also, set the **Sprite Renderer** component's **Order in Layer** to 1. That way, these objects will always appear above the map, as shown in the following screenshot:

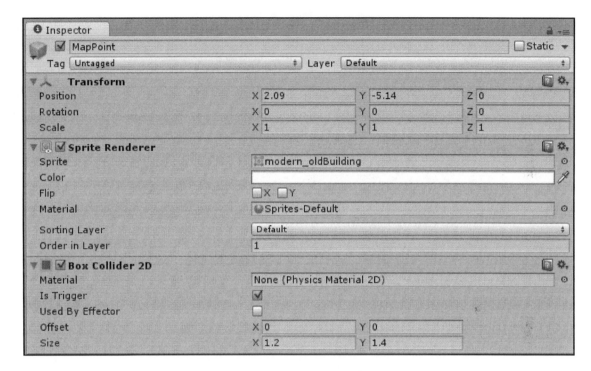

With a collider set as a trigger, it will cause the `OnTrigger` functions (`OnTriggerEnter2D` and `OnTriggerExit2D`) to be called in scripts as opposed to the normal `OnCollision` functions (`OnCollisionEnter2D` and `OnCollisionExit2D`). Bear this in mind when applying scripts that rely on a collider.

Now drag the town object to the `Assets\Prefabs\Environment` folder to create a prefab of the object.

Once the prefab is created, we can start to use it since this game object has now become the first instance of our `MapPoint` prefab. So, rename the instance on the scene `Town`, and then create a new tag called `Town`. Assign the tag to the object, as shown in the following screenshot:

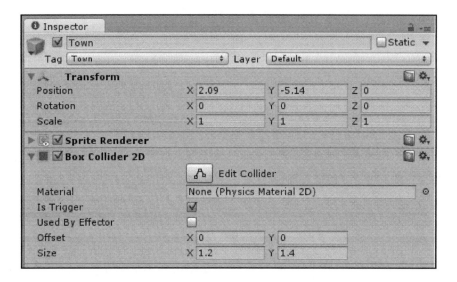

We will create a second place on the map that will represent a camp site. Add the following image, `hexagon-pack/PNG/Tiles/Modern/modern_campsite.png`, to your project by placing it in the `Assets\Sprites\Environment` folder:

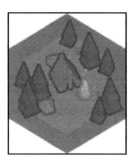

Next, create a new instance of our `MapPoint` prefab by dragging the prefab on to the scene, as shown in the following screenshot:

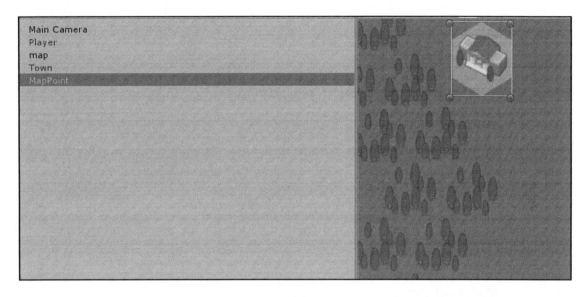

Rename it `Campsite` and create/set a tag with the same name. Now, replace its image with the `modern_campsite.png` image by dragging the new image to the `Sprite` slot of the `Sprite Renderer` component, as shown in the following screenshot:

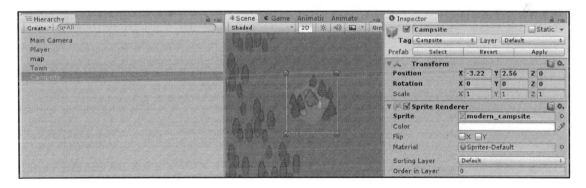

Due to the scope of this book, we are going to limit the character's movement on the map to the area visible by the camera. We could easily allow the character to walk further by removing the blockades we are about to include and adding a script to the camera that follows the player. In the same manner that we added borders to our town, we will now add them to our overworld, as shown in the following screenshot:

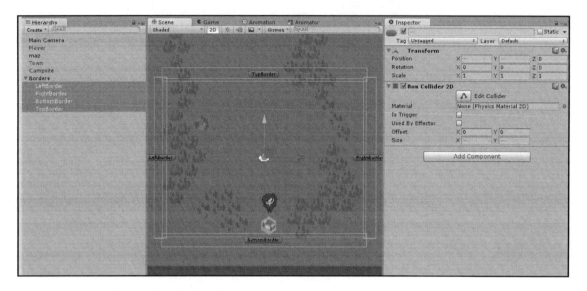

As you can see from the preceding screenshot, I made the box colliders overlap slightly with the bounds of the camera. That way, the player stops before she reaches the absolute edge of the screen.

 Do not let these colliders overlap with the colliders of the town or campsite. Doing so will make the scene transition code trigger instantly.

# Leaving town

Currently, our character can walk back and forth in the town and walk around in the map, but she can't go between the two scenes. Since the game will start off in the town, let's begin by allowing the character to leave the Town and enter the Overworld.

# Creating a NavigationManager script

To navigate between scenes, we could add a simple SceneManager script that says when you hit this collider, go to a specific scene, but if you are planning a larger world with a large number of interactions, it is better if we build a separate navigation system so that we have everything in one place; it's just easier to manage that way.

This separation is a fundamental part of any good game design. Keeping the logic and game functionality separate makes it easier to maintain in the future, especially when you need to take internationalization into account (but we will learn more about that later).

In Chapter 4, *The Town View*, we created a NavigationPrompt script that we will rewrite and tie into a manager script. As you may recall, we added the tag Borders to the LeftBorder and RightBorder. This allowed the NavigationPrompt text to output the message "leave town" in the console.

Let's return to our Town scene and change these tags. Create new tags called Construction and Overworld. Apply the Construction tag to the LeftBorder and the Overworld tag to the RightBorder, as shown in the following screenshot:

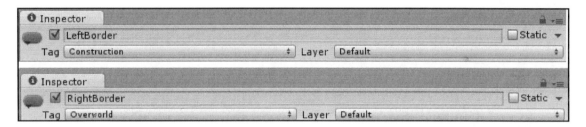

Next, let's create a new C# script called NavigationManager in Assets\Scripts\Navigation and then replace its contents with the following lines of code:

```
using System.Collections.Generic;

public static class NavigationManager{

    public static Dictionary<string, string> RouteInformation = new
      Dictionary<string, string>() {
        { "Overworld","The big bad world"},
        { "Construction", "The construction area"},
    };

    public static string GetRouteInfo(string destination){
        return RouteInformation.ContainsKey(destination) ?
```

```
            RouteInformation[destination] : null;
    }

  public static bool CanNavigate(string destination) {
    return true;
  }

  public static void NavigateTo(string destination){
    //we'll talk about this in a second :)
  }
}
```

Notice the ? and : operators in the following statement:

RouteInformation.ContainsKey(destination) ?
RouteInformation[destination] : null; These operators are C#
conditional operators. They are effectively the shorthand of the following:

```
if(RouteInformation.ContainsKey(destination))
{
return RouteInformation[destination];
}
else
{
return null;
}
```

Shorter, neater, and much nicer, don't you think?

For more information, see the MSDN C# page at
http://bit.ly/csharpconditionaloperator.

The script is very basic for now, but contains several following key elements that can be expanded to meet the design goals of your game:

- `RouteInformation`: This is a list of all the possible destinations in the game in a dictionary

  This is a static list of possible destinations in the game, and it is a core part of the manager as it has everywhere you can travel in the game in one place.

- `GetRouteInfo`: This is a basic information extraction function

  This is a simple controlled function to interrogate the destination list. In this example, we just return the text to be displayed in the prompt, which allows more detailed descriptions that we could use in tags. You could use this to provide alternate prompts, depending on what the player is carrying and whether they have a lit torch, for example.

- `CanNavigate`: This is a test to see if navigation is possible

  If you are going to limit a player's travel, you need a way to test if they can move, allowing logic in your game to make alternate choices if the player cannot. You could use a different system for this by placing some sort of block in front of a destination to limit choice (as used in the likes of Zelda), such as an NPC or rock. As this is only an example, we can always travel and add logic to control it if you wish.

- `NavigateTo`: This is a function to instigate navigation

  Once a player can travel, you can control exactly what happens in the game: does navigation cause the next scene to load straight away or does the current scene fade out and then a traveling screen is shown before fading the next level in? Currently, there is nothing here, because we have a few more things to take care of before we can navigate to new scenes.

You will notice that the script is a static class. This means it sits in the background, only exists once in the game, and is accessible from anywhere. This pattern is useful for fixed information that isn't attached to anything; it just sits in the background waiting to be queried.

With this class now created, we will update the `NavigationPrompt` script to communicate with our `NavigationMananger` script. Update the collision function in the `NavigationPrompt` script to now reference the `NavigationMananger`, rather than looking directly at the object's tags, as the shown in the following code:

```
void OnCollisionEnter2D(Collision2D col){
    if(NavigationManager.CanNavigate(this.tag)){
        Debug.Log("attempting to exit via "+ tag);
        NavigationManager.NavigateTo(this.tag);
    }
}
```

We will also remove this script from the `Player` and add it to the `LeftBorder` and `RightBorder`. To remove it from the `Player`, remove it from the `Player` prefab in the `Assets/Prefabs/Characters` folder. You will notice when the prefab is changed, it updates in the scene. This will also be true of the `Player` in the `Overworld` scene.

Now when you run into the borders, a message will appear in the console telling you that the player is attempting to leave town and the tag of the exit the player is attempting to use. Because there is no code in the `NavigationManager.NavigateTo` function, nothing else happens yet.

# Blocking off paths

We still have a bit of work to do to our `NavigationManager` script. Let's add code that enables us to have a simple mechanism to say whether a route is traversable or not. (In real scenarios, this should be serialized or it should have a manager for the player to remember where the player has traveled; otherwise, it is never going to get unlocked.)

Open up the `NavigationManager` script and create a new `struct` method as follows at the top of the class:

```
public struct Route{
    public string RouteDescription;
    public bool CanTravel;
}
```

Next, we need to update the `RouteInformation` variable to use this new `struct` method and update the information for the two destinations that we have already configured in our manager. This should enable us to state that you can travel to the big bad world but not to the construction area, as follows:

```
public static Dictionary<string, Route> RouteInformation = new
Dictionary<string, Route>() {
  { "Overworld", new Route { RouteDescription = "The big bad world",
    CanTravel = true}
  },
  { "Construction", new Route { RouteDescription = "The construction area",
    CanTravel = false}
  },
};
```

As we are now using a `struct` method for our destination information, we also need to update the `GetRouteInfo` method to access the dictionary correctly and return the routes' description if found; we do this using the following code:

```
public static string GetRouteInfo(string destination)
{
  return RouteInformation.ContainsKey(destination) ?
    RouteInformation[destination].RouteDescription :
    null;
}
```

With that in place, all we need to do is check whether the `CanTravel` flag is `true` when the system requests, and if you're allowed to travel, update the `CanNavigate` method with the following code:

```
public static bool CanNavigate(string destination)
{
  return RouteInformation.ContainsKey(destination) ?
    RouteInformation[destination].CanTravel :
    false;
}
```

Here, we simply look at the destination from our route information and return with information on whether the player is allowed to travel there or not.

Now, when you try to go to the construction area, you won't get the prompt from `NavigationPrompt` about attempting to leave.

# Updating build settings to include new scenes

Before we can have code send us from scene to scene, we must update our build settings. To add new scenes, we need to set up the **Build Settings** options for our project to tell it we have some additional scenes to choose from. Open **Build Settings** by navigating to **File** | **Build Settings** from the main menu or using *Ctrl + Shift + B* on the keyboard. The **Build Settings** window looks this:

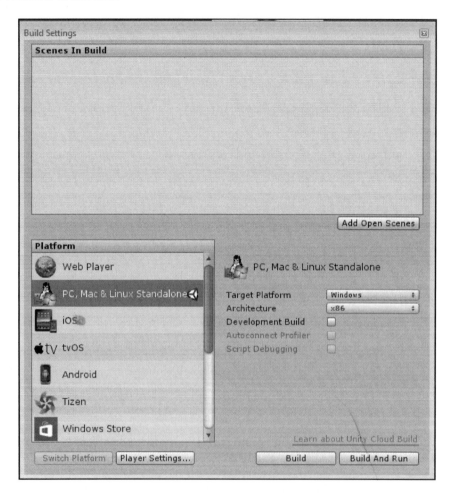

As you can see in the preceding screenshot, the **Scenes In Build** list is currently empty. So, when we run the game, it will just run the current scene in the editor.

To update this list, either drag the scenes from the project Hierarchy or use the **Add Current** button to add the scene you are currently viewing. So, add the two current scenes into the **Scenes In Build** list, as shown in the following screenshot:

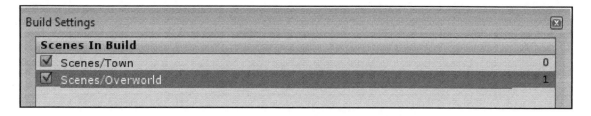

Now, one important thing to note is the order of the scenes. As you may expect, Unity will always start the project with scene 0, so be sure that the town is the first scene in the list. You can do this by simply dragging the scenes up or down.

> This ordering of scenes is very useful and powerful. Some developers like to put levels in order so that they can use the index to progress through.

> However, if you are having trouble with a particular scene in your game when running on a device, another trick is to reorder the scenes in the build so that the troublesome one is the starting scene. This saves you from having to keep playing through until you get to that scene or writing code to accelerate you. Granted, you need to ensure that whatever settings required for the scene are set on load if you debug this way.

# Changing scenes

Now that both of our scenes are in the **Build Settings**, we can write code to navigate between them. Return to the `NavigationManager` script and add the following code at the top of the script:

```
using UnityEngine.SceneManagement;
And update the NavigateTo function as such:
public static void NavigateTo(string destination){
    SceneManager.LoadScene(destination);
}
```

> In older versions of Unity, you could transition between scenes using `Application.LoadLevel ("name of level");` however, this code is now depreciated and will no longer work.

Now when you exit toward the left side of the `Town`, you immediate enter the `Overworld`.

# Returning to town

Since the town and campsite have their **Box Collider 2D** components set as triggers, we need to swiftly update our `NavigationPrompt` script to work with triggers. So, open the `NavigationPrompt` script and add the following function to it:

```
void OnTriggerEnter2D(Collider2D col){
    if(NavigationManager.CanNavigate(this.tag)){
        Debug.Log("attempting to exit via "+ tag);
      NavigationManager.NavigateTo(this.tag);
    }
}
```

The function in the preceding code does exactly the same as the `OnCollisionEnter2D` function, which we already have, but this will now respond to the colliders that have been set as triggers using the `is Trigger` flag.

# Updating the NavigationManager script

As the player can now venture out of town, we need to update our `NavigationManager` script with additional places to visit, including our town. We can do this simply by adding additional highlighted routes to our `NavigationManager` script as follows:

```
public static Dictionary<string, Route> RouteInformation = new
  Dictionary<string, Route>() {
  { "Overworld", new Route {
    RouteDescription = "The big bad world", CanTravel = true}},
  { "Construction", new Route {
    RouteDescription = "The construction area", CanTravel = false}},
  { "Town", new Route {
    RouteDescription = "The main town", CanTravel = true}},
  { "Campsite", new Route {
    RouteDescription = "The campsite",
      CanTravel = false}},
};
```

Now, attach the `NavigationPrompt` script to the `MapPoint` prefab in the
`Assets/Prefabs/Environment` folder. Since you added it to the prefab, when you select
the **Town** and **Campsite** objects in the scene, you will see they now contain the script. If you
play the game, you will see you can quite easily navigate between the `Overworld` and the
`Town`.

# Going further

If you are the adventurous sort, try expanding your project to add the following:

- Make map bigger and allow the character to walk further
- Add a camera-tracking script similar to the camera script we have already
  created, so that the player can move further around the map
- Create new scenes for the places to visit and get some more characters and
  conversations going
- Update the player's starting position when she enters the town from the map
- Create a transition animation to add fading between scenes

# Summary

Hopefully, you can appreciate by the end of this chapter how even a simple map-like
interface has its own flavors and complexities, but there is so much more you could do to
enhance this area. Depending on your style of game, the player could spend quite a lot of
time on the map exploring (such as Zelda) or they could just be zipping through. So, plan
time accordingly to decide how much you want to invest.

If you target mobile platforms, then other input strategies are very important. On handheld
devices, it doesn't really make sense to have the player move around the scene with a
keyboard.

In this chapter, we covered the following topics:

- Building the wider world using textures, texture generation tools, map tools, and
  some hints at procedural generation
- Adding the ability to transition between scenes

In the next chapter, we are going to start building our turn-based battle system!

# 8
# Encountering Enemies and Running Away

At the heart of most RPG-style games are the bad guys. How they think and how they confront and challenge you will mark your game as either too hard or too easy. Sadly, there isn't any real middle ground (you can't please everyone all the time). However, we can ensure a fair system and engage the players with systems that will surprise and entertain them as they move around in the big bad world.

The following topics will be covered in this chapter:

- Planning for event systems
- State machines
- Basic AI techniques

## Event systems

When you're looking to engage the player roaming around in your game, it is best to throw them off guard and challenge them when they least expect it; this ensures that the player is paying attention while playing and also serves to keep them on their toes at all times.

The following methods help to achieve this:

- **Fixed systems**: This is where the places and interactions are actually planned in advance by forcing the player to be drawn in to an event at prescribed times/places

- **Random generation**: This involves using random systems to challenge the player within a given time frame or occurrence, giving the player a chance of an event but not a certainty of one

There are merits and demerits with either approach for the player as they interact with your game. Fixed systems are easy to implement but limit replayability (game becomes dull in the second or subsequent runs), whereas random systems can be trickier to get the balance right but also means the player will likely keep playing longer or get irritated very quickly.

Finding the balance between implementing events is a tricky process, as you will have to find the right sweet spot for in your particular game, and inevitably all games implement this differently.

Also, remember that there is no silver bullet and no reason not to use both systems together—using fixed systems to tell a story and random events to keep it interesting.

# Exploring randomness

Now one strange thing to keep in mind is that there is no such thing as a completely random system, especially in gaming and computing. You can get close with some really complex mathematical systems but nothing is truly random. The best we can do is make it random enough to fool the player, making them believe it is random.

The reason for this is simple: computers are not random and don't think in random terms. When they generate a random number, they are using a seed (a unique number to base their random generation on) to work out what number to give you. But every time you generate a number based on that same seed, it will always be the same sequence; this is known as **pseudo-random**.

Most basic systems try to balance this out by also randomly generating the seed number, but this again falls under the same pattern. However, it does make the random pattern a little more random. A lot of systems use the date or current clock tick as the seed. It's important to know and remember this when you are planning to use random systems.

There is also a drawback to trying to make your random system even more random: you end up spending more time computing the random number in your game and stealing resources from other systems such as physics, AI, and so on. It's always a balancing game to ensure you plan where your precious system resources are going to be spent.

In most cases, developers use other effects to try to create randomness by using noise generating systems (**Perlin/fractals/Gaussian drift**) and other techniques to try to make the best use of low-cost generation systems with as few passes needed. By combining two or more systems, you can create an approximate and fairly complex random system.

 If you want to read up more on random and pseudo-random systems, you can get a full history on RANDOM.ORG at http://www.random.org/randomness/, which also features some examples of free and paid random systems.

There is another side to this predictability of basic random number generation systems: these can be used in various procedural techniques to build game items. If you can predict a sequence of numbers based on a particular seed, you can use that sequence to always build the same thing each and every time.

So, if you want a set of events to always occur in a particular order, you can actually use the basic random system to create a fixed event system; just use the seed you need to generate the sequence you need to use.

# True randomness

There is another course of logic in random generation systems called **True Random Number Generators** (**TRNGs**). They go to great lengths to guarantee the randomness of a generated number with greater and greater precision, but these also come at a heavy cost (if you really need them, however, they are worthy of study).

In games, however, it is usually sufficient to rely on pseudo-random systems, both for their efficiency as well as their predictability. Another reason is that you often don't want 100 percent randomness; you want something like a shuffle bag or similar to ensure that the event happens randomly enough within a time frame.

# Planning for random code/generation

A key point of any good game design when you even start to think about adding random code/generation to your game is to stop, look, and listen. Never rush into using random systems in your game, or you may end up rewriting it multiple times.

Start working from a simple base and ask yourself the following questions:

- Do I actually need it to be random or will it get configured?

  This is the first and most important question: are you trying to add random code/generation because it's easier to throw in, or will a fixed configuration be more suitable (is it really random you're after)?

  Never use randomization lightly, even when it is just a range of numbers you want to pick from; always question whether it is the right tool for the job. Inevitably, using randomization is always going to be more expensive in terms of processing than a simple mathematical equation to approximate the values you are after. Do your research.

- Where in your design do you see the need for randomization?

  Be specific! What do you actually need to be randomized or sampled?

  For example, in this RPG project for the random battle events on the map, we need to figure out the following:

  - The chance of an event occurring on a journey
  - Where on the journey the event will occur
  - What will be the starting condition of the battle, number of enemies, their strength, and who fights first

- In each area, how frequently will you need a random sample?

  Because of the cost of random selection, you need to decide when and where the generation will take place. If you need a single random for each frame, that might be okay (depending on what else is happening in each frame); but if you have many, then it may be better to prefill an array of random numbers at the start of the scene and perform a predictive selection of numbers in that array (either stepping through or selection based on other factors).

- What level of complexity does the random sampling/generation need?

  So once you've decided where you need randomization and how often you need it, only then do you decide on how complex that generation needs to be. Is it simply picking a random number or do you need a more accurate random number predication by using one of the aforementioned complex techniques, such as Perlin noise or fractal sampling?

In a lot of cases, only testing will tell how random you need to be. When testing, ask yourself if the current technique's pattern seems to obvious or if it hampers gameplay.

For the purposes of this book, I will keep the use simple; this section is mainly to highlight all the complexities of using random systems in games. This might sound like a nice idea to begin with, but beware, here be dragons, even if it's just as simple as a single random number picked in a range in each frame.

 Another important consideration is that random generation is not free. Depending on the system you use, it could also generate garbage and hamper the performance of your game that may not seem obvious at first glance.

# Basic Artificial Intelligence

**Artificial Intelligence** (**AI**) is a term bandied around most game systems and is a general bucket for several techniques for machine-based learning systems. Its sole aim is to fool the user/player into believing that the system is behaving like any living being. AI usually presents itself in the form of characters that challenge the player in head-to-head battles or helpful supporting characters.

Some systems used to achieve this are as follows:

- **Path-finding**: This helps AI-controlled entities navigate through levels to a specific destination
- **Flocking**: This orders how multiple AI entities will relate to each other within a given area
- **State machines**: These are fixed and basic sensor-driven intelligence to drive AI actions
- **Rule-based expert systems**: These are the defined logic systems for an AI entity to derive action from and aid decision-making
- **Neural networks**: These are advanced learning networks for AI entities, typically used to predict the performance of the AI and also understand the predictable behavior of opponents
- **AI algorithms** (reinforced learning/simulated annealing/genetic calculations): These are many different ways to reinforce neural networks and decision engines for better predictable behavior

The area of AI can be a very complicated minefield. It is often seen by some as a nice thing to have; however, getting it right is a very long and drawn out task no matter the size of the project.

My advice, especially if you are just starting out, is to lean on existing implementations, either through the asset store or the Unity wiki, to begin with and learn from there. The whole subject of AI has spawned numerous books and entire sites such as `http://aigamedev.com/` (a fantastic general resource).

Start simple and move from there. For the purposes of this book and the RPG game, we will focus on a simple state machine implementation using basic sensors to help drive the AI.

# State machines

In life, as well as in game development, state machines (or **Finite State Machines** as they are more commonly called) are a core component for day-to-day running. At a basic level, they tell us exactly what we are doing right now, what we were doing previously, and what we can do next.

They are commonly used for the following:

- Menu systems
- Game-level transitions
- AI/behaviors

We can implement these within games in various ways, from the very basic (and generally hard to manage) to a more ordered system and beyond with full state managers.

A basic state machine is like a flowchart and looks something like the following diagram:

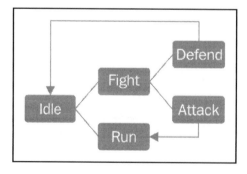

# Defining states

In all implementations, we start with a collection of states, which define both what conditions/states are in the game and what we do when that state changes.

These states describe both what can happen when that state is active and what other potential states could result in an action from the current state. If we look at an example that describes a simple case using a television (TV), we would end up with the states listed in the following table:

| State | Description | Actions |
|---|---|---|
| TV off | No activity is present and nothing is displayed. | The power button turns the TV on. |
| TV on | The TV displays images and plays sound. | The power button turns the TV off. The up button selects the previous channel. The down button selects the next channel. The menu button displays the menu. |
| Menu displayed | The TV displays the menu, overlaying the normal display. | The power button turns the TV off. The menu button turns the TV on (menu hidden). The up button highlights the previous menu item. The down button highlights the next menu item. The ok button activates the menu item. |

So from each individual state, there are a number of options; in some cases, the same action will lead to the same result (such as the power button) and some actions will do different things based on what the current state is (such as the up and down buttons).

It's important to note that in any game, you will likely use many state systems, from menus to in-game controls and AI.

So, once you have your collection ready, the next step is to define an enumeration in C# as follows, for example, using the previous states:

```
enum TvState
{
  Off,
  On,
  Menu
}
```

# Simple singular choice

The simplest way to implement a state system is using the C# switch statement; the benefit here is that there can only be a single result:

```
if (Input.GetButtonDown("Up"))
{
    switch (currentTvState)
    {
        case TvState.Off:
            //Nothing, tv is off
            break;
        case TvState.On:
            //Channel Up
            break;
        case TvState.Menu:
            //Menu selection up
            break;
    }
}
```

So, as you can see in the preceding example, we have simply implemented the pattern for the Up button on the remote, and depending on what the TV is doing currently, it will act appropriately.

This is good for menus, but is limiting in situations where, based on the state, we might want to do multiple things.

# Planning for multiple cases

The alternate simple approach to state machines is to use the `if` blocks to test what a state is: the only downside is that this can become very cumbersome to manage very quickly. Consider a slightly more complex scenario (related to the game) where a group of thugs are battling with you, but they are only confident when they are in a group and will run if their health is not good. Such a system wouldn't be possible using the previous `switch` style (or at least will be difficult to do so), so by using several `if` blocks, as shown in the following code, we can achieve something like the following:

```
if (EnemyState == State.Idle)
{
    //Check for player
    // If player found EnemyState == State.Attacking
    //Check for fellow enemies
}
if (EnemyState == State.Attacking && PlayerState == State.Idle)
{
    //Enemy Sneak attack
}
if (EnemyState == State.Attacking)
{
    //Play Attacking Music
}
if (EnemyState == State.Attacking && Health < 5)
{
    //Run away
}
if (EnemyState == State.Attacking && PlayerState ==     State.RunningAway)
{
    //Give Chase
}
```

Now, although the previous code can be nested or transformed into `switch` statements, writing it this way gives us other advantages. For one, we control when and under what conditions certain things will happen, for example:

- Battle music will always be played when the battle begins
- Enemies will chase the player unless they have low health
- At any point that the player is idle, the enemies will have a sneaking advantage

However, with either system, you are going to end up with a lot of code-making decisions around your game, such as the player, enemies, **Non Player Characters (NPCs)**, and so on. This will make it hard to manage and even worse to try debug; perhaps Unity offers us another way?

# State managers

Following on from the animation tutorial in `Chapter 3`, *Getting Animated,* we have seen that Unity has a very powerful state machine system built in it already using **Mecanim**. We have only used it for animation so far, but like **AnimationCurves**, we can use this to build a nice graphical system that is easier to maintain.

 Although the state machine is very powerful for controlling what states are available and how they transition between states, it can't actually implement actions (other than animation). There are triggers built into the state system, but these are not fully supported on all platforms. So if you use them, keep it limited.

To achieve this properly, you need to separate out the responsibilities for what does what within the state system into the following parameters:

- **Inputs**: What factors will be fed into the state system to affect change
- **The decision engine**: The core logic that drives the state machine
- **Outputs**: What the game will do based on the current state

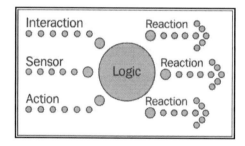

The preceding diagram shows an example of how you would componentize your state machine; this pattern is very extensible because it means you can apply separate scripts for each of the inputs, which also means many areas of the game can have an input to the state system. The outputs/reactions to states or state changes can also be componentized (but don't have to be) so that you can swap and change AI behaviors to the different states based on what you are implementing them on. Enemy 1 may be very brave and just act, and Enemy 2 might be a bit more cautious and require other enemies close by before attacking.

Implementing this in Mecanim animation controllers is very simple since at its heart it is a state machine itself, as shown in the following screenshot:

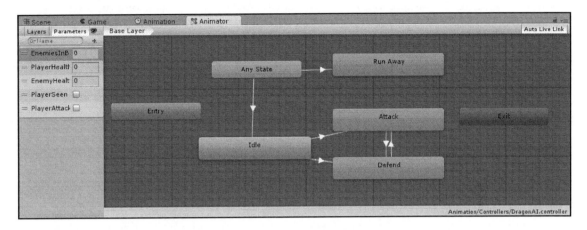

The preceding screenshot is a preview of the state manager we will create later in this chapter.

In the preceding screenshot, we can see a simple example of this: there are no animations connected to any of the states. We are just using them to track and control what drives our state machine. Using the parameters, it's easy to configure the following settings:

- If the player is seen, the enemy attacks
- If the player is seen and is attacking, the enemy should defend
- If the player attacks when the enemy is attacking, the enemy should defend
- If the player stops attacking, then the enemy should attack back
- If at any time the enemy health is less than 2 and the player's health is greater than 2, the enemy should run away
- If at any time the enemy loses sight of the player, then go back to idle

So, by controlling the input, we know how the enemy will behave, and this is completely configurable within the controller without any complex scripting.

# Sensors

Using the Mecanim state machine in this way is very powerful and just having scripts update the parameters of the state machine through input (user taps a key, or scene loads) is simple enough. However, if you want reactive AI, you might want to think about sensors.

Sensors are effectively the AI's eyes and ears and whatever else it wants to use to detect action within a scene (even if it's an alarm or trip wire). Generally, they are self-contained components that look after themselves and inform whatever they are attached to. They can be as complex or as simple as you need them to be.

A basic sensor might be an empty GameObject with a trigger collider (the trip wire), which tells the enemy state machine that the player has come into view. Alternatively, you could use ray casting (yes, even in 2D) to check whether the target is in view.

One of the best examples of a sensor I've seen is a wandering GameObject with a sphere trigger that wanders round the screen to represent the point where the enemy was looking at. If it falls on the player or an object that has been moved in the scene, then all hell breaks loose.

# Setting up your battle scene

As you would expect, we need to create a new scene for our battles. You may want to create several scenes for different battle areas or you may want to define one generic scene and randomize the contents of that scene to add variation. Obviously, there are pros and cons to each approach, but ultimately the choice is up to you.

# Building the new scene

For now, we will keep things simple and just create a new scene and then configure it as our battle area. If you have not already made the scene called BattleScene in Chapter 2, *Building Your Project and Character*, do so now.

Make it look pretty with some additional background scene elements. I have added the ForestBackground.png image to the background with an *X* and *Y* scale set to 1.5 to better fit the camera, as shown in the following screenshot:

I also imported the `ForestForegroundElements.png` image in **Multiple Sprite** mode. I sliced it by hand so that the grass was in one long sprite and the bushes were in two separate sprites, like so:

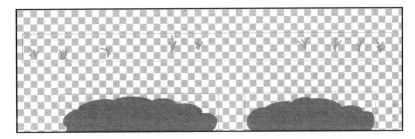

I placed these items in the scene with an *X* and *Y* scale set to 1.5 and their **alpha** values set to 168 so that they were semi-transparent, as shown in the following screen shot:

Notice that I lined everything up with the bottom of the camera.

> Remember to group your additional environmental assets under a single empty GameObject to keep them tidy in the **Project** Hierarchy. Also, set the sprite layer and order appropriately for all elements, including the background texture.
>
> If you're having trouble getting your background and foreground objects to display in the correct order, don't forget about sprite sorting layers and sorting order!

# Adding the first enemy

We need to create a prefab for our first enemy. Doing so is simple. First, let's start with the Dragon character in the asset pack (`dragon.png`):

1. Split its sprite up using the Automatic **Sprite Editor.**
2. Drag sprite image `dragon_0` on to the scene .
3. Rename the new GameObject `Dragon`.
4. Set its Sprite Sorting Layer to Middleground.
5. Change its *X* and *Y* scale to `0.5`.
6. Set its *X* and *Y* position to 0.

The enemy should look like this:

I created the sprite sheet for the Dragon by combining Flappy Dragon sprite sheets provided by bevouliin on OpenGameArt.Org found at `http://opengameart.org/content/flappy-dragon-sprite-sheets`. If you are interested in more enemy sprite sheets, check out the other resources provided by bevouliin at `http://opengameart.org/users/bevouliin`.

With the enemy in place, it's time to give the nasty little fellow some logic; we won't use this just yet in this chapter, but it's good to have it from the beginning (see `Chapter 10`, *The Battle Begins*, for the applied AI).

Create a new animator controller called `DragonAI.controller` by right-clicking in your `Assets\Animation\Controllers folder` and selecting **Create | Animator Controller.**

Double-clicking on the new controller brings up the basic Animator view, as shown in the following screenshot:

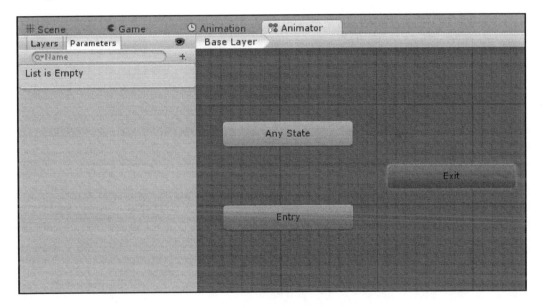

Next, we need some parameters to control the state machine, so add the following parameters to the controller by clicking on the + symbol on the parameters bar and selecting the correct data type, as shown in the following screenshot:

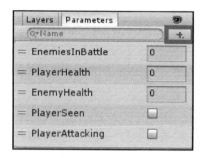

The parameters to be added and their data types are as follows:

- EnemiesInBattle: Int
- PlayerHealth: Int
- EnemyHealth: Int
- PlayerSeen: Bool
- PlayerAttacking: Bool

Now that we have some input parameters, we need our states. So, create the states shown in the following screenshot on the current animation layer by right-clicking within the window and navigating to **Create State | Empty**:

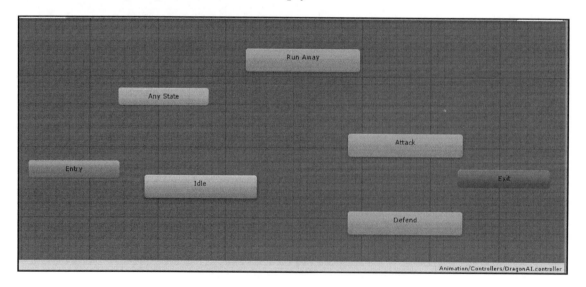

The states to be added are as follows:

- Idle
- Run Away
- Attack
- Defend

 You should note that the first state will be colored orange, whereas the rest are colored gray. This is simply because the first one you create becomes the default state (the state the state machine will start with). You can change the default state at any time by right-clicking on it and selecting **Set As Default**.

With the parameters and states in place, all that is left is to connect everything up and finalize the state machine. So, as we did in Chapter 3, *Getting Animated*, we need to create some transitions between the states along with the conditions for those transitions, as shown in the following screenshot:

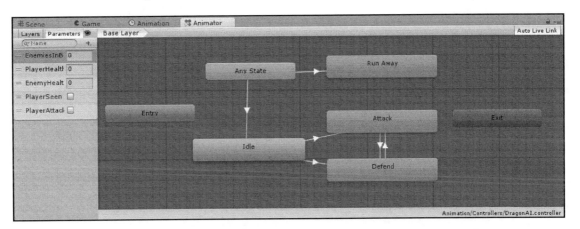

As seen in the preceding screenshot, the states and their transitions are as follows:

- *Idle -> Attack – PlayerSeen = true*

  Dragon attacks the player when she sees him

- *Idle -> Defend – PlayerSeen = true and PlayerAttacking = true*

  If the player attacks first when they are seen by the Dragon, then defend

- *Attack -> Defend – PlayerAttacking = true*

    Switch to defend if the player attacks

- *Defend -> Attack – PlayerAttacking = false*

    As soon as the player stops attacking, switch back to attack

- *Any State -> Idle – PlayerSeen = false*

    If the Dragon loses sight of the player at any time, go back to idle

- *Any State -> Run Away – EnemyHealth < 2 and PlayerHealth > 2*

    The Dragon is basically a coward; if at any time its health drops too low and the player is a lot healthier, then it will fly away as fast as its little wings will take it

Now that we have an AI state machine for our Dragon, select the **Dragon** GameObject in the **Scene** Hierarchy and add a new **Animator** Component in the **Inspector** menu by dragging the newly created animator to it, which should now look like the following screenshot:

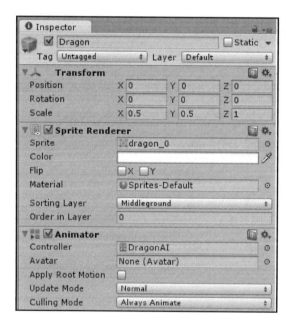

Now that we have our Dragon set up, we just need to create a prefab from it. So, drag the **Dragon** GameObject from the **Scene** Hierarchy and place it in the `Assets\Prefabs\Characters` folder. You can now delete the original in the scene as we don't need it anymore.

 If you ever need to change or add to a prefab, you can do this at any time by selecting the prefab and updating it in the **Inspector** menu. This will automatically update any scene object created from the prefab. However, if you add the prefab to the scene and then change it, the changes you make will only be for that instance in the scene and will not update the prefab.

As noted previously, you can also update the prefab from the instance by clicking on the **Apply** button.

# Spawning the Dragons

Now that we have our Dragon enemy, we need to be able to randomly drop some Dragons into the battle. For this, we need to set up some spawning points (because we don't want them to appear just anywhere) and a script to manage them.

First, create a new empty GameObject in the scene and call it `SpawnPoints`. Position it at (0,0,0). This is just a container to keep the spawn points all together. Create an empty child object of the `SpawnPoints` GameObject by right-clicking on `SpawnPoints` in the Hierarchy and selecting **Create Empty**. Rename it `Spawn1`. Change its display icon to the blue diamond, as shown in the following screenshot:

Duplicate this object eight times (by pressing *Ctrl + D*) so that you have a total of nine children of SpawnPoints. Now name them Spawn1, Spawn2, and so on, as shown in the following screenshot:

Now, position each spawn point in the scene where you want a Dragon to appear.

 While doing this, I find that adding the prefab manually to each spawn point and then positioning it makes it a lot easier to find the right spot. However, remember that the order in which you add them to the scene is important as it affects what order they are drawn in.

After a bit of tinkering, I ended up with the following (I also added the Protagonist_4 sprite for effect):

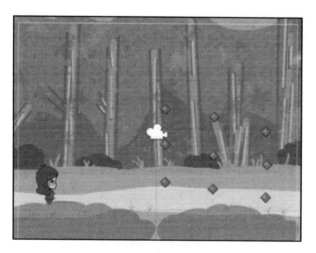

The spawn point markers

The following screenshot is an example scene where all nine Dragons have spawned in:

An example scene where all nine Dragons have spawned in

 If you added prefabs of the Dragons to each of your spawn points to help with position the points correctly, don't forget to delete the Dragons from the scene at this point.

Now that we know where the Dragons are going to appear, we just need to get them there, so we'll manage this with a `BattleManager` script.

The purpose of this script is to manage the life cycle of the battle scene—from setting up the battle scene, to taking turns to attack, and to finalizing the battle once complete.

We start off by creating a new `BattleManager` C# script and placing it in the `Scripts` folder along with the other managers (if you wish, you can create a separate `Managers` folder and organize them there). As this script only works when we are in a battle, there is no need to make it a singleton. Battles come and go and they should only last for the length of the current battle.

 For now, we will just set up the framework for the battle scene and get it populated. Our poor hero has no chance to defend herself yet, so we'll just let her run away.

First, we'll add some variables that we can configure from the scene using the following code:

```
public GameObject[] EnemySpawnPoints;
public GameObject[] EnemyPrefabs;
public AnimationCurve SpawnAnimationCurve;
```

The lines in the preceding code maintain the spawn points the battle manager knows about, the possible enemy prefabs it can spawn into the scene, and a curve that we can use later to control how we animate the Dragons. We'll set up the animation curve shortly.

Next, we have some control variables to manage the battle as it ensues. This is done using the following code:

```
private int enemyCount;
enum BattlePhase
{
    PlayerAttack,
    EnemyAttack
}
private BattlePhase phase;
```

These states are only temporary. In Chapter 9, *Getting Ready to Fight*, and Chapter 10, *The Battle Begins*, we will build on this for a more full-fledged system using Mecanim.

We keep a count of how many enemies are active in the scene as well as what phase the battle is in at the moment (along with our own enumeration of the states the battle can be in; you can always add more). Finally, we have a flag to monitor whether the enemy characters have actually started fighting.

Now when the script runs, it needs to initialize the battle arena; so add the following code to the Start method:

```
void Start () {
    // Calculate how many enemies
    enemyCount = Random.Range(1, EnemySpawnPoints.Length);
    // Spawn the enemies in
    StartCoroutine(SpawnEnemies());
    // Set the beginning battle phase
    phase = BattlePhase.PlayerAttack;
}
```

Keeping things simple for now, we generate a random number of Dragons who will attack (or be found wandering around the wood waiting to be chopped). Then, we spawn them in using a coroutine and start the battle with the player going first.

Since we simply need a fixed random number and we are only doing it at the beginning of the scene, we are just using the Unity Random function. If we needed a more complex random selection or more frequent selection, we would change this to something more complex or preloaded.

Now that we know how many Dragons we need in the battle, we can spawn them in. I've used a coroutine here so we can animate them one by one as follows:

```
IEnumerator SpawnEnemies()
{
    // Spawn enemies in over time
    for (int i = 0; i < enemyCount; i++)
    {
        var newEnemy =
            (GameObject)Instantiate(EnemyPrefabs[0]);
        newEnemy.transform.position = new Vector3(10, -1, 0);

        yield return StartCoroutine(
            MoveCharacterToPoint(
                EnemySpawnPoints[i], newEnemy));
        newEnemy.transform.parent =
            EnemySpawnPoints[i].transform;
    }
}
```

Here, we loop through how many Dragons we'll need, create a new instance using the prefab we created earlier, set its position off screen, and then animate it on to the screen using yet another coroutine (shown in the following code). When the coroutine finishes animating, we anchor it to the spawn point it was meant for.

I put the Enemy prefabs into an array so we can support multiple types of enemies in the battle.

So that the Dragons don't just appear at their spawn points, but rather move in to their spawn points, we use the AnimationCurve parameter we added to the script and a co-routine. This will move the Dragon from off-screen to its intended spawn point with the following code:

```
IEnumerator MoveCharacterToPoint(GameObject destination,
GameObject character)
```

```
{
    float timer = 0f;
    var StartPosition = character.transform.position;
    if (SpawnAnimationCurve.length > 0)
    {
        while (timer < SpawnAnimationCurve.keys[
            SpawnAnimationCurve.length - 1].time)
        {
            character.transform.position =
                Vector3.Lerp(StartPosition,
                    destination.transform.position,
                        SpawnAnimationCurve.Evaluate(timer));

            timer += Time.deltaTime;
            yield return new WaitForEndOfFrame();
        }
    }
    else
    {
        character.transform.position =
            destination.transform.position;
    }
}
```

In the preceding code, we work out where the GameObject is starting from and then use a `while` loop to keep the GameObject moving until it finally reaches its destination. However, to improve things, we will base the loop on the length of the `AnimationCurve` parameter we have defined for this transition.

This allows greater flexibility and allows us to have more complex and longer animations as follows:

- First we check whether there are animation steps (keys) within `AnimationCurve` (if you want something to just pop in to place, then don't configure a curve)
- If there are keys in the animation, then we keep iterating until we reach the last key in the animation based on the time of that step and our current iteration time

Then, within the loop, we use `Lerp` for the position of the object from start to finish using the animation curve to control its time and rate.

 We only go to the next animation step when the next frame is ready (using the `WaitForEndOfFrame` function), else the animation would happen all at once; so we do it gradually each frame.

You could use `yield return null`; however, this happens indeterminately and could cause the coroutine to be called several times per frame depending on how long the last render/draw took. Since this is a smooth animation, we need to process it for each frame. If it is another operation that just needs controlled cycles/iterations, returning `null` may be preferred.

# Creating the BattleManager

Now we need to create an object in the scene on which the `BattleManager` script will be attached. Add a new empty GameObject to the battle scene, name it `BattleManager`, and then attach the new script to it. The following screenshot shows the script with the `EnemySpawnPoints` and `EnemyPrefabs` arrays expanded:

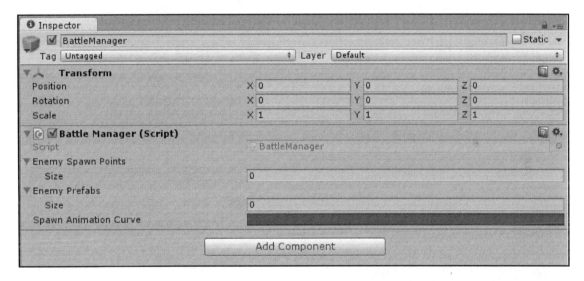

Once the script is attached to the empty GameObject, it is time to add the spawn points we created earlier to `EnemySpawnPoints`, the Dragon prefab to the `EnemyPrefabs` parameter, and the **Spawn Animation Curve**. You'll notice the two arrays are empty and there is currently just an empty gray box for the `SpawnAnimationCurve`.

Let's start by adding the spawn points we created earlier to the EnemySpawnPoints array. This is achieved by dragging the individual spawn points from the Hierarchy over the words, **Enemy Spawn Points**. Once you have dragged all nine spawn points to the array, you should see the following:

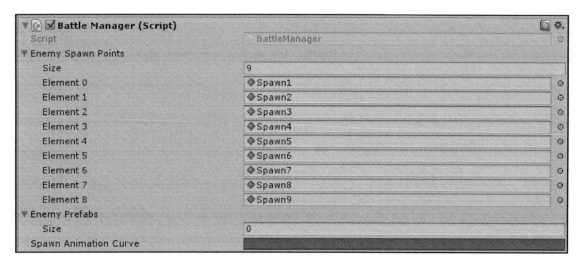

Now, from the **Project** view, drag the Dragon prefab over the words **Enemy Prefabs**. Even though we only have one type of enemy right now, an array was used so that multiple enemies could be added. You should see the following:

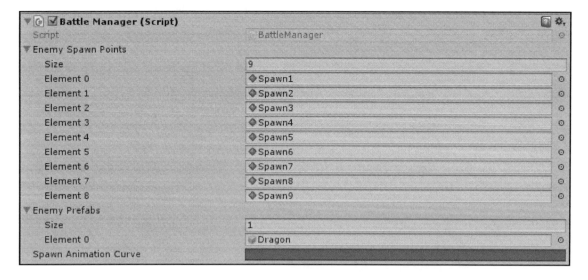

The last thing we are going to do is set up the animation curve. If you click on the gray box, the **Curve** window should pop up. Select the last curve option, as shown in the following screenshot:

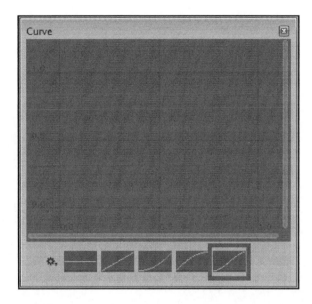

Now that you have everything set up, your `BattleManager` script should appear as follows:

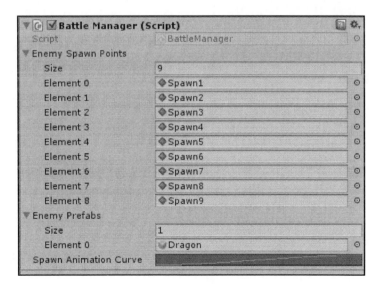

# Allowing the player to run away

To start with, we are only going to give the player the option to run away. We will achieve this by adding a button to the scene and then creating code that will execute when that button is pressed.

To make the button, select **Create | UI | Button**. Then, set its anchor and pivot point to the top-left corner. You'll notice that a text object is a child of the button object. Change the Text property to say **Run Away**. Your Game view should now look like the following:

Add a CanvasGroup component to the Canvas so that we can adjust its interactivity and visibility later. For now, set the alpha to 0, and deselect **Interactable** and **Blocks Raycasts**. The button should now longer be visible in your game view.

> Remember, we used a **CanvasGroup** component on the dialog box in Chapter 6, *NPCs and Interactions*.

We now need to write some logic for this button to follow. We want this button to only be visible during the player's battle phase and we want it to have the player return to the Overworld scene.

Return to your `BattleMananger` script and add the following to the top of the script:

```
using UnityEngine.UI;
```

The preceding line of code will allow us to have a variable related to a `CanvasGroup`.

Add the following variable declaration:

```
public CanvasGroup theButtons;
```

Now add the following code:

```
void Update(){
    if (phase == BattlePhase.PlayerAttack){
        theButtons.alpha=1;
        theButtons.interactable=true;
        theButtons.blocksRaycasts=true;
    }else{
        theButtons.alpha=0;
        theButtons.interactable=false;
        theButtons.blocksRaycasts=false;
    }
}
public void RunAway() {
    NavigationManager.NavigateTo("Overworld");
}
```

The `Update` function will turn the buttons on and off depending on whether or not it is the player's turn. The `RunAway` function will exit to the `Overworld` scene.

When you save the code, you should see a new public variable displaying in the `BattleManager` Inspector. Drag and drop the Canvas in to the slot next to **The Buttons**, to assign it to the `CanvasGroup theButtons` variable.

Currently, the `RunAway` function is not linked to the button we created earlier. To have this function activate whenever the button is pressed, we need to view the Button's Inspector. You will see at the bottom of the Button's Inspector the following:

This list being left empty means that nothing happens when the button is clicked. Click on the + sign at the bottom:

In the first drop-down, select **Editor and Runtime**. The slot below it that says **None (Object)** tells the button on which object the script it needs to look at is attached. Since our RunAway function is on the BattleMananger object, we will drag and drop that BattleMananger to this slot.

Once you do that, the drop-down that says **No Function** will now be interactable. The drop-down will now list all public scripts that are attached to the BattleMananger. From this drop-down, select **BattleMananger | RunAway**, letting the button know it needs to look at the BattleMananger script and run the RunAway function when clicked, as shown in the following screenshot:

# Starting the battle

We have our battle scene up and running, and when the player runs away, she will return to the Overworld. Wouldn't it be nice to also enter the battle scene? So let's add that.

We don't want the player to enter a battle when she is right on top of a town and want different areas to have higher probabilities of encountering a battle. So, to begin with, we will create some battle areas.

Return to the Overworld scene. Create an empty GameObject and call it BattleZones. As always, when creating empty GameObjects that will act as a holder, set its X and Y position to 0. Now, create an empty GameObject as a child of BattleZones and call it Zone. Add a BoxCollider2D component to it and set IsTrigger to true. Give it a red oval icon.

Leave the Zone GameObject as is for now, as we will come back to it in a minute. First, we have to write a script to attach to it.

Create a new C# script in the Scripts folder and call it RandomBattle.

We'll start by declaring some variables:

```
public int battleProbability;
int encounterChance=100;
public int secondsBetweenBattles;
public string battleSceneName;
```

Three of the preceding defined variables are set to public so that we can easily change them for individual battle zones. The first variable, battleProbability, represents the probability of encountering a battle within the given zone. The second variable, encounterChance, will hold a randomly generated number. If this number is less than or equal to battleProbability, a battle will occur.

The third variable, secondsBetweenBattles, will determine how much time will pass between each *try* at a battle. So, if encounterChance is assigned a random number and it is greater than battleProbability, the amount of time designated by secondsBetweenBattles will pass before a new random number is assigned to encounterChance, thus, creating another attempt at battle.

The last variable, battleSceneName, will be the string name of the scene that should load. Right now we only have one scene, but if you wanted to add multiple battle scenes, this will allow you to easily change the scene that loads.

> If you had multiple battle scenes, you could make things more interesting by making a battleSceneName array variable and randomly selecting between multiple scenes similar to the way we selected spawn points for the dragons.

To be able to load scenes through code, we need to add the following to the top of our script:

```
using UnityEngine.SceneManagement;
```

We are going to continually check if a battle should occur while the player is within the specific zone. To do so, we will use `OnTriggerEnter2D`, `OnTriggerStay2D`, and `OnTriggerExit2D` methods:

```
void OnTriggerEnter2D(Collider2D col){
    encounterChance=Random.Range(1,100);
    if(encounterChance>battleProbability){
        StartCoroutine(RecalculateChance());
    }
}
IEnumerator RecalculateChance(){
    while (encounterChance>battleProbability){
        yield return new WaitForSeconds(secondsBetweenBattles);
            encounterChance=Random.Range(1,100);
    }
}
void OnTriggerStay2D(Collider2D col){
    if(encounterChance<=battleProbability){
        Debug.Log("Battle");
        SceneManager.LoadScene(battleSceneName);
    }
}
void OnTriggerExit2D(Collider2D col){
    encounterChance=100;
    StopCoroutine(RecalculateChance());
}
```

When the player enters the zone (`OnTriggerEnter2D`), a random number (`encounterChance`) will be generated to determine if a battle will occur. If the battle does not occur, a random number will be generated in the `RecalculateChance` function. As long as the player is within the zone (`OnTriggerStay2D`), battles will be continually attempted. If a random number is successfully within the probability range, the appropriate scene will load. Once the player exits the zone (`OnTriggerExit2D`), battles will no longer be attempted until the player reenters the zone.

Now we can attach the `RandomBattle` script to the `Zone` object we created earlier. I'm going to set the `RandomBattle` values, as shown in the following screenshot:

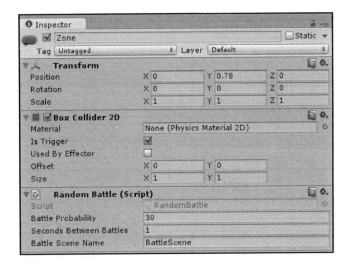

Now save this zone as a prefab in the `Prefabs/Environments` folder so that we can easily reuse it. Do not delete the current zone from the scene; we are just going to rename it now and change its parameters a bit so that it appears as shown in the following screenshot:

Let's make another zone that has a higher chance of battle. Drag the zone prefab to the `BattleZones` holder to make it a new child. Rename it and changes its values, as shown in the following screenshot:

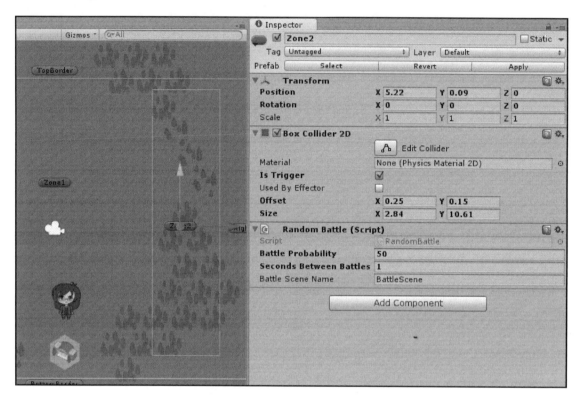

Before this will work, we need to add `BattleScene` to our build settings. Now, random battles will occur when the player walks in these zones.

# Saving the map position

So, the player will pop back and forth between the overworld and battles. As the player hits the button to run away, we see a very obvious problem: the map scene is starting afresh back at home. This is simply because we are not tracking where the player left the previous scene.

There are two ways to handle this: either we record where exactly everything is in every scene and where the player enters and exits or we can simply track the last known position (or possibly a mixture of the two?).

For now, let us simply implement the last known position method. To do this, we are going to need a central place to remember everything about our game world (well, at least the important bits we want to track), such as the player's stats, options and preferences they have set, and where they have been in the world. Some of these will need saving for the next time the player runs the game and some are just for the current instantiation, but we will cover saving and loading later in Chapter 13, *Putting a Bow on It*.

The settings we need don't have to be part of any scene, actively tracked in the scene, or even interact with other game components. So, we don't need a class that implements MonoBehaviour or ScriptableObject; however, we do need it to be around all the time and not be reloaded in every scene. For this, we need a very simple static class (we implemented one of these earlier in Chapter 7, *The World Map*, with NavigationManager).

Create a new C# script in Assets\Scripts\Classes called GameState and populate it with the following code:

```
using System.Collections.Generic;
using UnityEngine;

public static class GameState {

    public static Player CurrentPlayer =
        ScriptableObject.CreateInstance<Player>();
    public static Dictionary<string, Vector3> LastScenePositions = new
        Dictionary<string, Vector3>();
}
```

Here, we have some simple properties that do the following:

- Track the player's stats
- A flag to note whether the player is running home away from a battle
- A dictionary to record the scenes the player has been to and the last position they were in that scene

This was simple enough, but to avoid unnecessary code duplication, I have also added some helper methods to the GameState class to manage and simplify the use of the LastScenePositions dictionary (to save time later).

So, add the following code to the end of the GameState class:

```
public static Vector3 GetLastScenePosition(string sceneName)
{
    if (GameState.LastScenePositions.ContainsKey(sceneName))
    {
        var lastPos = GameState.LastScenePositions[sceneName];
        return lastPos;
    }
    else
    {
        return Vector3.zero;
    }
}

public static void SetLastScenePosition(
    string sceneName, Vector3 position)
{
    if (GameState.LastScenePositions.ContainsKey(sceneName))
    {
        GameState.LastScenePositions[sceneName] = position;
    }
    else
    {
        GameState.LastScenePositions.Add(sceneName, position);
    }
}
```

The preceding code is fairly similar but it ensures simple and effective use of any dictionary class, checking the following:

- When you request a value from the dictionary, it checks whether it exists first and then returns it
- If the value doesn't exist in the dictionary yet, it returns a default value
- When you add a new value to the dictionary, it checks whether it already exists, and if it does, then it updates the existing value
- If the value does not exist when you try to add it, it just adds it to the dictionary

Dictionaries are powerful when used correctly: you can find values by index (in this case a string) or you can find them by ID (like in arrays). You can even loop over dictionaries with for or foreach loops.

However, depending on how you use them, they may not perform well and can also generate garbage, so use them carefully.

For more details, see the C# article at

http://blogs.msdn.com/b/shawnhar/archive/2007/07/02/twin-paths-t
o-garbage-collector-nirvana.aspx. The article is based on XNA but
rings true for any C# platform.

There are also considerations when you need to serialize the values from a
dictionary since they are handled differently on some platforms and, in
some cases, are not even supported for serialization.

With the `GameState` class in place, we will create a `MapPosition` script for the map to load
the last position if one exists, and save the last position when exiting the scene (and in any
other scene that will need the logic).

Add the following `Awake` method to the newly created `MapPosition` script:

```
void Awake()
{
    var lastPosition =
        GameState.GetLastScenePosition(SceneManager.GetActiveScene().name);

    if (lastPosition != Vector3.zero)
    {
        transform.position = lastPosition;
    }
}
```

The preceding code simply looks for a last position for the current scene, and if there is one,
it moves the player to it.

Similarly, when closing the scene, we just need to store the last position. To do so, we add
an `OnDestroy` method as follows and save the player's current position:

```
void OnDestroy()
{
    GameState.SetLastScenePosition(
        SceneManager.GetActiveScene().name, transform.position);
}
```

Attach the `MapPosition` script to the player in the Player prefab so that it updates to all
instances of the player. This will allow the player to appropriately spawn in both the town
and the overworld.

Initially, it seems like this works very well. But, as is common with programming,
sometimes you add a new feature and it breaks something else (or multiple other things).

# Stop immediately re-entering battle

The first thing you may notice was affected by saving our map position is that since we spawn in a battle zone, it's possible that we immediately re-enter battle. This can be fixed by adding a new Boolean variable to the `GameState` script:

```
public static bool justExitedBattle;
```

We will turn this value on and off with the `BattleManager` and `RandomBattle` scripts.

Update the `BattleManager` script in the following way:

```
public void RunAway() {
    GameState.justExitedBattle=true;
    NavigationManager.NavigateTo("Overworld");
}
```

Update the `RandomBattle` script in the following way:

```
void OnTriggerEnter2D(Collider2D col){
    if(!GameState.justExitedBattle){
        encounterChance=Random.Range(1,100);
        if(encounterChance>battleProbability){
            StartCoroutine(RecalculateChance());
        }
    }else{
        StartCoroutine(RecalculateChance());
        GameState.justExitedBattle=false;
    }
}
```

Now if `GameState.justExitedBattle` is true, the value that checks if an encounter happens will not be calculated until after the time between battles has elapsed.

# Going back to town

Since adding in the ability to save the map positions, the game goes crazy if you try to enter and exit the town. Now, since the player's last position is being saved, when the player exits town, she continuously goes back and forth between the town and the overworld. This is because when the scene loads, she is touching the collider that loads the previous scene.

This is a little more complicated to fix, but not by too much. The big problem is that our colliders are being instantly triggered when the scene loads. So, we will be changing the script associated with those colliders causing scene loads (NavigationPrompt) as well as our GameState and MapPositions scripts.

Reopen the GameState script and add the following variable:

```
public static bool saveLastPosition=true;
```

Now reopen the MapPosition script and adjust the code as follows:

```
void OnDestroy(){
    if(GameState.saveLastPosition){
        GameState.SetLastScenePosition(SceneManager.GetActiveScene().name,
            transform.position);
    }
}
```

The last script we need to change is the NavigationPrompt script. Add the following variable:

```
public Vector3 startingPosition;
```

Open it and add the following to both the OnCollisionEnter2D and OnTriggerEnter2D methods:

```
GameState.saveLastPosition=false;
GameState.SetLastScenePosition(SceneManager.GetActiveScene().name,
    startingPosition);
```

Now we're done with changing code! Essentially what these changes have done is create a Boolean variable that tells us if we will or will not save the last game position. If we do not save the last position, we load a specific Vector3 value instead of grabbing the player's last position when in the scene.

For this to work appropriately, we need to adjust the parameters of the GameObjects in our Town and Overworld scenes that have the NavigationPrompt script attached to them.

 If you forget which objects in a scene have a specific script attached to them, right-click on the script in the Project view and select **Find References in Scene**.

In the `Overworld` scene, select the `Town` GameObject. Change the `StartingPosition` values of the `NavigationPrompt` script to the position at which you want the player to start. I used the following properties that place the player where she appears in the screenshot:

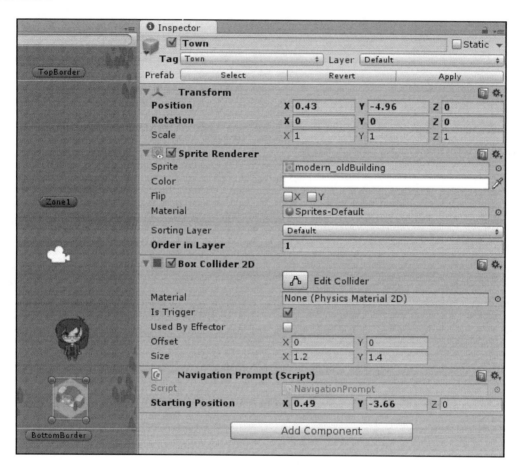

In the `Town` scene, select the `RightBorder` GameObject. Change the `StartingPosition` values of the `NavigationPrompt` script to the position you want the player to start at. I used the following properties that place the player where she appears in the screenshot:

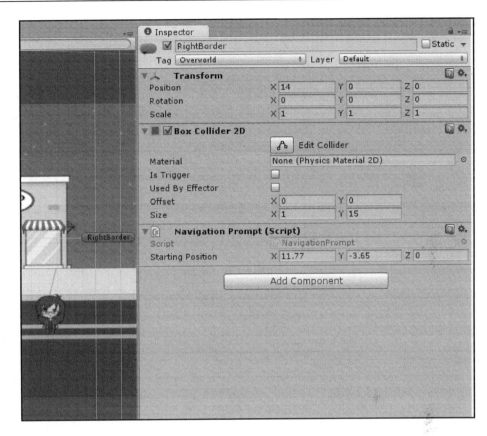

Now the player's position will be appropriately saved when entering and exiting the town.

# Going further

If you are the adventurous sort, try expanding your project to add the following:

- Add a few more enemy types and integrate the enemy class into the
- Animate the enemy
- Try putting together another battle scene and update the battle logic to pick a random scene
- Separate the random logic into its own manager class and try a few different patterns
- Increase the randomness of battles by making time between battles random as well

# Summary

Picking when and how often a player will enter battles is a tricky balance between fun and engagement. Do it too often and they will get annoyed, too infrequently and they will get bored. Also, the battles need to be achievable and challenge the player at the same time. It is a complex paradox that, if planned wrong, can ruin your hard work. The best solution, when all is said and done, is to get your game play tested by as many people as possible and genuinely consider feedback, no matter how harsh.

Alongside random generation, of course, is predictive planning: if you have a story to tell, you also need to have a framework to replay that story over a period of time, balancing when you need a random event or picking up the next page in your book.

In this chapter, we covered random generation, what it means, and when to use it effectively; covered some very simple uses of randomness; built a battle scene and planned for expansion; covered basic AI concepts and State Engines; and enabled the player to run away to fight another day.

In the next chapter, we will set up the UI for our battle system so our player can actually do things other than run away.

# 9
# Getting Ready to Fight

One of the hardest parts of any game development is engagement. This centers on how you can keep the players playing the game, how the game balances out to keep them challenged, and how to deliver enough varied content so they feel they are always experiencing something new.

This chapter will start out by laying the main foundation for the battle system of our game. We will create the **Head-Up Display (HUD)** as well as design the overall logic of the battle system.

The following topics will be covered in this chapter:

- Creating a state manager to handle the logic behind a turn-based battle system
- Working with **Mecanim** in the code
- Exploring RPG UIs
- Creating the game's HUD

## Setting up our battle state manager

The most unique and important part of a turn-based battle system is the turns. Controlling the turns is incredibly important and we will need something to handle the logic behind the actual turns for us. We'll accomplish this by creating a battle state machine.

## The battle state manager

Starting back in our `BattleScene`, we need to create a state machine using all of Mecanim's handy features. Although we will still only be using a fraction of the functionality with the RPG sample, I advise you to investigate and read more about its capabilities.

Navigate to the `Assets\Animation\Controllers` folder and create a new **Animator Controller** called `BattleStateMachine`, then we can begin putting together the battle state machine. The following screenshot shows you the states, transitions, and properties that we will need:

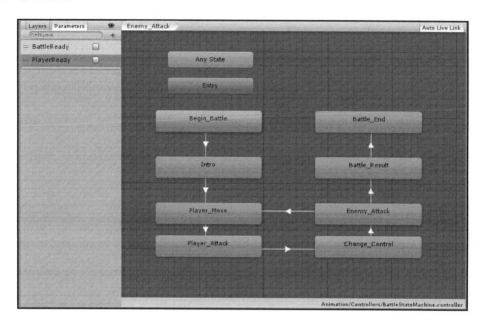

As shown in the preceding screenshot, we have created eight states to control the flow of a battle with two Boolean parameters to control its transition.

The transitions are defined as follows:

- From **Begin_Battle** to **Intro:**

  - **BattleReady** set to `true`
  - **Has Exit Time** set to `false` (deselected)
  - **Transition Duration** set to 0

- From **Intro** to **Player_Move:**

  - **Has Exit Time** set to `true`
  - **Exit Time** set to `0.9`
  - **Transition Duration** set to 2

- From **Player_Move** to **Player_Attack:**

    - **PlayerReady** set to `true`
    - **Has Exit Time** set to `false`
    - **Transition Duration** set to 0

- From **Player_Attack** to **Change_Control:**

    - **PlayerReady** set to `false`
    - **Has Exit Time** set to `false`
    - **Transition Duration** set to 2

- From **Change_Control** to **Enemy_Attack:**

    - **Has Exit Time** set to `true`
    - **Exit Time** set to `0.9`
    - **Transition Duration** set to 2

- From **Enemy_Attack** to **Player_Move:**

    - **BattleReady** set to `true`
    - **Has Exit Time** set to `false`
    - **Transition Duration** set to 2

- From **Enemy_Attack** to **Battle_Result:**

    - **BattleReady** set to `false`
    - **Has Exit Time** set to `false`
    - **Transition Time** set to 2

- From **Battle_Result** to **Battle_End:**

    - **Has Exit Time** set to `true`
    - **Exit Time** set to `0.9`
    - **Transition Time** set to 5

Summing up, what we have built is a steady flow of battle, which can be summarized as follows:

- The battle begins and we show a little introductory clip to tell the player about the battle
- Once the player has control, we wait for them to finish their move
- We then perform the player's attack and switch the control over to the enemy AI
- If there are any enemies left, they get to attack the player (if they are not too scared and have not run away)
- If the battle continues, we switch back to the player; otherwise, we show the battle result
- We show the result for five seconds (or until the player hits a key), then finish the battle and return the player to the world together with whatever loot and experience gained

This is just a simple flow, which can be extended as much as you want, and as we continue, you will see all the points where you could expand it.

With our animator state machine created, we now just need to attach it to our battle manager so it will be available when the battle runs; the following are the steps to do this:

1. Open up `BattleScene`.
2. Select the `BattleManager` game object in the project Hierarchy and add an **Animator** component to it.
3. Now drag the `BattleStateMachine` animator controller we just created into the **Controller** property of the **Animator** component.

The preceding steps attached our new battle state machine to our battle engine. Now, we just need to be able to reference the **BattleStateMachine** Mecanim state machine from the `BattleManager` script. To do so, open up the `BattleManager` script in the `Assets\Scripts` folder and add the following variable to the top of the class:

```
private Animator battleStateManager;
```

Then, to capture the configured `Animator` component in our `BattleManager` script, we add the following to an `Awake` function placed before the `Start` function:

```
void Awake(){
        battleStateManager=GetComponent<Animator>();
        if(battleStateManager==null){
            Debug.LogError("No battleStateMachine Animator found.");
        }
```

```
}
```

We have to assign it this way because all the functionality to integrate the **Animator Controller** is built into the `Animator` component. We cannot simply attach the controller directly to the `BattleManager` script and use it.

Now that it's all wired up, let's start using it.

# Getting to the state manager in the code

Now that we have our state manager running in Mecanim, we just need to be able to access it from the code. However, at first glance, there is a barrier to achieving this. The reason being that the Mecanim system uses hashes (integer ID keys for objects) not strings to identify states within its engine (still not clear why, but for performance reasons probably). To access the states in Mecanim, Unity provides a hashing algorithm to help you, which is fine for one-off checks but a bit of an overhead when you need per-frame access.

You can check to see if a state's name is a specific string using the following code:

`GetCurrentAnimatorStateInfo(0).IsName("Thing you're checking")` But there is not way to store the names of the current state to a variable.

A simple solution to this is to generate and cache all the state hashes when we start and then use the cache to talk to the Mecanim engine.

First, let's remove the placeholder code from Chapter 8, *Encountering Enemies and Running Away*, for the old `enum` state machine. So, remove the following code from the top of the `BattleManager` script:

```
enum BattlePhase
{
    PlayerAttack,
    EnemyAttack
}
private BattlePhase phase;
```

Also, remove the following line from the `Start` method:

```
phase = BattlePhase.PlayerAttack;
```

There is still a reference in the `Update` method for our buttons, but we will update that shortly; feel free to comment it out now if you wish, but don't delete it.

Now, to begin working with our new state machine, we need a replica of the available states we have defined in our Mecanim state machine. For this, we just need an enumeration using the same names (you can create this either as a new C# script or simply place it in the `BattleManager` class), as follows:

```
public enum BattleState
{
    Begin_Battle,
    Intro,
    Player_Move,
    Player_Attack,
    Change_Control,
    Enemy_Attack,
    Battle_Result,
    Battle_End
}
```

It may seem strange to have a duplicate of your states in the state machine and in the code; however, at the time of writing, it is necessary. Mecanim does not expose the names of the states outside of the engine other than through using hashes. You can either use this approach and make it dynamic, or extract the state hashes and store them in a dictionary for use.

Mecanim makes the managing of state machines very simple under the hood and is extremely powerful, much better than trawling through code every time you want to update the state machine.

Next, we need a location to cache the hashes the state machine needs and a property to keep the current state so that we don't constantly query the engine for a hash. So, add a new `using` statement to the beginning of the `BattleManager` class as follows:

```
using System.Collections;
using System.Collections.Generic;
using UnityEngine;
```

Then, add the following variables to the top of the `BattleManager` class:

```
private Dictionary<int, BattleState> battleStateHash = new Dictionary<int,
    BattleState>();
private BattleState currentBattleState;
```

Finally, we just need to integrate the animator state machine we have created. So, create a new `GetAnimationStates` method in the `BattleManager` class as follows:

```
void GetAnimationStates()
{
  foreach (BattleState state in (BattleState[])
    System.Enum.GetValues(typeof(BattleState)))
  {
    battleStateHash.Add(Animator.StringToHash(state.ToString()), state);
  }
}
```

This simply generates a hash for the corresponding animation state in Mecanim and stores the resultant hashes in a dictionary that we can use without having to calculate them at runtime when we need to talk to the state machine.

Sadly, there is no way at runtime to gather the information from Mecanim as this information is only available in the editor.

You could gather the hashes from the animator and store them in a file to avoid this, but it won't save you much.

To complete this, we just need to call the new method in the `Start` function of the `BattleManager` script by adding the following:

```
GetAnimationStates();
```

Now that we have our states, we can use them in our running game to control both the logic that is applied and the GUI elements that are drawn to the screen.

Now add the `Update` function to the `BattleManager` class as follows:

```
void Update()
{
  currentBattleState = battleStateHash[battleStateManager.
GetCurrentAnimatorStateInfo(0).shortNameHash];

  switch (currentBattleState)
  {
    case BattleState.Intro:
```

```
      break;
  case BattleState.Player_Move:
      break;
  case BattleState.Player_Attack:
      break;
  case BattleState.Change_Control:
      break;
  case BattleState.Enemy_Attack:
      break;
  case BattleState.Battle_Result:
      break;
  case BattleState.Battle_End:
      break;
  default:
      break;
  }
}
```

The preceding code gets the current state from the animator state machine once per frame and then sets up a choice (switch statement) for what can happen based on the current state. (Remember, it is the state machine that decides which state follows which in the Mecanim engine, not nasty nested if statements everywhere in code.)

Now we are going to update the functionality that turns our GUI button on and off. Update the line of code in the Update method we wrote as follows:

```
if (phase == BattlePhase.PlayerAttack){
```

Change it so that it now reads as follows:

```
if (currentBattleState == BattleState.Player_Move){
```

This will make it so that the buttons are now only visible when it is time for the player to perform his/her move. With these in place, we are ready to start adding in some battle logic.

# Starting the battle

As it stands, the state machine is waiting at the Begin_Battle state for us to kick things off. Obviously, we want to do this when we are ready and all the pieces on the board are in place.

When the current **Battle** scene we added in Chapter 8, *Encountering Enemies and Running Away*, starts, we load up the player and randomly spawn in a number of enemies into the fray using a coroutine function called SpawnEnemies. So, only when all the Dragons are ready and waiting to be chopped down do we want to kick things off.

To tell the state machine to start the battle, we simple add the following line just after the end of the `for` loop in the `SpawnEnemies IEnumerator` coroutine function:

```
battleStateManager.SetBool("BattleReady", true);
```

Now when everything is in place, the battle will finally begin.

# Introductory animation

When the battle starts, we are going to display a little battle introductory image that states who the player is going to be fighting against. We'll have it slide into the scene and then slide out. The following screenshot shows the end result:

 You can do all sorts of interesting stuff with this introductory animation, such as animating the individual images, but I'll leave that up to you to play with. Can't have all the fun now, can I?

Start by creating a new Canvas and renaming it `IntroCanvas` so that we can distinguish it from the canvas that will hold our buttons. At this point, since we are adding a second canvas into the scene, we should probably rename ours something that is easier for you to identify.

It's a matter of preference, but I like to use different canvases for different UI elements. For example, one for the HUD, one for pause menus, one for animations, and so on.

You can put them all on a single Canvas and use Panels and `CanvasGroup` components to distinguish between them; it's really up to you.

As a child of the new `IntroCanvas`, create a **Panel** with the properties shown in the following screenshot. Notice the **Color** property **of the Image component** is set to black with the alpha set to about half:

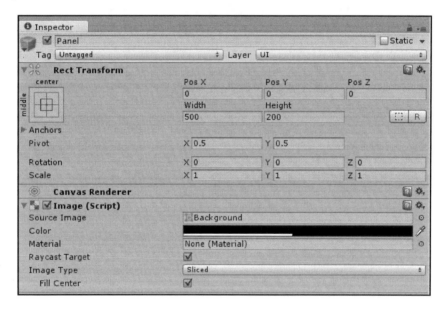

Now add as a child of the Panel two UI Images and a UI Text. Name the first image `PlayerImage` and set its properties as shown in the following screenshot. Be sure to check the **Preserve Aspect** property:

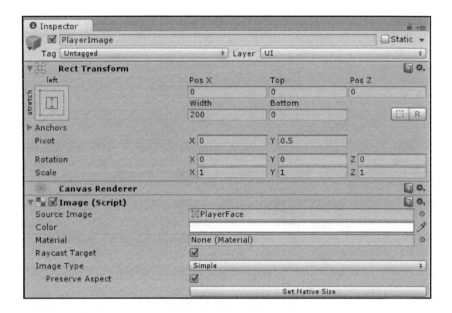

Name the second image `EnemyImage` and set the properties as shown in the following screenshot:

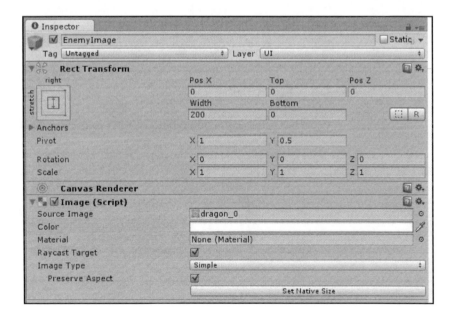

For the text, set the properties as shown in the following screenshot:

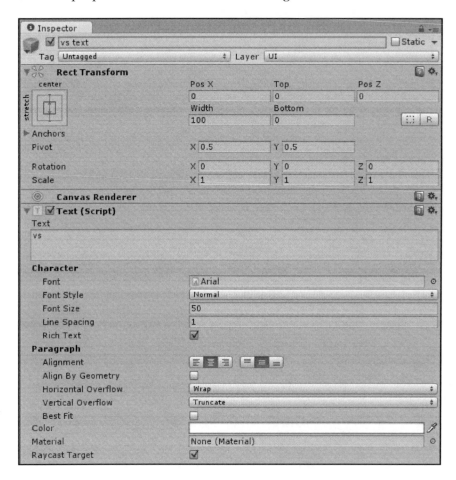

Your Panel should now appear as mine did in the image at the beginning of this section.

Now let's give this Panel its animation. With the Panel selected, select the **Animation** tab. Now hit the **Create** button. Save the animation as IntroSlideAnimation in the Assets/Animation/Clips folder.

At the **0:00** frame, set the Panel's *X* position to 600, as shown in the following screenshot:

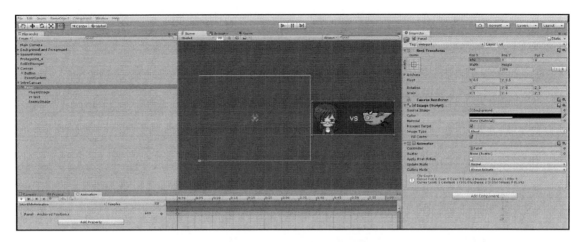

Panel moved outside of camera's view at animation frame 0:00

Now, at the **0:45** frame, set the Panel's *X* position to 0. Place the playhead at the **1:20** frame and set the Panel's *X* position to 0, there as well, by selecting **Add Key**, as shown in the following screenshot:

Create the last frame at **2:00** by setting the Panel's *X* position to −600.

When the Panel slides in, it does this annoying bounce thing instead of staying put. We need to fix this by adjusting the animation curve. Select the **Curves** tab:

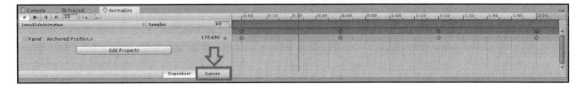

When you select the **Curves** tab, you should see something like the following:

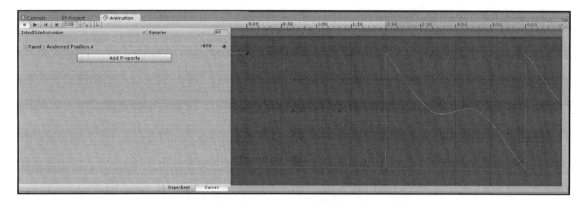

The reason for the bounce is the *wiggle* that occurs between the two center key frames. To fix this, right-click on the two center points on the curve represented by red dots and select **Flat**, as shown in the following screenshot:

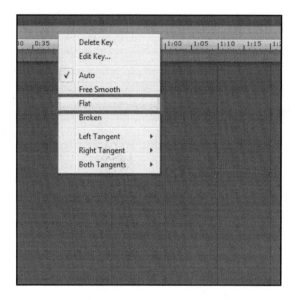

After you do so, the curve should be constant (flat) in the center, as shown in the following screenshot:

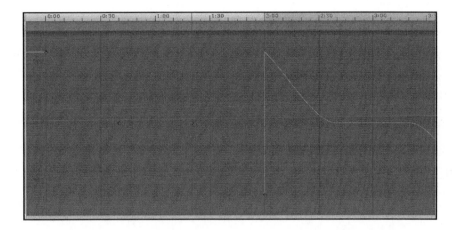

The last thing we need to do to connect this to our `BattleStateMananger` is adjust the properties of the Panel's Animator.

With the Panel selected, select the **Animator** tab. You should see something like the following:

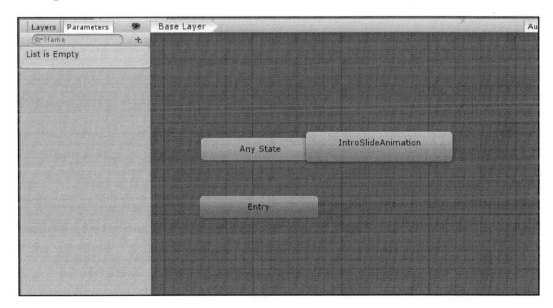

Right now, the animation immediately plays when the scene is entered. However, since we want this to tie in with our `BattleStateManager` script and only begin playing in the `Intro` state, we do not want this to be the default animation.

Create an empty state within the Animator and set it as the default state. Name this state `OutOfFrame`. Now make a Trigger Parameter called `Intro`. Set the transition between the two states so that it has the following properties:

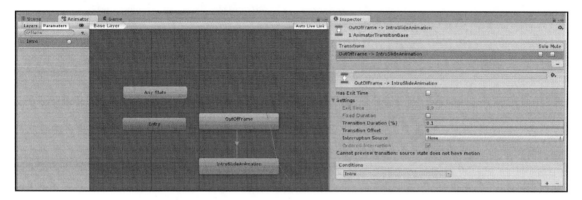

The last things we want to do before we move on is make it so this animation does not loop, rename this new Animator, and place our Animator in the correct subfolder. In the project view, select `IntroSlideAnimation` from the `Assets/Animation/Clips` folder and deselect **Loop Time**. Rename the Panel Animator to `VsAnimator` and move it to the `Assets/Animation/Controllers` folder.

Currently, the Panel is appearing right in the middle of the screen at all times, so go ahead and set the Panel's *X* Position to `600`, to get it out of the way.

Now we can access this animation in our `BattleStateManager` script.

Currently, the state machine pauses at the `Intro` state for a few seconds; let's have our Panel animation pop in.

Add the following variable declarations to our `BattleStateManager` script:

```
public GameObject introPanel;
Animator introPanelAnim;
```

And add the following to the `Awake` function:

```
introPanelAnim=introPanel.GetComponent<Animator>();
```

Now add the following to the `case` line of the `Intro` state in the `Update` function:

```
case BattleState.Intro:
    introPanelAnim.SetTrigger("Intro");
    break;
```

For this to work, we have to drag and drop the Panel into the **Intro Panel** slot in the `BattleManager` Inspector.

As the battle is now in progress and control is being passed to the player, we need some interaction from the user. Currently, the player can run away, but that's not terribly interesting. We want our player to be able to fight! So, let's design a graphic user interface that will allow her to attack those adorable, but super mean, dragons.

# Efficient RPG UI overlays

Researching various designs that have been implemented in RPG games, conveying important information such as health, stats, and other important details, is crucial to any gameplay. If the information is too obscure, the player won't understand when they are close to death (and should run far away) or will struggle to understand why their favorite magic trick just isn't going as well as it should. Similarly, if you make the UI too obtrusive, draw players' attention away too much, and obscure the real estate on the screen too much, then the result will be the same.

This balance is hard to maintain in any game, especially in RPG games, because we want to give as many capabilities as possible to our budding adventurer. It gets even harder once you start adding companions and hundreds of available skills and instant use items.

# The adventurer's overlay

Games such as *Baldur's Gate* (developed by Black Isle Studios) and games from the 1980s took the style of surrounding the player with everything at hand:

In the preceding screenshot, we see all the party members to the right, all the menu options to the left, and quick use items/skills laid at the bottom of the screen. Although functional, this style of design leaves only a small portion of the screen for the actual gameplay. Since these were mostly PC titles and large screens were available, this wasn't too much of an issue.

Today, with smartphones and 10-inch tablets being the norm, this would create a large issue. Put simply, it doesn't scale well.

# A context-sensitive overlay

The developers of *Fallout* (developed by Interplay Entertainment) took a slightly different approach; taking a similar style to that of *Baldur's Gate*, they opted for an onscreen approach but were a bit more clever about the use of it:

In the preceding screenshot, we see a smaller overlay screen at the bottom of the screen, taking up a lot less real estate. In this game, it was possible to change the overlay based on what was selected, allowing the selection of a character of the player's party to be displayed on the screen; this helped to change the details shown to that character.

Buttons were added to provide pop-up sections for skills, character attributes, and the map.

It also provided two modes, one for traveling and one for battle, each distinctly different based on what the player would need at the time.

# Modern floating UI approach

A popular pattern that fits more modern titles is to use floating elements on the player's screen, taking advantages of the improvements that *Fallout* implemented and extending them much further:

Mobile games, such as *Pylon* (developed by Quantum Squid Interactive), follow the standard of breaking up the important UI for the player and scaling/placing them on top of the main gameplay's screen. With this, the player can easily see their important stats, such as health/magic, and has easy access to actions and skills. Additionally, the map is informative and tapping on it brings out a full screen version.

Each of these elements only becomes active when the player needs them and are appropriately sized, so they don't get in the way too much.

# Balancing the need

As you can see, there are many choices as to how you can layout the important game UI; however, every game is different, so you will need to match up what the player needs to do against what they need to know in order to progress.

Above all, do not sacrifice the core of the gameplay at each point in the game just for a flashy screen element, unless it adds true value to the player.

# Bring on the GUI

Before we can start acting on the state machine, we first need to add something for the player to interact with, namely the buttons to select the attacks, items, and so on.

To do this, we will add a HUD that will hold the player's health and have buttons for the various actions. The following is a general example of the layout we will be placing the items:

In the preceding image, the last button will not be visible if there is not action tied to it, and the arrow button will only be visible in submenus. The UI elements are all provided on a sprite sheet, and we will need to do some work with the layout to get them to display, as shown in the preceding screenshot. Import the sprite sheet `BattleGUI` to the `Assets/Sprites/UI` folder. Import it in **MultipleSprite Mode** and automatically slice it.

# Laying out the HUD

Right now we have two Canvases, one holding our introduction animation and one holding the **Run Away** button. Eventually, we will delete the Canvas holding the current button. So, let's create a new Canvas and name it `HUDCanvas`. Right-click on it and create a new **UI | Panel**. Rename it `Background`. Change its properties so that you have the blue-stripped rectangle as the background and it is anchored at the top of the screen, as shown in the following screenshot:

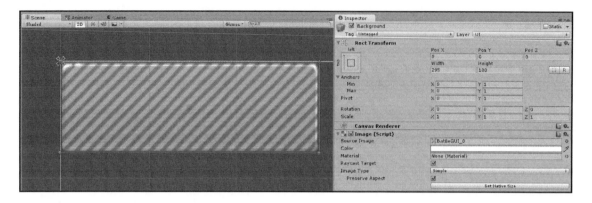

To get the other pieces to line up correctly, we will actually use two more Panels that will be children of this larger Panel. Right-click on the `Background` Panel and create two new Panels. Name the first Panel `HP`:

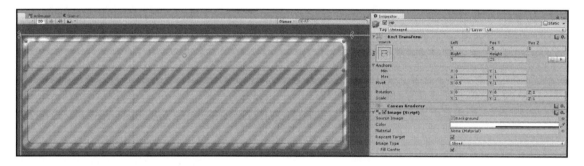

And name the second Panel `Bottom`:

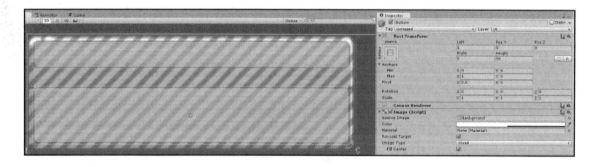

We're using these two Panels to help keep all of the items that will be within these areas contained together, as well as we use these as the holders in which we have to set our position and pivot points.

Now let's set up the top Panel that will hold our HP information. Start by setting the background of the HP Panel to the BattleGUI_1 image and settings its **Alpha** value to 256 so that it is fully opaque:

Now add, as a child of the **HP** Panel, a **UI | Text** object. Left align it, but also give it a little padding so it is not right up against the edge:

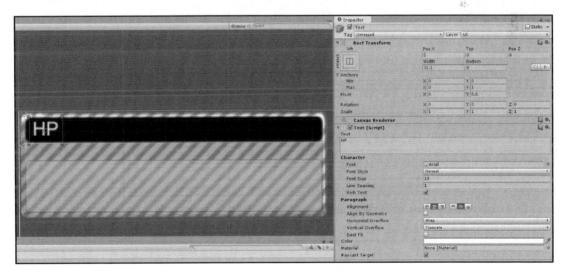

Add another **UI** | **Text** object, but put it on the right side. Later, we will get this text to update so that it appropriately displays the player's current health and total possible health:

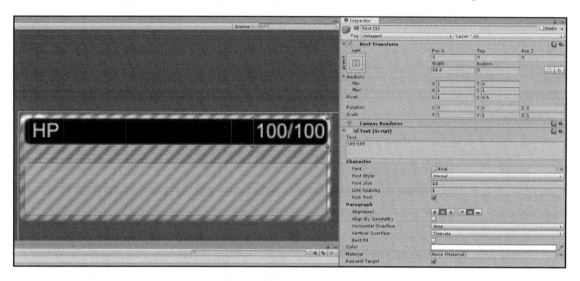

Now add, as a child of the HP Panel, a **UI** | **Slider**. Sliders are great for representing health bars. Position as shown in the following screenshot and set the **Value** to 1:

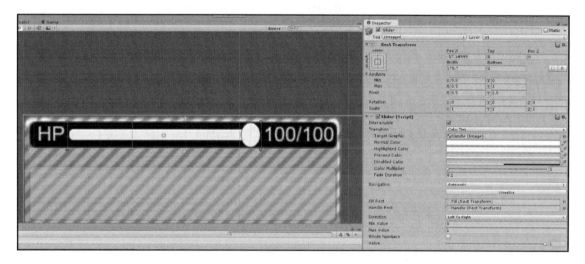

When you expand the **Slider** in the hierarchy, you will see that there are a few child elements of the **Slider**. Go ahead and delete the **Handle** that is a child of the **Handle Slide Area**:

Now select the Background child and set its image to the BattleGUI_2 image:

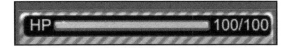

Now, for the **Fill**, which is a child of the **Fill Area**, set the image to the BattleGUI_2 image and align it appropriately:

Now if you change the value on the Slider component, you can watch the fill image increase and decrease.

Let's work on the Bottom Panel. We'll use a few Panels inside this to hold various buttons. Add a **Panel** as a child and name it Buttons. Align and position it as shown in the following screenshot:

This Panel is simply going to hold two other Panels of the exact same size. Create another Panel and call it `Button Menu`. Set its anchor and position so that it stretches both horizontally and vertically:

Add a **Layout | Horizontal Layout Group** component to the `Buttons Menu` Panel with the **Child Alignment** set to **Middle Left**. Add five buttons as children to this Panel and delete the text component from the last one:

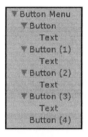

Now place the `BattleGUI_5` image as the background image for the first four buttons and the `BattleGUI_4` image as the background image for the last button. Also, set the text color for the buttons to white:

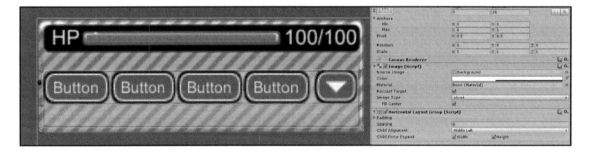

We added the layout component so that it would perfectly space all of our buttons, but we don't want it to be a component on our object anymore. The reason is if we try to delete a button, it will try to disburse the buttons, but we want them to be in the exact same place even if we only have less buttons. So, remove the layout component. Now save this Panel as a prefab in the `Assets/Prefabs/UI` folder so that we can easily reuse it.

Rename the Panel `Main Buttons`, delete the last two buttons, and change the text and button names as shown in the following screenshot:

Drag the `Button Menu` prefab in the Hierarchy so that it is also a child of the `Buttons` Panel and rename it `Attack Buttons`. Also, change the buttons' text and names as shown in the following screenshot:

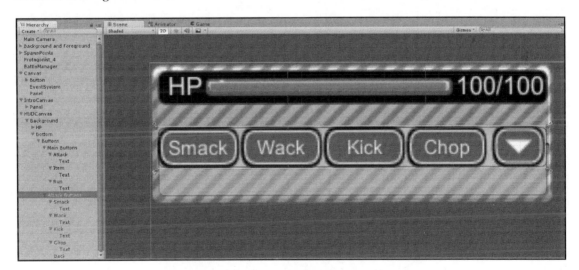

The last thing we want to do to set up the layout is get the status bar that will convey directions to the player at the bottom. Create a new Panel as a child of `Bottom` named `Text Holder` and give it the following properties:

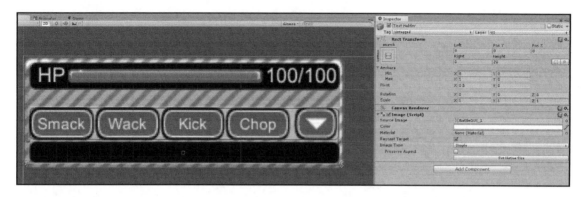

Now add a text component as a child of the `Text Holder` Panel with the following properties:

Now select all the Panels that have the whitish background displaying behind them and change their **Alpha** level to 0. After you are done, you should see the following:

Now that the buttons are all laid out correctly, we can start making them display at the correct time within battle.

## Displaying the correct buttons

The goal of this chapter is to have the `Attack`, `Item`, and `Run` buttons visible when it is the player's move and if the `Attack` button is selected, have the various `Attack Buttons` display on the screen. We'll also have the **Run** button perform appropriately.

In future chapters, we will make an item menu appear when the item button is selected, we will have the HP display correctly, have something actually happen when you hit the various attacks, and have information display in the status bar.

Right now, the `Attack Buttons` are displaying initially, but we actually want the `Main Buttons` displaying. Select the `Attack Buttons` Panel and add a **Canvas Group** component to it. Set the **Alpha** to 0 and deselect **Interactable** and **Blocks Raycasts**. Your gameplay scene should now appear as follows:

We want the Panel to display at all times, but we only want the buttons to display when it is the player's turn to move. So, we want these buttons to behave similar to the way the Run Away button is performing currently.

Instead of writing all new code for this, we will simply replace the Canvas holding the Run Away button with the Panel holding all of the buttons in the BattleManager script. Before we can do so, however, we need to add a **Canvas Group** component to the Buttons Panel. Set the **Alpha** to 0 and deselect **Interactable** and **Blocks Raycasts**, as shown in the following screenshot:

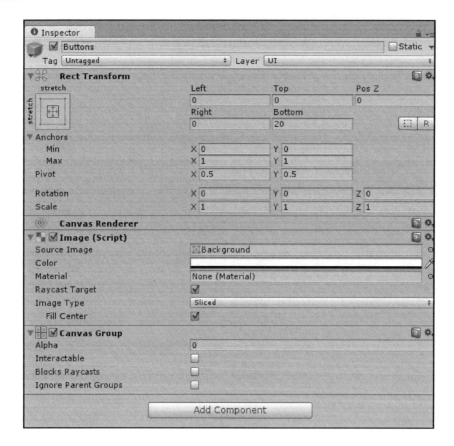

Now select the BattleManager object and drag the Buttons Panel to the the **Buttons** variable in the BattleManager script. Now you can delete the old canvas that held the **Run Away** button.

If you have the EventSystem GameObject as a child of the canvas that holds the Run Away button, be sure to move it before deleting the canvas.

We don't have anything that lets the Attack button access the Attack Buttons Panel, so let's write some code that will allow that to happen. Instead of putting this code in the BattleManager script, we are going to create a new script to hold this information. The reason for this is we can actually reuse this code with other menus that we make throughout the game and it will be easier to reuse it if we just make it its own script.

Create a new C# script and call it PopUpMenu. We'll write a pretty simple script that will have one function that turns on all the **Canvas Group** values and another that turns them all off:

```
using UnityEngine;
using System.Collections;
using UnityEngine.UI;

public class PopUpMenu : MonoBehaviour {
    public CanvasGroup popUp;

    void Awake(){
        popUp=GetComponent<CanvasGroup>();
    }
    // Use this for initialization
    public void EnableTheMenu () {
        popUp.alpha=1;
        popUp.interactable=true;
        popUp.blocksRaycasts=true;
    }
    public void DisableTheMenu () {
        popUp.alpha=0;
        popUp.interactable=false;
        popUp.blocksRaycasts=false;
    }
}
```

Attach this script to the `Attack Buttons` Panel and drag the `Attack Buttons` Panel to the **Pop Up** slot, as shown in the following screenshot:

 We could have written this code to grab the **Canvas Group** off of the object that it was attached to, but I felt this was more versatile for future uses.

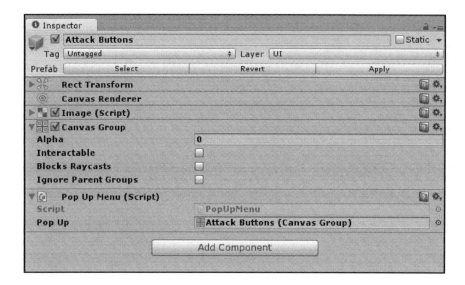

Now we just need to link all of the buttons up to the appropriate functions. Let's start with the `Attack` button. With the `Attack` button (in the `Main Buttons` Panel) selected in the Hierarchy, hit the + symbol in the **On Click()** event. Set it up so that the `EnableTheMenu` function from the `PopUpMenu` script that is attached to the `Attack Buttons` Panel will run:

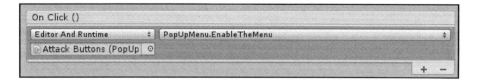

Now let's set up the Back button to hide this Panel. With the Back button (in the Attack Buttons Panel) selected in the Hierarchy, hit the + symbol in the **On Click()** event. Set it up so that the DisableTheMenu function from the PopUpMenu script that is attached to the Attack Buttons Panel will run:

Now when you run the game, the buttons do not appear until it is the player's turn. Once it is the player's turn, if you select the Attack button, the list of attacks are displayed (they don't actually do anything yet, though) and when you hit the arrow button, the original menu is redisplayed.

The last thing we need to do is get the new Run button to perform the way the old Run Away button did. With the Run button (in the Main Buttons Panel) selected in the Hierarchy, hit the + symbol in the **On Click()** event. Set it up so that the RunAway function from the BattleMananger script that is attached to the BattleMananger GameObject will run:

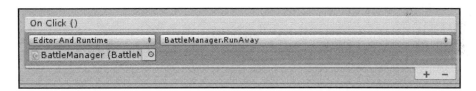

Now we can run away again.

Now that we have our UI and state machine set up, we have prepared the backbone for our battle system. Our poor hero still can't actually attack. However, we will implement her attacks and the enemies' attacks in the next chapter, Chapter 10, *The Battle Begins*. We'll also give the player some items to use in battle in Chapter 11, *Shopping for Items*.

# Going further

As we reach the halfway mark in the battle implementation, we can take stock of what we have and also look forward to more things we could include at this point.

Try expanding the battle to include the following:

- Add an animation that allows the `Attack Buttons` to roll in and out rather than just appear
- If you added other enemies in the scene, have the `IntroSlideAnimation` look for the types of enemies and generate the image from code rather than just using a static image for the dragons
- Hype up the `IntroSlideAnimation` particle effects and other interesting artistic elements

# Summary

Getting the battle right based on the style of your game is very important as it is where the player will spend the majority of their time. Keep the player engaged and try to make each battle different in some way, as receptiveness is a tricky problem to solve and you don't want to bore the player.

Think about different attacks your player can perform that possibly strengthen as the player strengthens.

In this chapter, we covered the following:

- Setting up the logic of our turn-based battle system
- Working with state machines in the code
- Different RPG UI overlays
- Setting up the HUD of our game so that our player can do more than just run away

In the next chapter, we will continue the battle and set out to teach those adorably vicious dragons a lesson or two.

# 10
# The Battle Begins

Creating a battle system is such a big endeavor, so we split ours into two chapters. In the previous chapter, we set up the general logic of the turn-based system and designed the HUD to allow our player to select an attack, but our player cannot actually attack any of the enemies yet and they do not attack her. Let's allow our player and our enemies to fight each other.

The following topics will be covered in this chapter:

- What it means to battle
- Planning for longevity
- Enhancing the enemy AI
- Particle systems in 2D

## Designing an interesting battle system

Before we begin fleshing out our battle system, it is important to consider various elements that we may want to include in our game. Designing an interesting and unique battle system is difficult. The battle system should be challenging and engaging. The challenge can be accomplished with enemies that level up as the player progresses or with enemies that acquire new and unique skills. The engagement can be achieved by quirky enemies, interesting animations, or many other ways.

There are several things you may wish to consider to include in your battle system:

- Animations
- Player actions
- Enemy defenses and reactions

- Special moves
- Interactions

Each of these provides an engaging experience for the player and makes the battle feel worthwhile. When developing an RPG, I highly recommend you play many different RPGs and study the different ways in which the battle system has been developed. Determine which preceding element listed is important to you and plan to include it.

# Leveling up

It's important to ensure that the player feels they are achieving something as they progress. This may be, for instance, how much gold they collect from the fallen enemies to buy swanky new gear. It could also be about increasing the statistics or skills of the player, enabling them to take on more powerful enemies with a wave of their wrist.

Invariably, it is a mix of all of the preceding things that makes a game stand out. In fact, in some titles, this is the whole focus of the game; you spend lots of time planning what skills to have or upgrade as you progress on to explore/fight.

One piece of advice I would give is to ensure that you have some sort of whole-world experience system. You can have skills and strengths the player can use to affect the whole game; it should be about the game experience and not just the fight. Many big RPG games spend a lot of their development effort getting this right, but that's not to say this cannot be applied to smaller or even episodic games.

# Balancing

By far the most difficult thing to implement in any game is balancing. If done right, you will spend over 50 percent of your development efforts testing, tweaking, retesting, and retweaking the game.

Don't use just one focus group to test your game, but use people from all walks of life. The more people you have test your game, the better the balance of the game will be.

Finding that sweet spot between difficulty, playability, engagement, and fun is always hard, so do not underestimate it. Remember, just because you play the game in a certain way doesn't mean everyone else will play in the same way.

# Preparing to attack a single enemy

Following on from the previous chapter, we will continue building our battle system.

Let's begin our focus on letting the player attack a single enemy. To do this, we'll add some variables to `BattleManager` to manage this.

We will also add some other elements to spruce up the battle, such as a selection circle or a target identifier, and add a variable to set a prefab for this.

So, open the `BattleManager` script and add the following variables to the top of the class:

```
private string selectedTargetName;
private EnemyController selectedTarget;
public GameObject selectionCircle;
private bool canSelectEnemy;

bool attacking = false;

public bool CanSelectEnemy
{
  get
  {
    return canSelectEnemy;
  }
}

public int EnemyCount
{
  get
  {
    return enemyCount;
  }
}
```

 We haven't created the `EnemyController` class yet, so it will show as an error. We will add that next.

So, we have added properties to hold the selected target, a flag, and a property to track whether we can actually select an enemy (as the player needs to select an attack first). Additionally, we've added a variable to maintain a record of just how many enemies are left in the battle.

Instantiating prefabs in the code requires the prefab to be in the `Resources` folder, because they are associated with the asset-bundling features.

For single objects, it's easier to attach a prefab to the editor via the Inspector and use it from there (either on an existing class or a static editor class).

# Beefing up the enemy AI

At the moment, `Dragon` is just a sprite drawn on the screen with an AI system that just sits idle in the background. So, let's expand on this and give our Dragons some muscle power.

As stated earlier, to keep the player engaged, you need to have a varied amount of enemies in the battle and they need to be challenging enough to make the player think and apply tactics.

# The enemy profile/controller

First, we'll create a new profile for the enemies, starting off with a new enumeration for the enemy class. Create a new C# script named `EnemyClass` in `Assets\Scripts\Classes` and replace its contents with the following code:

```
public enum EnemyClass
{
   Dragon,
   Blob,
   NastyPeiceOfWork
}
```

I've used just a couple of examples, as we will only be using the `Dragon` for now. Next, create a new `Enemy` class C# script in the same folder, as follows:

```
public class Enemy : Entity
{

   public EnemyClass Class;
}
```

The preceding code just extends the base `Entity` class for our enemies and adds the `EnemyClass` enumeration we just created.

Now that we have a profile for the enemy, we need a controller to make the enemy perform actions in a controlled way. So, create another C# script named `EnemyController` in `Assets\Scripts`, starting with the following variables:

```
using System.Collections;
using UnityEngine;

public class EnemyController : MonoBehaviour {

    private BattleManager battleManager;
    public Enemy EnemyProfile;
    Animator enemyAI;

    public BattleManager BattleManager
    {
        get
        {
            return battleManager;
        }
        set
        {
            battleManager = value;
        }
    }
}
```

The preceding code gives us the missing `EnemyController` class that we used in the `BattleManager` script with the following properties:

- A tight reference to the `BattleManager` script, which is needed because the enemies are directly affected by the battle as it is ensued
- The enemy profile
- A reference to the AI animator controller we created in Chapter 8, *Encountering Enemies and Running Away*

As the AI needs information about the battle, we need to ensure that it has kept each frame up to date. So, for this, we add an `UpdateAI` method and call it from the `Update` method to keep the AI up to date, as follows:

```
void Update()
{
    UpdateAI();
}

public void UpdateAI()
{
```

```
    if (enemyAI != null && EnemyProfile != null)
    {
       enemyAI.SetInteger("EnemyHealth", EnemyProfile.health);
       enemyAI.SetInteger("PlayerHealth",
    GameState.CurrentPlayer.health);
       enemyAI.SetInteger("EnemiesInBattle",           battleManager.EnemyCount);
    }
}
```

The preceding code just sets the properties of the AI to the current values.

Next, we need to grab the reference to the AI that is currently configured against the GameObject that will be used by the preceding UpdateAI function in the Awake method:

```
public void Awake()
{
  enemyAI = GetComponent<Animator>();
  if (enemyAI == null)
  {
    Debug.LogError("No AI System Found");
  }
}
```

There are several logging options in Unity, from the basic Log to the more detailed LogWarning and LogError. These logging options provide us with more detail while debugging our project, so use them wisely.

To save sanity when you are adding more content to the game, it is worthwhile to add Debug comments, surrounding them with important components or scripts required by an object. Using them this way does not affect the performance and can save you hours of searching for the reason for a crash because you forgot to add something.

However, do not use Debug.Log extensively or in the normal operation of your game, as it kills the performance!

# Updating the Dragon prefab

The following are the steps that need to be followed to update the **Dragon** prefab:

1. The **Dragon** prefab we created earlier now needs this new `EnemyController` class attached to it. Select the **Dragon** prefab from the `Assets\Prefabs\Characters folder,` click on the **Add Component** button in the **Inspector** window, and navigate to **Scripts | Enemy Controller** (notice it breaks your script's name it to two words based on your capitalization), as shown in the following screenshot:

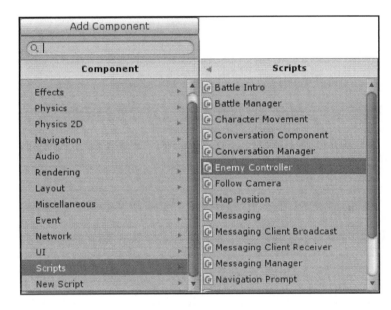

2. Once added, the updated **Dragon** will look like the following screenshot in the **Inspector** window:

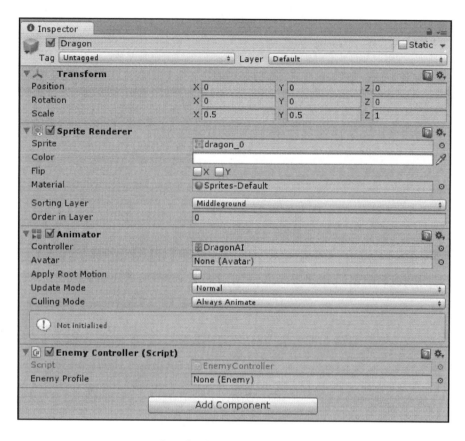

As you can see, we cannot currently edit the **Enemy Profile** tab from the editor (as this requires a custom Inspector. Hence, we are doing it through the code. You can use a scriptable object asset and assign it to the tab, and I've already shown you how to do this.

# Setting up the enemy profile in the code

Returning back to the `BattleManager` script, the area where we push our Dragons into action is in the `SpawnEnemies` coroutine. Now, instead of just throwing sprites at the screen, we can add some real danger to the mix for our humble player using the following code:

```
IEnumerator SpawnEnemies()
```

```
{
  //Spawn enemies in over time
  for (int i = 0; i < enemyCount; i++)
  {
    var newEnemy = (GameObject)Instantiate(EnemyPrefabs[0]);
    newEnemy.transform.position = new Vector3(10, -1, 0);
    yield return StartCoroutine(
    MoveCharacterToPoint(EnemySpawnPoints[i], newEnemy));
    newEnemy.transform.parent = EnemySpawnPoints[i].transform;

    var controller = newEnemy.GetComponent<EnemyController>();

    controller.BattleManager = this;

    var EnemyProfile = ScriptableObject.CreateInstance<Enemy>();
    EnemyProfile.Class = EnemyClass.Dragon;
    EnemyProfile.level = 1;
    EnemyProfile.damage = 1;
    EnemyProfile.health = 20;
    EnemyProfile.name = EnemyProfile.Class + " " + i.ToString();
    controller.EnemyProfile = EnemyProfile;
  }
  BattleStateManager.SetBool("BattleReady", true);
}
```

Now, as we loop through the number of enemies being added to the battle, we grab the `EnemyController` class attached to the **Dragon** prefab, create a new `EnemyProfile` class, give it some values, and, finally, initialize the controller with the new `EnemyProfile` class.

Ideally, you should change this generation to something that is a bit more structured instead of just initializing it this way, but you should get the picture.

Now that we have a stronger opponent, let's select an attack and then select the enemy we wish to attack.

# Selecting an attack

The player will select an attack and then select the enemy to perform the attack. To allow the player to select various attacks from the HUD, we will create a new script called `Attack` in the `Assets/Scripts` folder, as follows:

```
using UnityEngine;
using System.Collections;

public class Attack : MonoBehaviour {
```

```
public bool attackSelected=false;
public int hitAmount=0;

public void Smack(){
    hitAmount=5;
    AttackTheEnemy();
}

public void Wack(){
    hitAmount=10;
    AttackTheEnemy();
}

public void Kick(){
    hitAmount=15;
    AttackTheEnemy();
}

public void Chop(){
    hitAmount=20;
    AttackTheEnemy();
}

public void AttackTheEnemy(){
    attackSelected=true;
}
}
```

Essentially, when each button is hit, it will reference a different attack with a different hit amount. For this to work, we will need to have each button run is specified function when clicked. Attach this script to the **BattleManager** GameObject.

Now that it is attached to the **BattleManager** GameObject, we can easily set up the correct buttons to run the function `OnClick()`.

Select the first button, `Smack`, from the hierarchy and add a new `OnClick()` event. Drag the `BattleMananger` GameObject in to the **Object** slot and select **Attack | Smack** from the function list, as shown in the following screenshot:

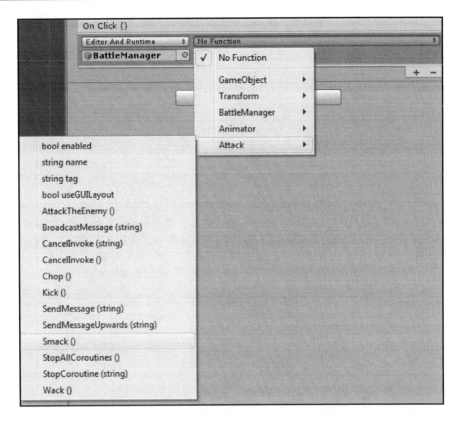

Complete the same process for the other three attack buttons, by assigning their appropriate functions.

This doesn't really do anything in particular yet, but sets the value of the attack that will be performed. In the `Attack` script, we have a function called `AttackTheEnemy()` that gets called whenever one of the buttons are selected. Within it, a Boolean variable, `attackSelected`, is set to `true`. This value will be used to turn on and off the player's ability to actually select an enemy to perform the attack. We will utilize this variable soon when we set up the player's ability to select an enemy.

# Adding a visual effect to attack selection

Now that we can select the attack, we want to provide some sort of feedback to the player to let him or her know what attack is currently selected. We'll do this by adding an outline to the button that represents the current attack.

For each of the attack buttons, add an **Outline** component to the button's Inspector. You can do this all at once by selecting all of the buttons.

To select all of the buttons, click on the first one in the Hierarchy, and then while holding down *Shift* click on the last one.

Make sure you do not select the Back button and only select the ones that designate attacks. With all attack buttons selected in the Hierarchy, select **Add Component | UI | Effects | Outline**, as shown in the following screenshot:

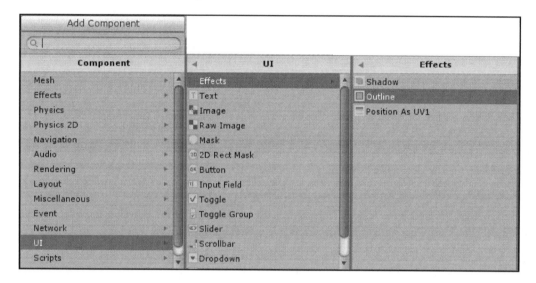

 Instead of navigating through the **Add Component** menus, you can also just type **Outline** in the search bar after selecting **Add Component**.

Now that the Outline component has been added, change the **Effect Distance** to 2 and −2, as shown in the following screenshot:

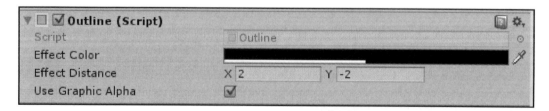

Now disable the **Outline** component from each button by deselecting the check box next to **Outline (Script)**.

Now, update the `Attack` script by including the following `using` statement:

```
using UnityEngine.UI;
```

And add the following variable declarations:

```
public Button smack;
public Button wack;
public Button kick;
public Button chop;
```

Now create the following function:

```
void HighlightTheButton(){
    if(hitAmount==5){
        smack.GetComponent<Outline>().enabled=true;
    }else{
        smack.GetComponent<Outline>().enabled=false;
    }

    if(hitAmount==10){
        wack.GetComponent<Outline>().enabled=true;
    }else{
        wack.GetComponent<Outline>().enabled=false;
    }

    if(hitAmount==15){
        kick.GetComponent<Outline>().enabled=true;
    }else{
        kick.GetComponent<Outline>().enabled=false;
    }

    if(hitAmount==20){
        chop.GetComponent<Outline>().enabled=true;
    }else{
        chop.GetComponent<Outline>().enabled=false;
    }
}
```

Lastly, add the following line to each of the attack functions:

```
HighlightTheButton();
```

The preceding code will highlight or unhighlight the appropriate button based on the current value of `hitAmount`. We could have used a new variable for this, but since the `hitAmount` is directly tied to which button was pressed, this seemed like a quicker solution.

Before this code will work, we need to assign the correct buttons to the `Attack` script in the `BattleManager` class' Inspector. So, drag and drop the buttons to their appropriate slots, as shown in the following screenshot:

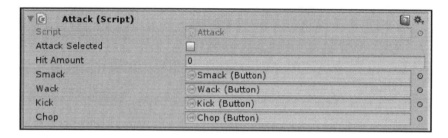

Now you can select the various attacks and they will remain highlighted with an outline until you select a different attack. The following screenshot demonstrates the **Wack** attack selected, because it has a thicker outline:

# Selecting a target

Before we can attack an enemy, we must select which enemy to attack. When an enemy is selected, the player needs some visual representation to confirm they have, in fact, selected an enemy. To do this, let's add some selection logic for our enemies and a nice visual effect in 2D. First, we'll create the prefab for this with a little animation and then get ready to attach our `BattleManager` script using the variable we added earlier.

# The selection circle prefab

To show the player which enemy is selected, the following circle will spin below the enemy:

So, add `SelectionCircle.png` to your project from the assets that accompany this title to the `Assets\Sprites\Props` folder.

Next, we'll create a prefab of this sprite in our scene for later use. This simply sets up how we want to use it visually, and since we are going to use it several times over in the scene, using prefabs means that there will only be one instance with many copies.

Now, drag the `SelectionCircle` image on to the scene (if it doesn't work, you are looking at the game view, which means that you need to switch to the **Scene** tab) and set the properties, as shown in the following screenshot:

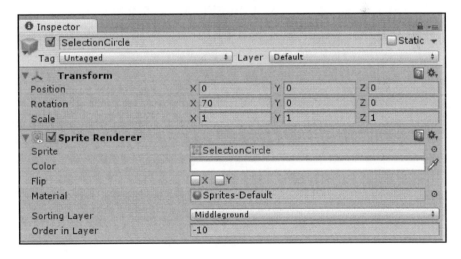

Finally, drag the object from the **Scene** Hierarchy into the `Assets\Prefabs\Props` folder to create the prefab, ensuring its name is `SelectionCircle`. Then, delete the object from the scene, as we no longer need it.

Now, in the `Battle` scene, in the editor, select the `BattleManager` GameObject in the **Hierarchy**; once you do this, drag the `SelectionCircle` prefab on to the **Selection Circle** property for the `BattleManager` script to attach it to the `BattleManager` GameObject.

# Adding selection logic to the EnemyController class

With everything set up in the `BattleManager` GameObject, we can now return to the `EnemyController` script and make it so that the `SelectionCircle` prefab highlights a Dragon if the player clicks on it.

First, we need a couple of properties in the `EnemyController` script to keep a reference to our `SelectionCircle` prefab and determine whether the current enemy is selected or not. So, add the following to the top of the `EnemyController` class:

```
private bool selected;
GameObject selectionCircle;
```

Now, to liven up the selection process a bit, let's add some spin to the selection circle when it is on the screen. To do this, we'll add a simple coroutine to constantly update the selection circles' rotation transform (simple and effective). We could have used the 2D animation system to do the same thing, but it's a bit too much for a simple rotation (unless you want to do more fancy things with the selection circle, such as add particles, have the circle jump up and down while spinning, and so on).

So, in the `EnemyController` script, add the following coroutine function:

```
IEnumerator SpinObject(GameObject target)
{
  while (true)
  {
    target.transform.Rotate(0, 0, 180 * Time.deltaTime);
    yield return null;
  }
}
```

Nothing fancy; you just need to rotate the object on its z axis over time.

If you want the circle to spin faster or slower, just alter the amount of z axis rotation you apply. Here, I have it set to spin 180 degrees every second, one full spin every 2 seconds.

Next, when the player clicks on a Dragon, we use the combination of the `BoxCollider2D` and `OnMouseDown` functions to select the Dragon and display the selection circle.

Add a new `BoxCollider2D` component to the `Dragon` prefab and then add the following function to the `EnemyController` script:

```
void OnMouseDown()
   {
       if (battleManager.CanSelectEnemy)
       {
           selectionCircle =
(GameObject)GameObject.Instantiate(battleManager.selectionCircle);
           selectionCircle.transform.parent = transform;
           selectionCircle.transform.localPosition = new Vector3 (0f,-1f,
0f);
           selectionCircle.transform.localScale = new Vector3 (4f, 4f,
1f);
           StartCoroutine("SpinObject", selectionCircle);
           battleManager.SelectEnemy(this, EnemyProfile.name);
           GetComponent<Attack>().attackSelected=false;
           battleManager.battleStateManager.SetBool("PlayerReady",true);
       }
   }
```

Now, once an enemy is selected, the selection circle should appear below it with the following logic:

1. Create a clone of the `SelectionCircle` prefab.
2. Set its parent to the selected Dragon.
3. Set its local position so that it is just below the Dragon.
4. Make it appear a bit bigger.
5. Start `SelectionCircle`, spinning with its coroutine.
6. Tell the **BattleManager** GameObject that we have selected a target to destroy.
7. Reset the `attackSelected` Boolean in the `Attack` script so that the next round will perform properly.
8. Change the state of the battle so that the attack will now be performed.

 The `SelectedEnemy()` function don't exist on the `BattleManager` script yet, so we will return to those shortly. So, you will see this function highlighted red within **MonoDevelop** and also get an error message in the console.

We are done with the `EnemyController` script now.

To finish off the selection logic, let's return to the `BattleManager` script and add the two missing functions as follows:

```
public void SelectEnemy(EnemyController enemy, string name)
{
    selectedTarget = enemy;
    selectedTargetName = name;
}
```

The preceding function is pretty simple. It sets the two variables we created earlier for the `selectedTarget` and `selectedTargetName` and gets the `EnemyController` component for the selected target.

However, we still can't select the enemy to attack yet, as our `BattleManager` script does not let us do it. Since we want to control the flow of what the player does, we do not enable this until they have first selected an attack.

To enable you to select an enemy and then progress on to the battle, we need to update the `case BattleState.Player_Move` as follows:

```
case BattleState.Player_Move:
    if (GetComponent<Attack>().attackSelected==true){
        canSelectEnemy=true;
    }
    break;
```

You'll notice that even though the game has changed over to the next state, you can still click on the enemies and add selection circles under them. So, to fix this, update the `case BattleState.Player_Attack` as follows:

```
case BattleState.Player_Attack:
    canSelectEnemy=false;
    break;
```

Now the battle can ensue. The player selects an attack and a target, and the battle moves on to the next phase. In this new phase, the player can no longer select attacks or enemies and will not be able to do so again until it is their turn.

Now, when you run the project, the flow of the battle will be as follows:

1. The battle begins.
2. The introduction is played, informing the player of the battle.
3. The player can select from a list of attacks.
4. When an attack is selected, the attack is highlighted by an outline.
5. The player is asked to select a target.

6. The selected enemy gets the red ring of death circling their feet, and they probably get a sense of foreboding.
7. The `Battle` state manager gets informed that the player has completed his/her move and is ready by setting the `PlayerReady` property in the state machine to `true`.

So, when you run the project, your scene should look like the following with the player no longer being able to select anything:

# Attack! Attack!

Now that the player has committed themselves into the fray, we can play through their selected action.

The attack phase will simply run for 1 second and then it will be the enemies' turn. To accomplish this, we use a simple coroutine to perform the attack itself. So, let's add the following function to the `BattleManager` script:

```
IEnumerator AttackTarget(){
    attacking=true;
    selectedTarget.EnemyProfile.health-=GetComponent<Attack>().hitAmount;
    yield return new WaitForSeconds(1);
```

```
    attacking=false;
    GetComponent<Attack>().hitAmount=0;
    battleStateManager.SetBool("PlayerReady", false);

}
```

The following is what the preceding code is doing:

1. Sets a variable that states the player is attacking.
2. Decreases the selected enemy's health based on the chosen attack.
3. Waits for 1 second to reset the values.
4. Changes over to the next state.

All that is left is to call this function now when the `Player_Attack` state is begun. In the `Update` function, update the `case BattleState.Player_Attack` section as follows:

```
case BattleState.Player_Attack:
    canSelectEnemy=false;
    if(!attacking){
        StartCoroutine(AttackTarget());
    }
    break;
```

Now that the attack has commenced and no doubt some Dragons were at least hurt in the ensuing battle, let us provide the player with some visual feedback.

# Using particle effects to represent an attack

The player has made his or her move, and the Dragon has been affected in some way; it would be nice to see what happened. We'll use a different particle effect to represent each of the attacks.

# Creating the materials for the particle effects

Add the `attacks.png` sprite sheet and the `smokeCloud.png` sprite to the `Assets\Sprites\FX` folder. Change its settings so that it is a multiple sprite sheet and slice it automatically.

For particle effects to work, they need a material defined, not just the raw texture/sprite itself. So, navigate to `Assets\Materials` (create it if you haven't done so already) and right-click on it to create a new material and name it `Attacks`.

Change the **Shader** material used to the **Particles/Vertex Lit Blended** shader. You can change the **Shader** by clicking on the drop-down menu next to the **Shader** property of the `Attacks` material and then navigate to **Particles | Vertex Lit Blended**.

Next, change the **Emissive Color** to **White**. Lastly, click on the **Select** button on the material properties in the **Inspector** window for the new `Attacks` material and select the `attacks.png` image we just imported.

Your material should now look like the following screenshot:

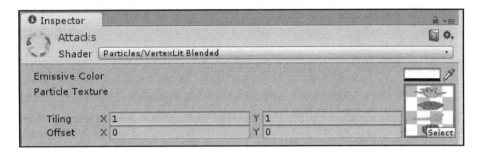

Repeat the preceding steps to create a material for the `smokeCloud.png` sprite.

# Adding the particles

Let's make our participle system. In the Hierarchy, select **Create | Particle System**. Change its transform position to 0,0,0. The particles will initially appear behind the 2D objects, as shown in the following screenshot, but this is an easy fix:

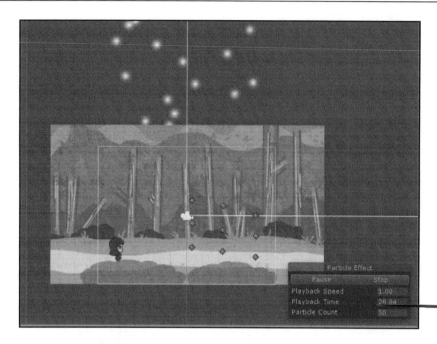

Expand the **Renderer** setting of the particle system and change the **Sorting Layer** to **Foreground**, as shown in the following screenshot:

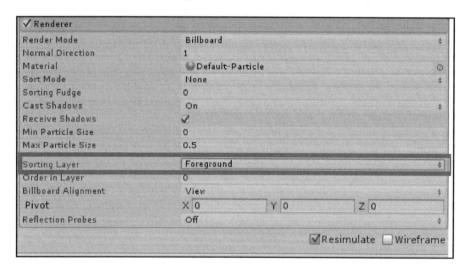

It will now display correctly in the **Scene** view and the **Game** view. The following is a screenshot of the **Game** view:

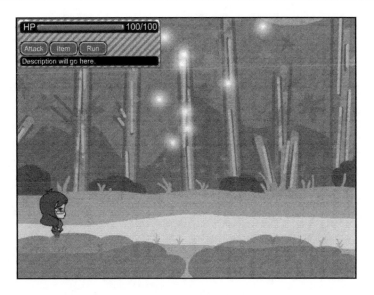

 This used to be not so easy to fix as the only way to change the particle's
sorting layer was through code.

Rename the particle system **Smack** and change its material to the `Attacks` material by
dragging the `Attacks` material to the **Material** slot within the **Renderer** options, as shown
in the following screenshot:

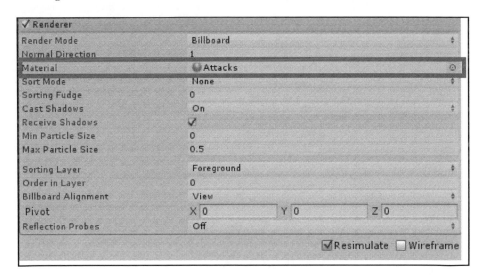

This initially is going to seem like a bad choice, because all of the images will now display and we only want the first image to display, as shown in the following screenshot:

But, check and expand the **Texture Sheet Animation** property. Change the values, as shown in the following screenshot:

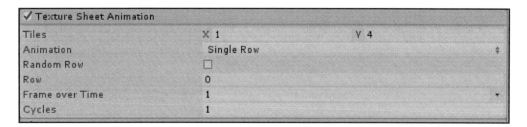

Texture Sheet Animation properties for the Smack attack

To get the 1 in **Frame over Time**, select **Constant** from the drop-down menu. You should now see the following:

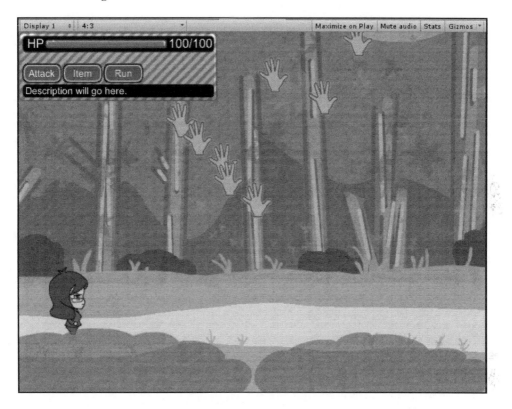

To get the correct shape, we now need to update the other properties, as shown in the following screenshot:

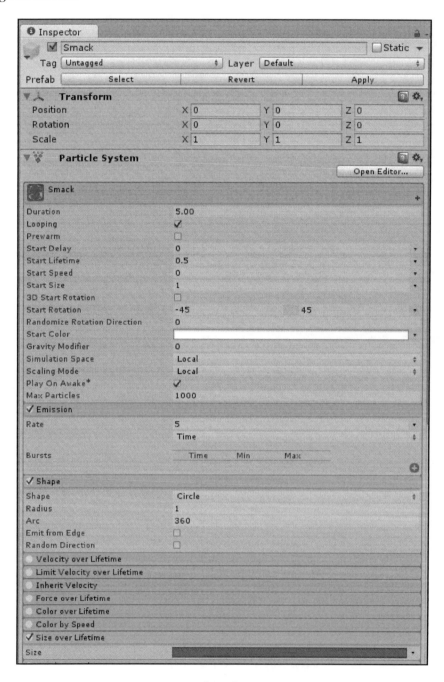

The hands should now be concentrated to a single area, as shown in the following screenshot:

Now, duplicate this particle system (*Ctrl + D*) in the Hierarchy and rename it `Smoke`. Deselect the **Texture Sheet Animation** property and change the **Renderer** | **Material** to Smoke. All other properties will remain the same, as shown in the following screenshot:

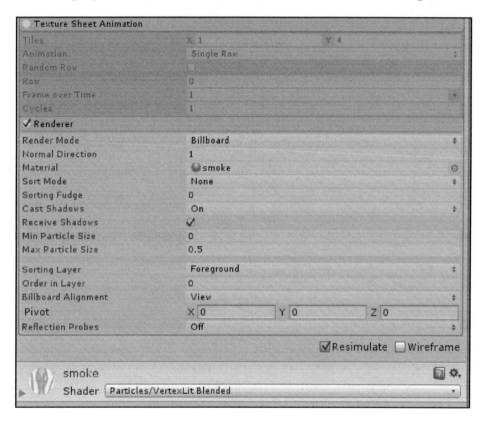

Now we will group these two particles together by creating an empty GameObject to hold them. In the Hierarchy, select **Create** | **Create Empty**. Position it at 0,0,0 and rename it `Smack and Smoke`. Now, drag the two new particle systems to `Smack and Smoke` so that they are children of the empty GameObject.

Duplicate `Smack and Smoke` three times and rename the other three `Wack and Smoke`, `Kick and Smoke`, and `Chop and Smoke`. Rename the first particle system within each appropriately. Now to get each to display the correct image for the attack material, change the **Texture Sheet Animation** | **Row** value. The following screenshot shows the properties for `Wack and Smoke`:

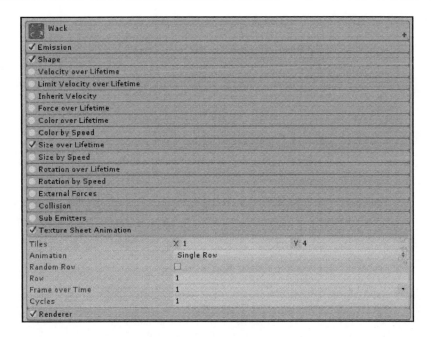

The following screenshot shows the properties for `Kick and Smoke`:

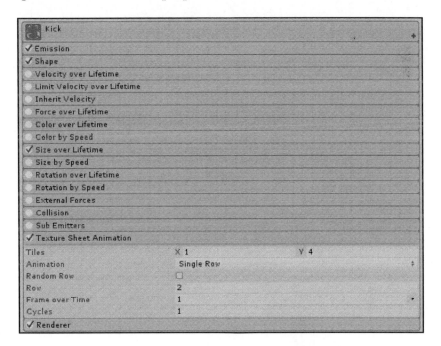

The following screenshot shows the properties for Chop and Smoke:

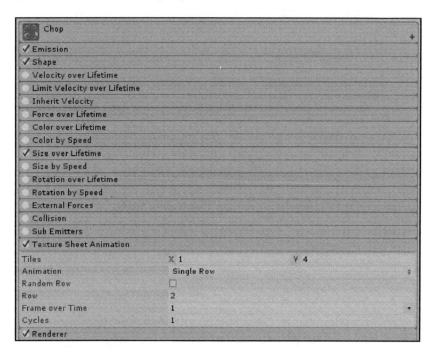

Now drag Smack and Smoke, Wack and Smoke, Kick and Smoke, and Chop and Smoke into the Assets/Prefabs/FX folder, as shown in the following screenshot:

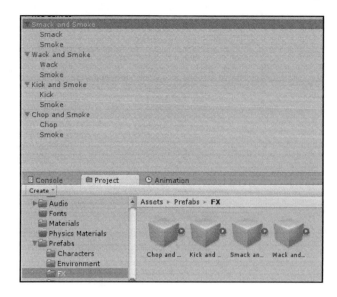

You can now delete the particle systems from the scene.

# Displaying the particles upon attack

Now we will update our `BattleManager` script to instantiate these particle systems when the attack is performed.

Add the following variable declarations to the top of your `BattleManager` script:

```
public GameObject smackParticle;
public GameObject wackParticle;
public GameObject kickParticle;
public GameObject chopParticle;
private GameObject attackParticle;
```

Now, update your `AttackTarget()` function to appear as follows:

```
IEnumerator AttackTarget(){
    attacking=true;
    var damageAmount=GetComponent<Attack>().hitAmount;
    switch (damageAmount){
        case 5:
        attackParticle = (GameObject)GameObject.Instantiate(smackParticle);
        break;
    case 10:
        attackParticle = (GameObject)GameObject.Instantiate(wackParticle);
        break;
     case 15:
        attackParticle = (GameObject)GameObject.Instantiate(kickParticle);
        break;
    case 20:
        attackParticle = (GameObject)GameObject.Instantiate(chopParticle);
        break;
    }

    if(attackParticle!=null){
        attackParticle.transform.position=selectedTarget.transform.position;
    }

    selectedTarget.EnemyProfile.health-=damageAmount;
    yield return new WaitForSeconds(1f);
    attacking=false;
    GetComponent<Attack>().hitAmount=0;
    battleStateManager.SetBool("PlayerReady", false);
    Destroy(attackParticle);
}
```

This will look at the amount stored for the attack and select the correct particle system to instantiate. It will place the particle system where the selected Dragon is located. Then it will destroy the newly created particle system when the battle phase has changed.

The last thing we need to do is place the correct particle systems in the correct variable slot of the `BattleManager` script. Drag and drop your particle systems, as shown in the following screenshot:

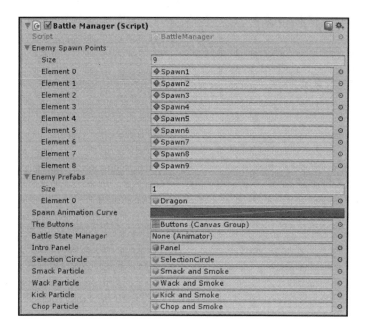

# Finishing up the battle

Now, you are probably thinking at this point, *What about the rest of the battle?* Put simply, I leave that up to you.

You are now armed with everything you need to know to be able to complete the rest of the battle scene. You should not just stop there, however, and you should see just how far along you can get.

To complete the battle system, include various states using the following steps:

1. Destroy enemies with health less than 1.
2. Loop through the Dragons and let them attack the player; rough her up a bit.
3. Update the player's health bar to display the correct HP.
4. Check whether the battle is complete and, accordingly, either transition back to the **Player Move** state or set the `BattleReady` state variable to `false` to transition to the **Battle Result** state.
5. Display a UI element to summarize the battle results and grant the user some reward, perhaps with some gold, after the battle has completed.
6. Transition back to the map when the battle is over.
7. Update the description text to tell the player what to do next or what is currently happening in the battle.

The best way to learn is through re-enforcement and testing yourself.

# Going further

You can add a lot of fancy elements to this battle system that could really make it shine. A few recommendations are as follows:

- Have the player and Dragons animate when attacking by moving them forward slightly
- Give the Dragons floating health bars
- Give the more powerful attacks a time limit or use limit of some sort, so that the player doesn't spam the highest level attack

# Summary

This is a chapter with lots of new code, features, and tips and tricks. Hopefully, you have learned a lot.

We covered the factors that make a battle, adding display elements to help the player know what is happening, and working with particle effects.

In the next chapter, we will create an inventory system so that the hero can heal herself.

# 11

# Shopping for Items

Arguably, the inventory system in any good RPG game is one of the most important components. Depending on the style or background of your design, it may be even more important than the story or battle system. The reason I say this is because the way in which you design and implement your shopping and inventory system will alter how your game is played and how quickly the player will progress through your creation.

The topics that will be covered in this chapter are as follows:

- Exploring the inventory and items
- Building a shop and an inventory UI layer

## Why do we shop?

The motivation to buy things is strong, and we have come to expect this in almost any game. From a simple adventure game where we just pick things up off the street that may come in useful later, to full-fledged RPG games where the inventory is everything, this motivation is indispensable. Even **First Person Shooter** (**FPS**) games aren't immune to this phenomenon.

It is important to keep all of this in mind and look at the real-world when designing any shopping/inventory system for your RPG game. The more it feels like something that someone would do in real life, the more at home they will feel with it, and the easier they will find to use it.

You should always be asking the following questions of yourself while designing such a system:

- How does an item add value?
- Does it seem affordable?
- Is it going to improve the play?
- Is it desirable?
- Is it better to know what the player will already have and why?
- Is it single-use (consumable) or fixed (durable/non-consumable)?
- Will it break or wear out over time?

A lot of this leads us beyond just what is good for the game; it leads us to what is good for the player. Another factor that can lend weight to this is whether we are going to monetize certain powerful items. However, we will cover this in more detail later.

# The power of an item

At the core of any inventory/shopping system are the individual items themselves. They need to be designed in a way that will not only set each item apart from every other item, but will also ensure that they work together to benefit the player as they travel through your world.

Items generally have their individual properties. Refer to the following table:

| Item/property | Description |
|---|---|
| Slot | Can this only be used in a certain slot for the player or in general? |
| Stackable | Can items, such as ammo or potions, be stacked on top of each other? |
| Strength or damage | What is the effect on the player's health? Does it restore the player's health (like with health potions) or damage the player's health (like with poison)? |
| Defense | Does the item protect the player at all, even if only a little bit? |
| Power | Does the item have its own source of power/ammunition? Is it limited? |
| Recharge rate | Does the item recharge itself or not? Can it be recharged? |
| Size | Is the item bulky and cumbersome? |
| Weight | Is it light or heavy? Will it encumber the player and slow them down? |

| Storage | Similar to a backpack, does it enable the player to carry more? Negative would mean that they will carry less. |
|---|---|
| Cost | What is the value of an item? |
| Trade-in value | In some systems, the item's health will impact this. |
| Perks | Does the item have bonuses that will also enhance the player? |
| Abilities | Similar to perks, does the item grant a special action to the player? |
| Use/type | Is it a weapon, armor, potion, and so on? |
| Category | Does it have a specific category within its type? |
| Level | Can the item be leveled up, making it stronger, or is it a fixed level? |
| Durable or consumable | Is the item non-consumable, durable, purchasable, or one-time consumable? |
| Rarity | Is the item one of a kind, simply hard to find, or a commonplace object? |

A lot of the preceding items will just depend on the style of the game you are making; not all will fit, but you should review each of them in turn as you design the shopping/inventory system.

# Building your shop

Once you have decided on the types of item to provide in your game, you need to start thinking about how the player can be provided with these items. Do they need to be bought from a shop? Are they found somewhere, and can they be sold later? Or does the player simply throw them away once done with them and move on to the next shiny thing? In some games, the previous item fuse with the new one to highlight a progression.

The next thing that should come to mind once you have settled on some sort of shopping system is how the player will access it. In most RPG games, it is the traditional roadside shop or wandering peddler. The player has to travel to a certain location in order to buy items. In the case of some of the rarer items, they have to travel to a specific shop or a mystic seer guarding the item in order to acquire it.

Laying out the shop's design is fairly easy, simply because it is a shop. You don't have to worry about loads or size; it is just a storefront.

Some examples of different shop layouts are as follows:

**Final Fantasy** has a very basic text layout where each shop or shop owner only stocks a single type of item.

**World of Warcraft** employs a much more graphically rich still a very basic system with few categories to choose from.

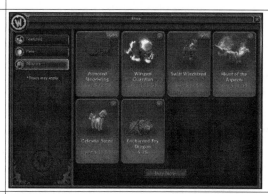

Other titles, such as **DaggerVale** from Concept Softworks use a simple grid-based approach showing all the wares that a shop stocks.

The pattern you choose will entirely depend on the style of your game.

Some games, however, take a different approach. They make the storefront available from anywhere in the game; it can simply be accessed through the player's inventory. Items can be bought and sold anywhere in such games.

# Laying out your inventory

Your character's layout is usually a lot more restricted as compared to that of a storefront. However, the character's layout needs to follow the same design pattern you are using in your game.

These systems usually fall into a couple of patterns.

## Rule of 99'

Players are limited to a certain number of each item. The number can vary based on the item (for instance, you can have only one weapon) or its effect on the player's load. As a rule of thumb, 99 should be the maximum number. However, it's up to you how your game will use the item to denote its maximum number.

In the **Final Fantasy** series of games, Rule of 99' was used throughout its inventory system, allowing the player to carry no more than 99 potions at a time, or anything else for that matter, as shown in the following screenshot:

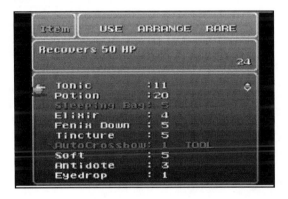

## Encumbrance systems

A system based on the strength, endurance, and energy of a player is a faux-style system. It ensures that the player cannot carry more than he/she is able to; generally though, it doesn't take into account the size of the item, just its weight. This provides a more taxing system for the player, forcing them to only carry what they need.

**Skyrim** implements this system very well; it not only forces the player to manage his/her load when looting but also focuses on leveling up the player to increase what they can carry, as shown in the following screenshot:

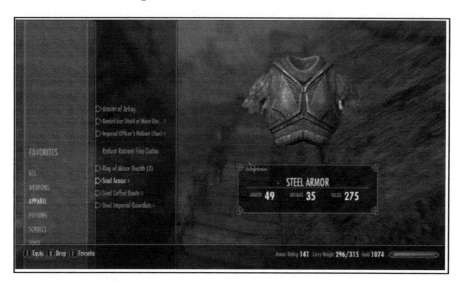

# Slot-based systems

A slot-based system is a variation of the preceding encumbrance system. Instead of weight, it uses a grid system for the player's inventory and assigns a certain number of those grid points to an item. These points relate to how bulky or awkward a particular item is going to be. This generally limits the player more than other systems because it forces the user to reserve enough space to carry the items they really need.

The **Fallout** series implement a very effective slot-based system.

It gets tricky for the player when large mission items require a lot of slots. Refer to the following screenshot:

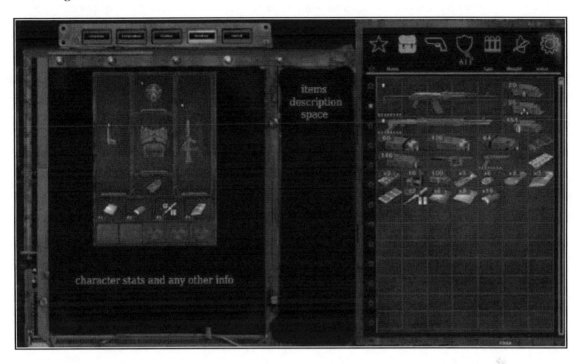

# A mini game

Another approach is to go a step further with an inventory system and evolve it into a mini game in itself. Generally, players don't just move things around or sort them; instead, they start combining items within the inventory to create or craft new items or just upgrade them. A crazy idea I saw involved turning the inventory screen into a game of Tetris with new items being dropped; if you could place them, you would be successful.

It certainly brings a new challenge. Moreover, if the bandwidth of your game can allow it, it's certainly another opportunity to make use of.

# Real world

The most complex system to implement is a real-world or a simulated kind of inventory pattern to use. Attempting to make a player carry things around needs to be as real as possible. It embodies all of the preceding systems and adds rules around the need for special belts to carry axes/swords. Hooks and backpacks have to be carefully packed. In some games, the player carries lots of items on their belt or back; this generates noise, making them less stealthy.

# Creating a shop and inventory

As with other areas in this book, we will just keep things simple when implementing the sample project. You can always extend or replace it later if you wish.

We will also look at two slightly different approaches: using a scene for the shop and a layer system for the inventory.

# Gathering shop assets

The shop will contain various healing items for the player to purchase. To create the shop, we'll just create a new scene to keep things simple as we expect to enter a shop and leave it when we are done.

I altered the assets I used to make the HUD for the battle system to create a new menu that will be used for the shop. I also added a talk bubble, which we will use for the shopkeep to speak to us and show us what we are buying. We'll layout the individual buttons and slots within Unity. The following screenshot shows the buttons, bubbles, and other things that we are going to use:

For items to show in the shop, I turned back to Kenney on OpenGamAart.Org (who made the awesome Hexagon Pack we used for the map) and got the **Generic Items** set at `http://opengameart.org/content/generic-items`. Instead of using the provided sprite sheet, I combined the `.png` files of the healing items I planned on using into one sprite sheet to make it easier to sort. I also used Photoshop to add a slight drop shadow to each item so that the items will be easier to see when implemented.

The following screenshot shows the sprite sheet containing the healing items:

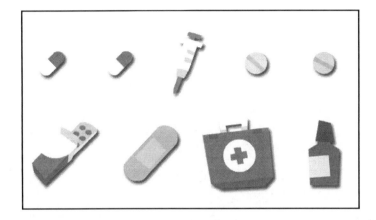

This gives us a nice array of healing items. We will only use a few of these for the shop, but the others would be great to use in the hospital.

We're also going to use the sprite sheet for the `Shopkeep` that we imported in `Chapter` 6, *NPCs and Interactions*, as shown in the following screenshot:

Go ahead and import `Inventory.png` into the `Assets/Sprites/UI` folder and
`healing_items.png` into the `Assets/Sprites/Props` folder. Change their **Sprite Mode**
to **Multiple** and automatically slice them. If you did not bring the `Shopkeep.png` image
into the project in `Chapter 6`, *NPCs and Interactions*, import it now with a **Sprite Mode** of
**Multiple** and automatically slice it.

# Building the shop scene

In `Chapter 2`, *Building your Project and Character*, we made a scene named `Shop`; open it to
view the blank scene.

We will build out the entire shop scene using the UI system. You should be sufficiently
versed in setting up images and panels by now to create the following in your scene:

We're now going to change the background color using the camera setting because right now it is the generic blue, as shown in the following screenshot, and leaving it as it is just shows that we put no thought into the scene's design:

We'll make the background color black by selecting the **Main Camera** in the **Hierarchy** and changing the **Background** color to black, as shown in the following screenshot:

We need to add some text, a back button, and a buy button. Add the text and buttons, as shown in the following screenshot:

We're just going to add a few slots for the inventory items. However, we will use a panel to contain all of the inventory items. This will allow us to easily add more of them and even add a scroll-bar if necessary.

Right-click on the `Inventory` Panel in the **Hierarchy** and select **UI** | **Panel**. Rename this panel `Items`. Position it so that it takes up the area between the buttons and the `Inventory` text, as shown in the following screenshot:

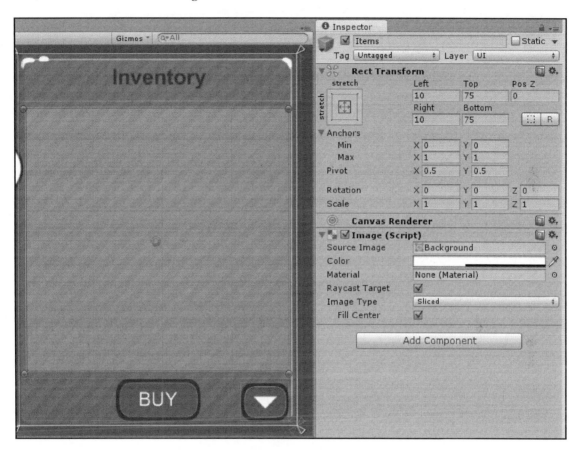

Add a UI Image as a child of the `Items` panel and name it `Slot`. Give it the properties shown in the following screenshot:

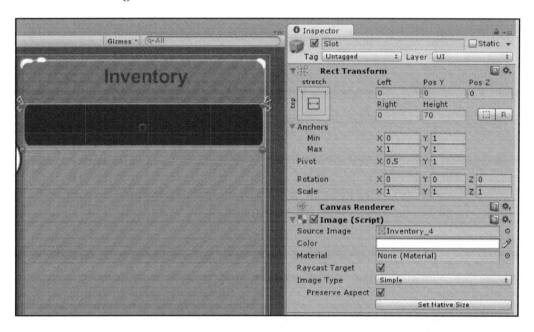

Now add a UI Image as a child of `Slot` and name it **Item Image**. Give it the properties shown in the following screenshot, making sure that **Preserve Aspect** is selected:

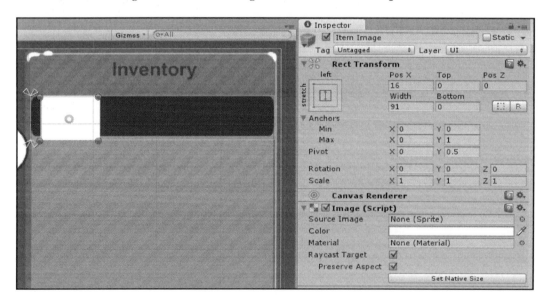

Lastly, add a UI Text object as a child of `Slot` and give it the properties shown in the following screenshot:

Duplicate `Slot` three times by selecting it in the Hierarchy and hitting *Ctrl + D*, as shown in the following screenshot:

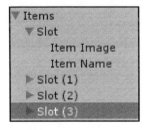

All four of these slots will now appear right on top of each other. To make them line up appropriately, we will add a **Vertical Layout Group** component to the Items Panel. To do so, select the Items panel from the **Hierarchy** and select **Add Component**. Next select **Layout | Vertical Layout Group** and deselect **Child Force Expand Height** from the **Vertical Layout Group** component.

Doing this will actually mess up the alignment of the image and text objects that are children of each of the Slots. This is because the **Vertical Alignment Group** has made the slots taller and their child images are stretching appropriately. The reason why the slots don't look taller is we selected **Preserve Aspect Ratio** on the slot's image, as shown in the following screenshot:

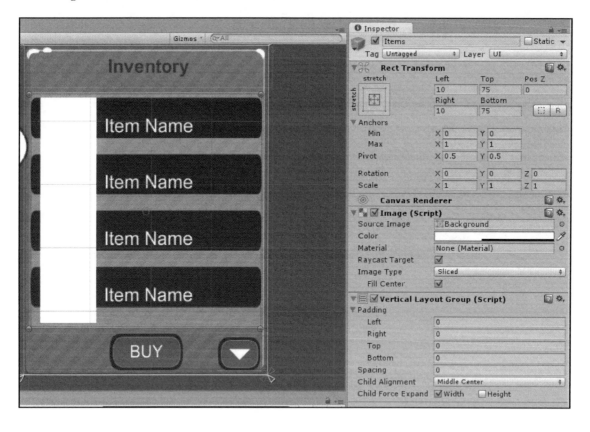

To fix this, we will simply change the height of the `Items` panel. The result is shown in the following screenshot:

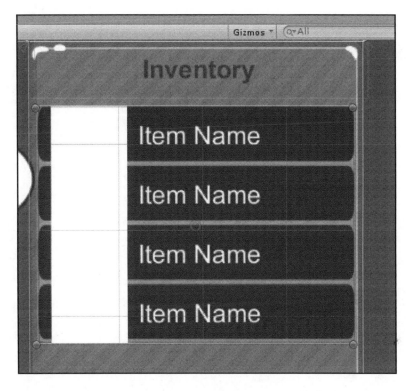

Now, if we wanted to add more inventory items, all we would have to do is duplicate the **Slot** again and change the height of the **Items** panel, and everything would automatically align.

The last thing we are going to do to set up our scene is add some elements to the Shopkeep's dialog bubble. In an ode to **Resident Evil 4**, he will ask *What are you buying?* when no item is selected. Then, when an item is selected, the image of the selected item will appear in his dialog bubble.

To achieve this, add an image as a child of the `Talk Bubble` and name it `Item Choice Image`; make sure **Preserve Aspect** is selected, as shown in the following screenshot:

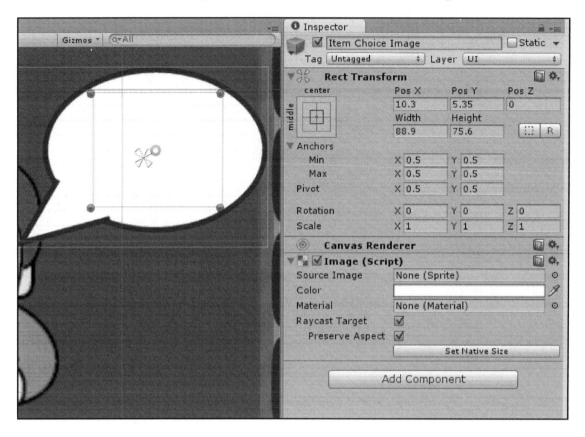

Now, add the following text as a child of `Talk Bubble`. The text should appear below the Image in the **Hierarchy** and in front of the Image in the Scene, as shown in the following screenshot:

When you have put all the GameObjects into the scene, you should have something like the following screenshot:

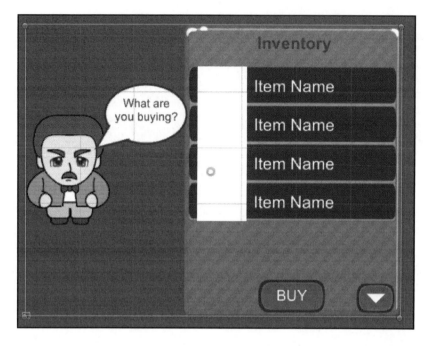

We will add all of the inventory items, their names, and the Shopkeep's reference to them through code.

With the layout in place, we need something for the screen to use. So, let's add some items.

# Creating inventory items

As with the conversation items we created in Chapter 6, *NPCs and Interactions*, we want to be able to simply manage items that can be used or bought in our game.

First, we need a scriptable object to describe our inventory items. So, create a new script in `Assets\Scripts\Classes` named `InventoryItem` and populate it with the following structure:

```
using UnityEngine;
using System.Collections;

public class InventoryItem : ScriptableObject
{
  public Sprite itemImage;
  public string itemName;
  public int cost;
  public int strength;
}
```

 Note that we haven't implemented all of the properties we described earlier, just a subset as an example. You can add more if you wish.

Now that we have our scriptable object, we need an editor script to create our inventory items. So, create another script named `InventoryItemAssetCreator` in the `Assets\Scripts\Editor` folder and populate it with the following structure (note that we are again using our generic utility class to make this very easy to implement):

```
using UnityEngine;
using UnityEditor;

public class InventoryItemAssetCreator : MonoBehaviour {

  [MenuItem("Assets/Create/Inventory Item")]
  public static void CreateAsset()
  {
    CustomAssetUtility.CreateAsset<InventoryItem>();
  }
}
```

With this in place, we can now create some inventory items. Create a new folder named `Inventory Items` in the `Assets\Resources folder`, navigate to that folder, and create a new `InventoryItem` class from the **Create** menu (right-click on **Create** or use the `Project` folder window's **Create** menu option).

With the `New InventoryItem.asset` created, we can configure our first item. Rename the asset to `RedCapsule` and then configure its properties, as shown in the following screenshot:

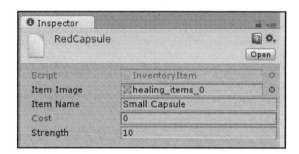

You can configure the properties using the following steps:

1. Set the **Sprite** property to the red capsule image from the `healing_items` Sprite Sheet (**healing_items_0**).
2. Give it a name through the **Item Name** field.
3. Set **Cost** to 0 to denote it's a free item (since we don't have a monetary system yet).
4. Set **Strength** to 10 so that it will heal 10 HP points.

Create three more `InventoryItems` in the same manner. I created `BlueCapsule`, `Bandaid`, and `MedPack`, as shown in the following screenshot:

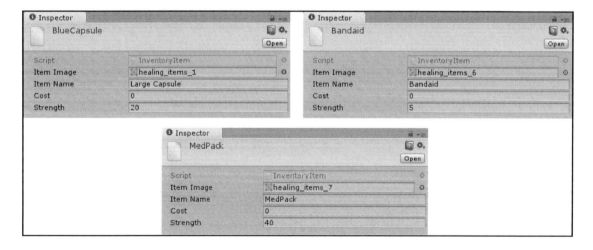

# Managing the shop

Now that we have our shop interface and some stock we can put in it, it's time to bring them together.

First, we need to set up a shop manager who looks after the day-to-day running of the shop, and then we will add shelves to the shop to manage where we can put the stock.

We will create two scripts, ShopSlot and ShopManager, in this section. The ShopSlot and ShopManager scripts will depend on each other, so we need to create them together. Until both are complete, you will most likely see errors; just keep this in mind as we progress.

The situation always applies when you are creating codependent classes.

First, we need the shop manager itself. To keep things neat, create a new folder named Shop in the project's Assets\Scripts folder and then create a new script named ShopManager in the Shop folder. This just ensures that any script related to shopping is stored here if you want to expand it later. The manager is only used in this one scene, so we don't need to make it a singleton.

To start off, we will just add some parameters so that we can control the shop we are creating and set it up as follows:

```
using UnityEngine;
using UnityEngine.UI;

public class ShopManager : MonoBehaviour {

  public Image PurchaseItemDisplay;
  public ShopSlot[] ItemSlots;
  public InventoryItem[] ShopItems;
  private static ShopSlot SelectedShopSlot;

  private int nextSlotIndex = 0;
  public Text shopKeepertext;
}
```

When the player enters the shop's screen, we want to be able to display the current selection of wares. So, when ShopManager starts, we need to configure those items as follows:

```
void Start () {
  if (ItemSlots.Length > 0 && ShopItems.Length > 0)
  {
    for (int i = 0; i < ShopItems.Length; i++)
```

```
    {
        if (nextSlotIndex > ItemSlots.Length) break;
        ItemSlots[nextSlotIndex].AddShopItem(ShopItems[i]);
        ItemSlots[nextSlotIndex].Manager = this;
        nextSlotIndex++;
    }
  }
}
```

The preceding code just loops through all the available slots in the shop and picks out items from its inventory to place in them, ensuring we only stock as many items as the shop can handle.

You will notice that the last function actually has an error. This is because we did not add the actions/behaviors for the ShopSlot script. We will fix that shortly.

Next, we need some helper functions to represent the actions/behaviors that the shop is capable of performing; first, we add the ability to select an item for purchase using the following function:

```
public void SetShopSelectedItem(ShopSlot slot)
{
    SelectedShopSlot = slot;
    PurchaseItemDisplay.sprite = slot.Item.itemImage;
    shopKeeperText.text=" ";
}
```

Finally, we add the ability to purchase the currently selected shop item using the following function:

```
public static void PurchaseSelectedItem()
{
    SelectedShopSlot.PurchaseItem();
}
```

Each of the preceding functions is self-contained and controls each step necessary to perform each action. They do so by enabling or disabling screen elements, such as PurchasingSection, to perform actions on dependent objects such as shop slots.

You will note that this last function is also set as static. This is to enable it to be accessed from anywhere in the code without referencing it or performing GetComponent for the ShopManager script.

As stated in the previous sections, it might seem as of you could make everything static and avoid using `GetComponent` altogether. However, using statics has certain overheads and can lead to messy and hard-to-diagnose code; this technique should not be overly used. If in doubt, don't use it unless necessary.

With `ShopManager` set up, we can now create the missing definition for `ShopSlot`. This will define slots in the shop that remember what is being stored on the shelf. Create a new script in the `Assets\Scripts\Shop` folder and name it `ShopSlot`, replacing its contents with the following code:

```
using UnityEngine;
using UnityEngine.UI;

public class ShopSlot : MonoBehaviour {

    public InventoryItem Item;
    public ShopManager Manager;
    Image image;
    Text name;

}
```

Now, to add other functions for the shop slots that will be used by the manager, add the following functions to the `ShopSlot` script:

```
public void AddShopItem(InventoryItem item)
{
    image = transform.GetChild(0).GetComponent<Image>();

    image.sprite = item.itemImage;
    Item = item;

    name=transform.GetChild(1).GetComponent<Text>();
    name.text=item.itemName;
}

public void PurchaseItem()
{
    //We'll do some stuff here later to add it to our inventory
}
```

The first function enables the ability to add an inventory item to the current slot and display it, and the second function controls how an item is purchased. Again, each function is distinct and is just related to the task that it is to perform. Wherever possible, you should follow this pattern, as it will make maintaining or extending your game much easier later.

Finally, we need to add one last piece of code in order to enable the player to click on items in the shop slots; so, add the following function to the ShopSlots script:

```
public void ItemSelected()
{
  if (Item != null)
  {
    Manager.SetShopSelectedItem(this);
  }
}
```

Now that we can stock our shop and purchase items from it, we just need the ability for users to buy items when selected, so add the following function to the ShopManager script:

```
public void ConfirmPurchase(){
    PurchaseSelectedItem();
  shopKeeperText.text="Thanks!";
}
```

The preceding code simply calls the static Purchasing function we created in the ShopManager script earlier to buy an item. We will tie these last two functions to our buttons and inventory items shortly.

# Updating the player inventory definition

Now that we have a definition for InventoryItem, we can update the Player class so that the player can carry the correct item. So, open the Player class under Assets\Scripts\Classes and update the script to use the new InventoryItem class instead of a string as follows:

```
using System.Collections.Generic;
public class Player : Entity
{
  public List<InventoryItem> Inventory = new List<InventoryItem>();
  public string[] Skills;
  public int Money;
}
```

# Stocking the shop

With all our scripts in place, let's return to the shop scene, start applying them, and, finally, get some stock displayed on the shelves.

So first, let's attach the following scripts:

- Attach the `ShopManager` script to the `Inventory` GameObject
- Attach the `ShopSlot` script to each **Slot** in the shop

Now, our shop is ready to receive its owner and some inventory items to stock. So, select the `Inventory` GameObject; once you do this, you should see the following configuration options in the **Inspector** pane:

I've preconfigured **Shop Manager** as an example. So, let's walk through the steps that are available:

1. Drag the `Item Choice Image` to the **Purchase Item Display** slot.
2. Next, set the **Item Slots** pane's **Size** to 4 and attached each of the available `Slots` in the shop by dragging them from the **Hierarchy** into the **Inspector** pane. You can also achieve this by using the circle icon to the right of each element and finding the `Slot` in the scene. Note that you cannot drag slots into this list if you do not have the `ShopSlot` script attached to them.

3. Finally, set the **Shop Items** pane's **Size** to 4 and dragged the four `Inventory Items` we created earlier in the `Assets\Resources\InventoryItems` folder into each element of the **Shop Items** array. The order in which you drag them into the array is the order in which they will appear on the screen.

If you now run the scene at this point, you should see the following:

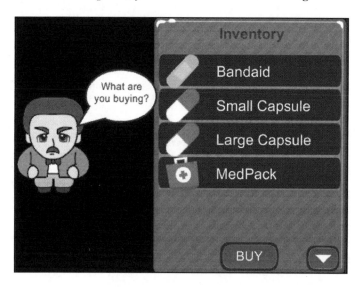

Now we need to get the buttons working appropriately and allow the player to select the items.

# Linking up the buttons

We created all of the slots as images, but we want them to perform as buttons. So, we can easily add a button script to each of the slots. Select all four of the slots and add **Commponent | UI | Button**.

We want each of these slots to perform the `ItemSelected()` function that is in the `ShopSlot` script attached to each of them. For each slot's `Button` script, set up the `On Click()` event, as shown in the following screenshot:

Make sure you drag the correct `Slot` to each.

Now, when you select an item, it should appear in the ShopKeep's dialog bubble, as shown in the following screenshot:

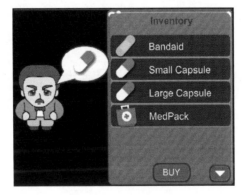

The last button we need to link up is the `Buy Button`. We want it to perform the `ConfirmPurchase()` function within the `ShopManager` script. So, add the function to the button's `On Click()` functionality, as shown in the following screenshot:

Now when you click the `Buy Button` after selecting an item, the Shopkeep will say *Thanks!* over the item to affirm that it has been purchased. Soon, we'll allow this to also add the item to our inventory.

# Turning off the Buy Button

Currently, there is one big problem with our shop. If you select the `Buy Button` before you select an object, an error message will appear. It doesn't break the game, but it isn't a good idea to let error messages (even if your game continues to run) show up. The best way to deal with this is to disable the `Buy Button` until after an item has been selected because, after all, it doesn't really make sense for this button to be there if the player hasn't selected anything.

To accomplish this, we will add a **Canvas Group** to our `Buy Button` by selecting **Add Component | Layout | Canvas Group** from the **Inspector**.

Change the **Canvas Group** values as follows:

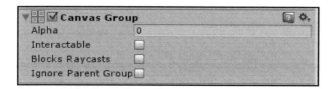

The `Buy Button` will now no longer be visible in the scene. Add the following variable to the `ShopSlot` script:

```
public CanvasGroup buyButton;
```

And update the `ItemSelected()` function as follows:

```
public void ItemSelected()
    {
        if (Item != null)
        {
            Manager.SetShopSelectedItem(this);

            if(buyButton.alpha==0){
                buyButton.alpha=1;
                buyButton.interactable=true;
                buyButton.blocksRaycasts=true;
            }
        }
    }
```

Now drag the `Buy Button` into the **Buy Button** variable for each of the `ShopSlot` scripts attached to the **Slot**, as shown in the following screenshot:

You can do this for all four slots at once by selecting all of the `Slots` in the **Hierarchy** while holding *Ctrl*.

# Entering the shop

We can buy items from the shop but we can't actually enter the `Shop` scene or leave the `Shop` scene. As we did in `Chapter 7`, *The World Map*, we just need to add trigger colliders in the `Town` where the user can enter the `Shop`. To do this, return to the `Town` scene.

Add a new empty GameObject named `Shop` as a child of the **WorldBounds** GameObject (because it takes us out of the scene) and add a **Box Collider 2D** component (set as a trigger), as shown in the following screenshot:

The collider just needs to be shaped or scaled enough so that our 2D character will collide with it when she passes in front of the shop.

Attach the `NavigationPrompt` script to the `Shop`.

Trying to enter the shop isn't going to get us very far if the game doesn't know it exists, so add the `Shop` scene to the project's **Build Settings**.

Also, update the `NavigationManager` script to include a new `Route` asset for the shop as follows:

```
public static Dictionary<string, Route> RouteInformation = new
   Dictionary<string, Route>() {
      { "Overworld", new Route{RouteDescription="The big bad world",
         CanTravel=true}},
         { "Construction", new Route{RouteDescription="The construction
area",
            CanTravel=false}},
         { "Town", new Route{RouteDescription="The main town",
CanTravel=true}},
         { "Campsite", new Route{RouteDescription="The campsite",
            CanTravel=false}},
         { "Shop", new Route{RouteDescription="The town shop",
CanTravel=true}},
      };
```

Finally, to ensure that we navigate to the new `Shop` scene, we need to add a new tag named `Shop` and assign it to the new `Shop` GameObject, as shown in the following screenshot:

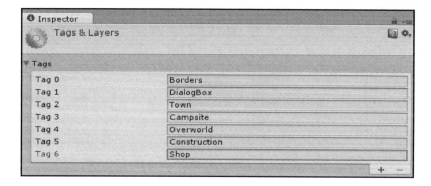

After you add the **Shop** tag, be sure to assign it to the shop.

# Leaving the shop

The hero can purchase items from the shop (she doesn't get to keep them just yet), but she is stuck in the shop, the doors and windows are barred, and the owner has a very stern face.

To allow the hero to leave, we just need to call the `NavigationManager` script. Instead of making a whole new script for this, I will just add it to the `ShopMananger` script.

Add the following function at the end of the `ShopManager` script:

```
public void LeaveTheShop(){
    NavigationManager.NavigateTo("Town");
}
```

Now just have the preceding function called from the **Back** button when clicked, as shown in the following screenshot:

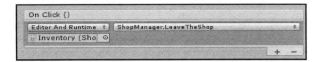

The hero should now be sent to the middle of town. Let's fix it so that she returns through the front door instead of returning to the middle of town.

Using the same method we used in Chapter 8, *Encountering Enemies and Running Away*, to get character to spawn in the correct location, we need to update the `StartingPosition` on the `NavigationPrompt` script that is attached to the `Shop`, as shown in the following screenshot:

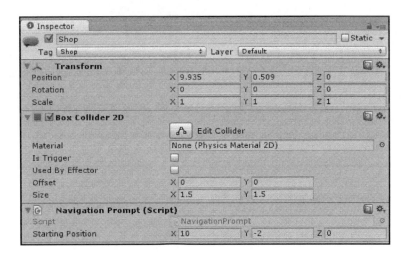

Now the player will spawn in front of the shop when leaving it.

# Managing your inventory

Now let's put an inventory window in our scene so that the player can view what he/she has purchased.

In the `Town` scene, create a new UI Canvas and name it `PopUpWindows`. Add a panel named `InventoryPanel` as a child of the new canvas with a width and height of `300` and give it the `Inventory_1` background image. Give it a text `Title` and add a `Close` button, as shown in the following screenshot:

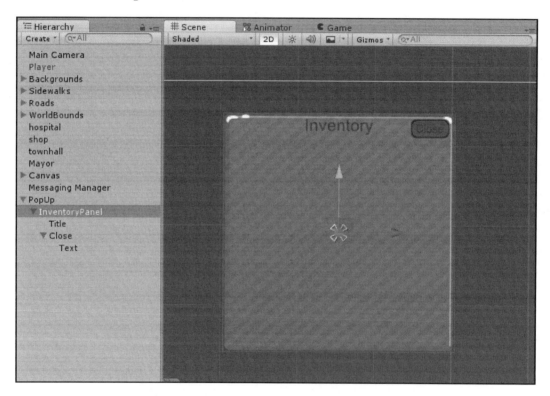

Add another panel as a child of `InventoryPanel` and name it `InventoryList`. Adjust its size so that it only takes up the bottom portion of `InventoryPanel`, as shown in the following screenshot:

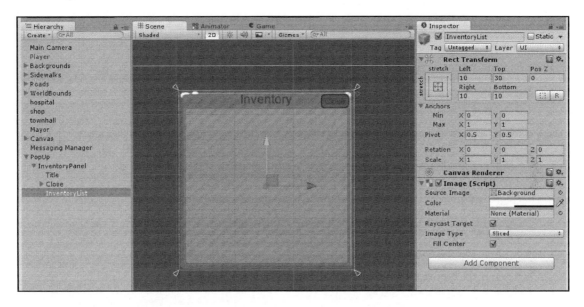

Now we'll give it the ability to pop up and close in the scene by adding a new button to access it. Add a new button to the `PopUp` Canvas and call it `ShowInventory`. Place it at the bottom corner of the canvas, as shown in the following screenshot:

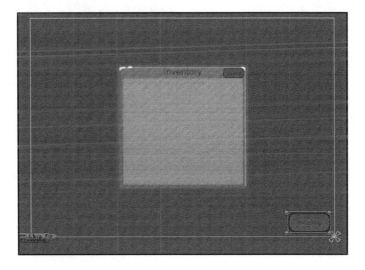

Now add a Canvas Group to the `InventoryPanel`. Set the **Alpha** to 0 and deselect **Interactable** and **Blocks Raycasts**.

In `Chapter 9`, *Getting Ready to Fight*, we created a `PopUpMenu` script. Attach this to the `InventoryPanel` and assign `InventoryPanel` to the **PopUp** slot.

Set up the `On Click()` events for the `ShowInventory` and `Close` buttons to run the `EnableTheMenu` and `DisableTheMenu` functions from the `PopUpMenu` script, respectively.

Now the inventory menu should open and close appropriately.

We are going to let the inventory populate within the panel area based on what the player purchases. We also want this to automatically display in a grid. So, add the **Grid Layout Group** component to the `InventoryList` panel by selecting **Add Component | Layout | Grid Layout Group** from the Inspector, as shown in the following screenshot:

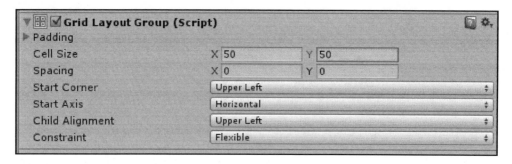

Return the **Alpha** of the `InventoryPanel` to 1 so that you can see what you are doing, for now.

Add a button as a child of `InventoryList` and delete its text component. Name this button `InventoryItemPrefab`. Set its anchor and pivot to the top left corner, as show in the following screenshot:

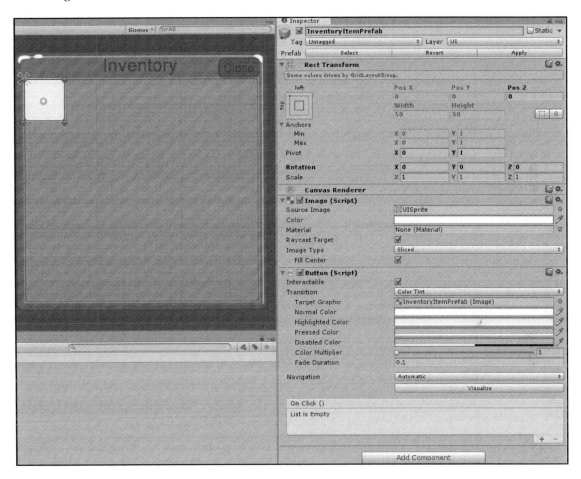

Save this button as a prefab and delete it from the scene.

Create a new C# script in the `Assets/Scripts` folder, name it `PlayerIventoryDisplay`, and populate it with the following code:

```
using UnityEngine;
using UnityEngine.UI;

public class PlayerInventoryDisplay : MonoBehaviour{

public Button invPrefab;
```

```
void Start() {

    foreach (var item in GameState.currentPlayer.Inventory)
    {
        Button inventoryChild = (Button)
            Instantiate(invPrefab,Vector3.zero, Quaternion.identity);
        inventoryChild.transform.parent=transform;
        inventoryChild.GetComponent<Image>().sprite=item.itemImage;
    }
  }
}
```

The preceding code loops through all the items in the player's inventory (if there are any) and displays them as buttons.

Attach the preceding code to the `InventoryList` panel and add `InventoryItemPrefab` to the **Inv Prefab** slot.

# Adding objects to the player's inventory

Right now, if the player character is holding inventory items, they display in the inventory. But, she doesn't actually have the ability to hold any items.

Open up the `Player` script under the `Assets\Scripts\Classes` folder and add the following additional function:

```
public void AddinventoryItem(InventoryItem item){
    Inventory.Add(item);
}
```

Now the player character will have a list of all objects that she is holding.

Now that we have our helper function to control a player's **Inventory** property, we just need to update the `ShopSlot` script we created earlier to use the following new function:

```
public void PurchaseItem()
{
   GameState.CurrentPlayer.AddinventoryItem(Item);
}
```

Now try playing the game and entering the shop. Buy some stuff, return to the town menu, and view all of your fancy items, as shown in the following screenshot:

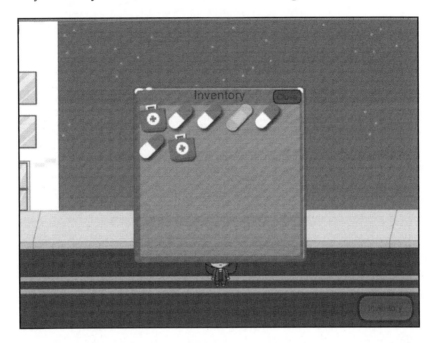

Now you have the basic inventory set up and each item is a button. You can easily have these buttons add health to the player and remove them from the list when used. The nice thing about using the **Grid Layout Group** is that the items will automatically lay out appropriately.

There is one issue with the current layout, if you exceed the number of items that can be held in the specified space, they will overflow the menu. You can fix this by adding a scroll bar and also by having repeated inventory items group together.

Remember, in Chapter 9, *Getting Ready to Fight*, we had a button for items in our HUD. Save the PopUp canvas as a prefab and bring it in to the Battle scene. Then link the InventoryPanel to the Item button in the HUD the same way you did in the Town scene. When you bring the Popup canvas prefab in to the Battle scene, be sure to delete the ShowInventory button, as it conflicts with the button already available in the HUD.

# Going further

If you are adventurous, try expanding your project to add the following features:

- Add the inventory menu to the battle scene, as previously discussed.
- Use a scroll bar to allow the inventory menu and shop inventory to exceed the current view.
- Group similar inventory items together by showing a single image with an item count.
- Add scripts to the inventory items to allow them to affect the player's health.
- Have a go at adding money into the equation by making things cost money. In the purchasing section, display and act on it if the player does not have enough.
- Put a second view in the shop to allow the player to sell items back to the shop.

# Summary

In this chapter, we added a new location for the player to visit, the shop, where the player character was able to purchase many different items and add them to her own personal inventory.

The next chapter discusses adding sound and music to your project.

# 12
# Sound and Music

Our character can do lots of things now. She can shop, she can fight, she can run away, and explore a map, but it's as if she is doing it in a soundless vacuum. Therefore, it's time to add some sound and music to our game.

Unity has a lot of built-in functionality when it comes to audio, much of it is beyond the scope of this book. You can mix audio, create 3D sounds, and do all sorts of fancy things with audio within Unity. We're going to cover the basic functionality of adding sound and music to get you started on your auditory journey.

The topics that will be covered in this chapter are as follows:

- Adding background music to your game
- Adding sound effects to your game
- Muting and unmuting audio

## Choosing the appropriate sound and music

Choosing the sound and music will likely be one of the last things you do for your game (unless, of course, you're making a music game).

It is important that the music *fits* with the tone that you have set with the art and overall feel of the game. For me, this is harder than choosing art, because I know that choosing the wrong music could drastically bring down the appeal of my game. If the player finds your music choice annoying, too loud, or overbearing, their experience will be far from ideal. I recommend playing the music you chose over and over for yourself. If it annoys you after a few loops, it will definitely annoy the player.

Appropriate sound effects are also important. You want to make sure that all appropriate actions have sound and that the sound fits the action that it accompanies. You don't want the sound of breaking glass to accompany the action of a character sighing, for example. Too few sound effects can make your game feel incomplete and too many (especially triggering at the same time) can make your game seem muddled. It's also important that the sound doesn't get too repetitive, as this will become annoying quickly.

Just remember to play-test your game with many different types of people from many different walks of life and specifically ask them their opinion on the sound and music. Many players will mute the sound of a game before they even hear it, so if you are testing for sound and music, make sure the players know ahead of time.

# Where to get sound and music for your game

There are a few different options for where you can get sound and music. You can make the audio yourself, you can hire composers, you can purchase stock audio, or you can even use free stock audio.

If you purchase stock audio or use free stock audio, be sure to check the licensing agreement. Purchasing audio does not automatically guarantee you unrestricted use and sometimes, even if you pay for it, you cannot use it in a commercial game.

## Free resources

If you're like me, free is probably the price range you are looking for. What follows is a list of a few places where you can get free resources to help you design your own audio or get pre-existing sound effects/music:

- Audacity is free software and can be downloaded at `http://www.audacityteam.org/`. This software can be great for recording your own sound effects and dialog.
- My favorite place to get music is `incompetech.com/`. You can sort the music by feel and genre and there is a huge selection of quality music available here. Make sure that you check the licensing info on this, because the artist does require credit when using his material.
- Free sound effects are a little harder to come by. `Freesound.org` is a good place to get sound effects. Each sound effect has a different license agreement, so make sure you check that out before downloading.

- Always check out the Unity Asset Store when you're looking for any resource, at `https://www.assetstore.unity3d.com`. While there aren't many free assets in terms of sound or music, there are a few and the store gets new items daily.

# Audio listeners and audio sources

To have audio in your scene you need at least two objects: an audio source and an audio listener. The audio source is the object that emits the sound and the audio listener is the object that receives the sound.

Any object in your scene can be turned into an audio source or listener by attaching the corresponding component to it. However, you will notice that the `Main Camera` always comes with an `Audio Listener` component automatically added to it when a new scene is created. The following screenshot shows the **Inspector** for the `Main Camera` from our `BattleScene`:

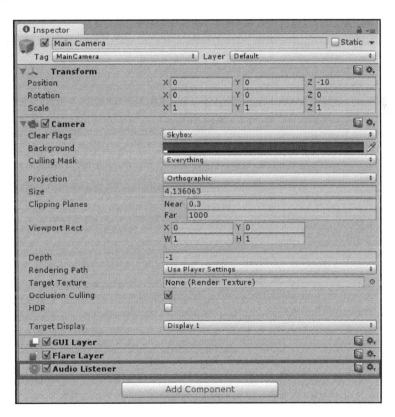

Since we will be working in a 2D game the object that we use as our audio source is not terribly important. If we were working in a 3D game and wanted our sound to be 3D (that is, the distance the object is away from the audio listener will affect the sound's volume), we'd want the object actually making the sound to be the audio source.

My preference is to have two objects in my game that are carried between scenes and act as audio sources. I use one object as the audio source for the music in the game and the other as the audio source for all sound effects. This allows me to easily mute the sound and music separately.

# Adding background music

To begin, I grabbed the song **Bit Shift** by Kevin MacLeod over at incompetech.com. If you go to the site, select **Get Started with Music** and you can search by mood, genre, and other properties. You can also search for the name of the song to download the one I am using. I chose this song because it reminds me a lot of **Phantasy Star** on the **Sega Master System**, which is one of my all-time-favorite games. But I digress. Add whichever song you choose to the `Assets/Audio/Music` folder.

We are going to just have this one song play throughout all of our scenes. This means that we need to create an object that starts playing the music at our initial scene and then doesn't destroy when a new scene loads. Placing this object in a scene and telling it not to destroy when we go to new scenes works great, except for one problem; if you return back to the initial scene, the sound will duplicate and each time you return to the scene it will add a new instance of the song. We could accomplish this with code, but I want to show you another way to handle it, and that's by adding a splash screen to our project.

# Creating a splash screen

A splash screen is the initial screen that displays before all others in a video game. It usually contains a logo, credits, copyright, and so on. When you build a game in Unity, a Unity splash screen will initially play. We will customize this screen in Chapter 13, *Putting a Bow on it*, but for now we will just have a blank splash screen that loads our audio sources.

The splash screen is a great place to load your objects that you want to carry on throughout the entire game because:

1. Everyone sees this screen when they first start playing.
2. You never return to this screen, so items will not duplicate.

To begin, create a new scene by navigating to the Assets/Scenes folder, right-clicking within the folder, and selecting **Create | Scene**. Name this new scene SplashScreen. Double-click on the scene to load it.

# Adding the audio source

Now, within the **Hierarchy**, select **Create | Audio | Audio Source**. Position it at 0,0,0 and rename it Music. Now, drag the song you downloaded into the **AudioClip** slot of the **Audio Source**. Also, make sure **Loop** is selected in the **Audio Source** component. As shown in the following screenshot:

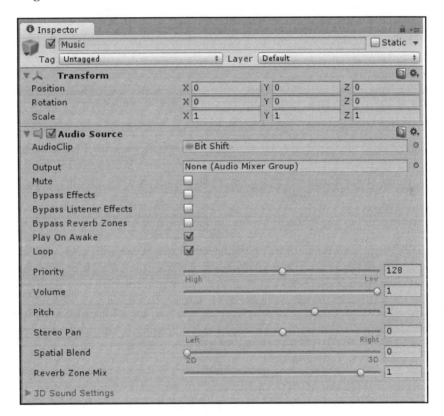

When you play the scene, the music should immediately begin playing.

# Transitioning to the next scene

We are going to write two small scripts: one that automatically transitions from this scene to the next and one that keeps the music from destroying when the next scene loads.

Before we begin writing these scripts, let's go ahead and add this scene to the **Build Settings**; otherwise, none of the code we are about to write will work. When you add it to the **Build Settings**, make sure it is the first scene in the list. This will cause this to be the first scene that loads when the game begins. As shown in the following screenshot:

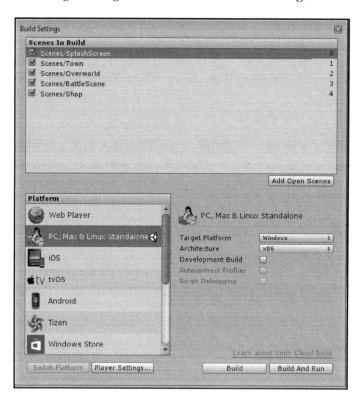

The first script we will write will make sure the game automatically transitions to the next scene. As you can see from the **Build Settings** dialog, the next scene is the Town. Create the following C# script in the Assets/Scripts folder and call it SplashScreen.cs:

```
using UnityEngine;
using System.Collections;
using UnityEngine.SceneManagement;

public class SplashScreen : MonoBehaviour {
```

```
public string sceneToLoadName;
public int timeToLoad;


void Start () {
    Invoke("NextScene", timeToLoad);
}
void NextScene () {
    SceneManager.LoadScene(sceneToLoadName);
}
}
```

This code simply loads a scene by name after a specified amount of time.

To get this code to work, we need to attach it to something. We don't want to attach it to the `Music` object, because that will be transferring to the next scene, so let's just add it to the `Main Camera`. Give the **Scene To Load Name** variable the value of `Town` and the **Time To Load** variable the value of 1. As shown in the following screenshot:

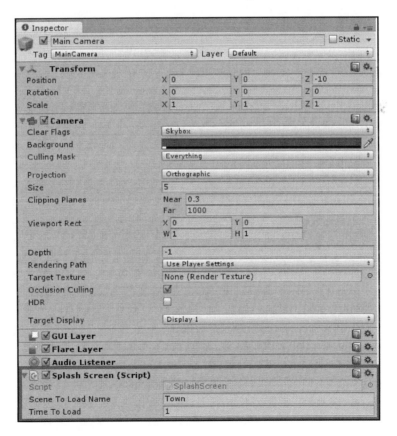

Play the scene, and after one second the `Town` scene will load. However, the music instantly stops playing, as it is not carried over to the `Town` scene.

# Keeping the music after the scene transition

Now that the scene automatically transitions, let's make our music come along for the ride.

Create the following C# script in the `Assets/Scripts` folder and call it `KeepAround.cs`:

```
using UnityEngine;
using System.Collections;

public class KeepAround : MonoBehaviour {
    void Update (){

        DontDestroyOnLoad(gameObject);

    }
}
```

This script simply states: when a new scene loads, don't destroy whatever GameObject to this script is attached to. Now attach this script to the `Music` GameObject.

Now, when you play the scene, the music will continue to play in the `Town`. It will also play in the `Shop`, `Overworld`, and any other scene you feel like having your character travel to.

# Adding sound effects

We will create another `AudioSource` to play all sound effects. The way in which we have the sound effect play will be handled through code instead of having it play instantly and continuously.

Now, within the **Hierarchy**, select **Create | Audio | Audio Source**. Position it at 0,0,0 and rename it `Sound`, as shown in the following screenshot. Since we don't want a sound to play the moment the game starts, deselect **Play On Awake**. Also drag and drop the `KeepAround.cs` script into the **Inspector**:

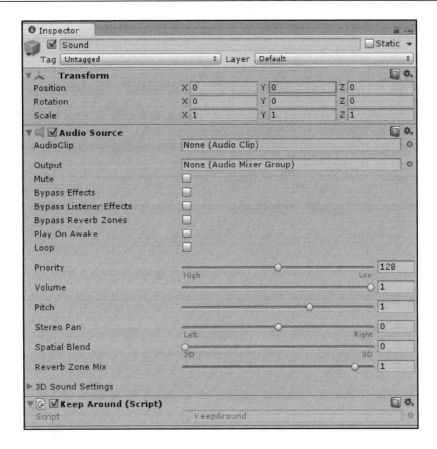

I chose to have this single audio source for my sound effects and to have it continue through each scene to make muting and unmuting the sound easier.

To easily access the Sound GameObject through code, we will use a **Tag**. Select the Sound GameObject and add the new tag Sound. As shown in the following screenshot:

# Adding a sound to the buy button

We can add all sorts of sounds to our game and the process will be the same throughout. For this text, to preserve the page count, we will only add one sound. We will add a nice coin sound that will play whenever the Buy Button in the shop is selected. I toyed with the idea of using a sound effect that was simply me saying *cha-ching*, because I thought it would be funny in a terrible way, but I decided against it. Instead, I went over to freesound.org and got the sound of coins being shaken in a bag, found here: http://freesound.org/people/D%2W/sounds/14382/. Place the sound in the Assets/Audio/FX folder.

Return to the Shop scene. If you recall, the functionality for the Buy Button was in the ShopMananger script attached to the Inventory GameObject. So, open the ShopManager script from the Assets/Scripts/Shop folder.

Create two new variables at the top of the script as follows:

```
GameObject soundEffectsSource;
public AudioClip buySound;
```

Now create a new Awake() function before the Start() function as follows:

```
void Awake(){
        soundEffectsSource= GameObject.FindGameObjectWithTag("Sound");
}
```

Now we just need to update the ConfirmPurchase() function by adding the following if statement:

```
if(soundEffectsSource!=null){
soundEffectsSource.GetComponent<AudioSource>().PlayOneShot(buySound);
        }
```

I made the buySound a public variable so that we could easily assign it through the **Inspector**. So, select Inventory from the **Hierarchy**, and drag the coin sound to the **Buy Sound** slot in the ShopMananger, as shown in the following screenshot:

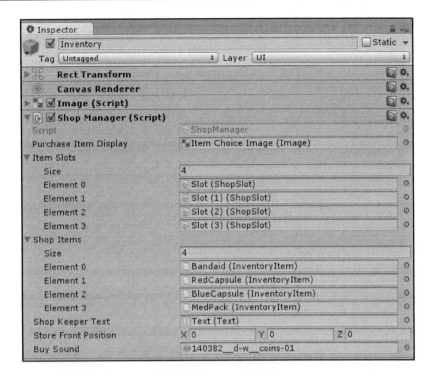

If we neglected to place the `if(soundEffectsSource!=null){}` condition in our function, we would be unable to buy objects unless we started playing our game at the splash screen, because we would get an error if we tried to buy something.

Now, since our sound effect source is created on the splash screen, the only way we can check to see if our sound effect works is by playing the game from the splash screen. Reload the splash screen, play the game, navigate to the Shop scene, and buy something. The sound should play whenever the Buy Button is pressed.

Having to always play from the splash screen is quite annoying when you are testing your game. I recommend adding an audio source with the Sound tag to each scene just for sound-testing purposes, but disabling them before building the final version of your game.

# Muting/unmuting audio

Before we proceed, we need to create a Music tag similar to the way we created a Sound tag. Return to the splash scene and select the Music GameObject in the **Hierarchy**. Create a Music tag and assign it to the Music GameObject, as shown in the following screenshot:

We need to add a few little UI elements to mute and unmute our audio. We'll add two buttons to our Town scene that will turn the sound and music on and off. We're going to use the image on the button to indicate to the player if the sound and music channels are on or off.

Add the following soundUI.png image to the Assets/Sprites/UI folder. Import it under **Multiple Sprite Mode** and slice it automatically:

Navigate to the Town scene and select the PopUp canvas from the **Hierarchy**. Add two buttons to the bottom left part of the screen, as shown in the following screenshot:

Name the first button `Music` and the second button `Sound`.

Now, create a C# script named `MuteUnMute` within the `Assets/Scripts` folder, and replace its code with the following:

```
using UnityEngine;
using System.Collections;
using UnityEngine.UI;

public class MuteUnMute : MonoBehaviour {
    public Button musicButton;
    public Button soundButton;
    Image musicImage;
    Image soundImage;
    public Sprite MusicOn;
    public Sprite MusicOff;
    public Sprite SoundOn;
    public Sprite SoundOff;

    GameObject soundEffectsSource;
    GameObject musicSource;
    AudioSource musicPlaying;
    AudioSource soundPlaying;
    void Awake(){
        soundEffectsSource=GameObject.FindGameObjectWithTag("Sound");
        musicSource=GameObject.FindGameObjectWithTag("Music");
        if(musicSource!=null){
            musicPlaying=musicSource.GetComponent<AudioSource>();
        }
        if(soundEffectsSource!=null){
```

```
            soundPlaying=soundEffectsSource.GetComponent<AudioSource>();
    }

    musicImage=musicButton.GetComponent<Image>();
    soundImage=soundButton.GetComponent<Image>();

    //show correct music image when starting scene
    //music is off
    if (musicPlaying.mute==false) {
        musicImage.sprite=MusicOn;
    //music is on
    }else{
        musicImage.sprite=MusicOff;
    }

    //show correct sound image when starting scene
    //sound is off
    if (soundPlaying.mute==false) {
        soundImage.sprite=SoundOn;
    //sound is on
    }else{
        soundImage.sprite=SoundOff;
    }

}
public void MuteAndUnMuteMusic(){
    //mute music if off
    if (musicPlaying.mute==false) {
        musicImage.sprite=MusicOff;
        if(musicPlaying!=null){
            musicPlaying.mute=true;
        }
    //unmute music if off
    } else {
        musicImage.sprite=MusicOn;
        if(musicPlaying !=null){
            musicPlaying.mute=false;
        }

    }
}
public void MuteAndUnMuteSound(){
    //mute sound if on
    if (soundPlaying.mute==false) {
        soundImage.sprite=SoundOff;
        if(soundPlaying !=null){
            soundPlaying.mute=true;
        }
```

```
        //unmute sound if off
        } else {
            soundImage.sprite=SoundOn;
            if(soundPlaying !=null){
                soundPlaying.mute=false;
            }
        }
    }
}
```

The preceding code does the following:

- Finds the audio sources and assigns them to the variables soundEffectsSource and musicSource based on their tags.
- Assigns the correct image to the button that controls music and the button that controls sound when the level starts. For example, if the music is muted when the player enters the scene, the muted music image will display.
- The MuteAndUnMuteMusic() function will be called when a button is clicked. It will turn the music on and off and change the button image depending on whether or not the music is already on or off.
- The MuteAndUnMuteSound() function performs similarly to the MuteAndUnMuteMusic() function.

Now, begin playing the game from the SplashScreen scene and you should have full control of your music and sound through these two buttons.

# Going further

If you are adventurous, try expanding your project to add the following features:

- Add sound effects to other events
- Tie sound effects to animations through animation events
- Instead of just muting and unmuting your sound and music, add a volume control by adjusting the Volume parameter on the Audio Source component

# Summary

In this chapter, we covered the basics of adding audio to a game. We started out by adding a blank splash screen to hold our audio sources, added background music to our game, added a simple sound effect, and finally learned how to mute and unmute the audio through code.

# 13
## Putting a Bow on It

You have a game; it looks good, plays well, and everyone loves it. The only problem is that it is still not a finished project.

In this chapter, we will package up the game and surround it with menus and other features to make it whole. We will then explore how we can extend Unity to make the content easier and better.

As they say, finishing a project can take up to 80% of the time needed to polish it. Be warned! This is usually right. To wrap up, we will look at an overview, persisting the player's data as they play both on the device and on the cloud.

The following topics will be covered in this chapter:

- Packaging your game with menus and additional screens
- The editor and how to make the most out of it
- Saving, loading, and persistence for your game

## Building in-game menu structures

Usually left as an afterthought or slapped on at the end, menu systems are just as important as your game in most aspects. How the user interacts/starts or walks through all the sections of your game leading to the actual gameplay can radically change how the user feels about your game. There's no point in having a world-beating game if the first thing the user sees on starting your game is a roughly drawn or shabby-looking menu system. The best menu systems I've seen are actually seamlessly built into the game mechanics themselves.

# The screens

First off, you need to work out the structure of your menu systems in advance; it doesn't need to be detailed, just understand the flow of your game from start to finish and then iterate on that design until it looks impressive and easy to use. The kinds of screens and areas that you need to focus on are covered in the next section.

## Splash screens

We discussed splash screens briefly in the previous chapter, but let's go a little further. Splash screens tell the user about you and your brand; it's always the first thing they see. If you animate a splash screen, try to keep it under three seconds; a good baseline is to aim for between 1-2 seconds. Anything shorter and users won't pay attention; longer and you could just annoy them by making them wait to start the game.

A big debate I've seen between studios is whether you should allow the user to skip splash screens, and there doesn't seem to be any firm view either way.

A general piece of advice though is to not allow skipping as it can devalue your brand.

Splash screens can either be separate screens or just a full screen UI Image displayed when the game loads. Either method will work; the direction you take will largely depend on the style of your game.

## Loading screens

Plan to have a loading screen in advance. You may not actually use it initially, but when your game runs on lower spec devices, you will find that the loading times will increase, sometimes dramatically. Be prepared!

A good example of a loading scene tutorial can be found at `http://chicounity3d.wordpress.com/2014/01/25/loading-screen-tutorial/`. This tutorial uses the older GUI system, but can be easily edited to fit with the new UI.

## The main menu

The main menu is the obvious focal point when the player starts your game. Ideally, this should flow in to your game rather than look like a bolt on. Try to use game elements and moving/animated features.

This screen will be the first true impression of your game the player gets.

Ensure that the player has a *Continue* option that returns them to their last point in the game so that they start playing in as few clicks/taps as possible. If you support the saving option, have a Continue button to jump on to the last save. If you use levels, jump on to the next level that they can play.

Don't force the player to wade through mountains of screens just to continue playing. I'm not saying don't have a new button or an option to select levels; just add an additional Continue option so they can jump straight in to the game.

## Save slots/level selections

The norm these days is just to have a grid array with masses of numbers plastered across the screen. These aren't bad per se; however, if you want to stand out, think differently. Surprise the player: stylize these screens as much as possible, animate them, and make them exciting/interactive.

## Settings pages

Every game usually has an array of settings to control various elements of the game itself. However, don't forget to check platform requirements with regards to these.

If you use audio, always have options to control the volume and a quick mute option; you may find you have to set this programmatically on some platforms.

If you use location services, then you must have an option to turn this on or off. It's a mandatory requirement on some platforms. Have a backup plan if the location is not available.

Try and support closed captioning; it is fairly easy to do this, and it means you open up your game to an even wider audience. Then, just have a setting to enable/disable it. Highlight it in your description on the store; you'll get extra credit for this from your users and reviewers.

## The About screen

There are so many games that leave out the About screen. This is not essential by any means, but you can have a page that describes your game studio, the developers, any extra credits for artists, resources, and so on. This screen generally doesn't have to be fancy, but it helps.

# Privacy policy

In an ever-growing world of security, privacy, and data protection, even if your game doesn't use any online features or store any data about the user, it is still essential to include a privacy policy.

On some platforms, it is becoming mandatory to have your policy stated somewhere in the app/game.

 Do not ship your game without some form of privacy policy.

Policies do not have to be extensive, and there are numerous examples of different types of policies out there; a quick search or a good lawyer will stand you in good stead.

The following site lists several generators; just pick the one that is right for you to get started: `http://www.applicationprivacy.org/do-tools/privacy-policy-generator/`

# Pause screens

Like a lot of common screens used throughout your game, from scene to scene, one of the most common panels the player will see is the Pause menu.

Whether it is a simple *on hold* screen or a full navigation system, you should devote some care to how you design it. Some games truly build the pause screen into the game and make it part of the game experience, while others just stop everything and throw up a panel.

When designing your pause screen think outside the box and don't just do what is necessary. Make it interesting!

If you are using a state machine (as in this book), you should then also progress it to a paused state as well.

 A simple way to stop all of the game updating (and effectively pause the game) is to set `Time.timeScale = 0`; but if you have logic that requires updates on the screen, then this may not work.

# Additional menus (purchasing, achievements, leaderboards, and so on)

Generally shown as big lists on screens, these areas are your main way to entice the player to keep playing, whether it's to compete with friends for the highest scores or work toward a number of achievements (for the completionists out there). You should try to make these screens fun and informative. For levels, think about linking them with friends of the player to see how they compete with each other, or offer deals/promotions. As per a repeated statement in this chapter, think about what makes your game different and go beyond the norm.

# Social

In an ever-increasing social world, games need to react to this and think beyond the boundaries of just the game. Whether you are enabling simple bragging on levels/scores or if you are using social networks to find friends online and suggest games, you have to consider social link-ins with your game to stay competitive.

Social integration is not required, but an ever increasing number of players now actively look for it, so you should consider it at some level.

# The flow

When you have decided on all the screens within your game, the next step is to visualize (before cutting code) how they will all fit together. It doesn't take long and can save you hours of head-scratching later.

You can either grab a piece of paper or download some of the many free tools out there such as FreeMind (a mind-map tool at
`http://freemind.sourceforge.net/wiki/index.php/Main_Page`) and Expression Design (now free from MS at
`http://www.microsoft.com/en-gb/download/details.aspx?id=36180`).

In the end, you want to have written down how each screen will connect to each other, what state the game will be in for that transition, and any key information that will need storing to prevent failure (since your game could be closed at any point by the user). At all states (based on how your game is intended to work), the player's current state should be preserved; whether you save it once or progressively will be impacted by how your screens fit together.

The following diagram shows a very simple example in a mind-map tool of a game screen flow:

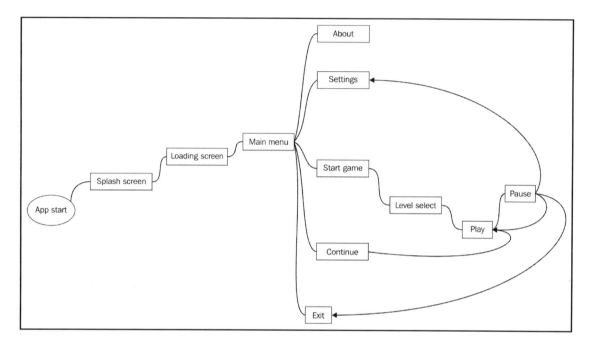

# Finishing our splash screen

Open the scene created in the last chapter that functioned as our splash screen, SplashScreen.unity. Currently, this screen simply displays for 1 second and starts playing the music. Let's get a little fancier and add a logo to the scene. Usually I use this screen to show my company's logo zooming in for 3 seconds.

For this example, I am going to just have the Packt Publishing logo display for 3 seconds. Add the following packt.png image to the Assets/Sprites/UI folder:

Now change the **Background** color of the Main Camera to white.

Drag the packt.png image to your scene and set its **Transform Position** to 0, 0, 0.

Right now, if we were to play the game, the image would show for 1 second and then the Town scene would open. We want this to transition to the StartScreen after 3 seconds. So, select the Main Camera, and change the settings on the SplashScreen script as follows:

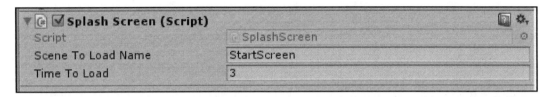

We have not yet added the StartScreen to our build settings, so do so now; otherwise, we will get an error when we attempt to play the game. It doesn't matter what position in the list you place the StartScreen, but I prefer to have it as my second scene. As shown in the following screenshot:

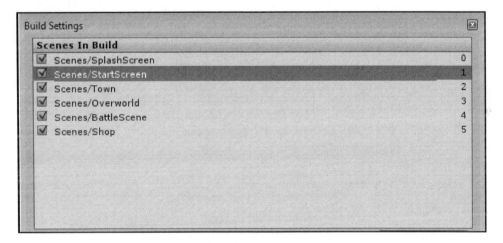

Now when we play the game, the Packt Publishing logo will display for 3 seconds, the music will begin, and we will be taken to the blank StartScreen.

# Building our start screen

As stated earlier, the start screen is the first screen the player will see and a lot of their opinion of your game will be derived from how good it looks. If you are not the artistic type and don't have an eye for layout, I highly recommend looking at the start screen of other games to get an idea of what to make it look like. Usually the start screen has its own unique game art.

We're going to make a very simple (and sadly, kind of ugly) start screen for now. You can adjust this later to make it more attractive and give it menus, but we are just going to have the title of the game, the town's background image, and a Play button.

Select StartScreen from the Assets/Scenes folder. Select Create | UI | Image from the **Hierarchy**. We want this background image to scale with the screen size, so select the Canvas and change the **Canvas Scaler** properties as the following shows:

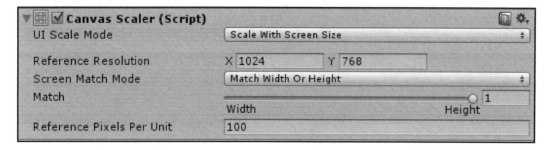

We used 1024×768 as the reference resolution, because the background image we will use has that resolution.

Now select the **Image** from the Hierarchy and change its anchor presets so that it stretches across the entire screen. Add the background image to the **Source Image** slot of the **Image** script. Do not select **Preserve Aspect**. Oddly enough we are OK with this scaling if we have a different screen size; we just want it to always fill the screen. As shown in the following screenshot:

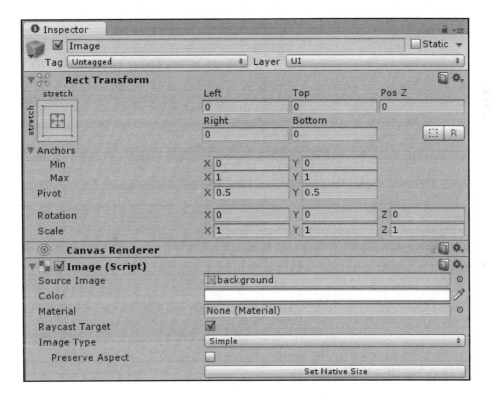

Now add text to the scene by right-clicking on the `Canvas` and selecting **UI | text**. Change the text to **Mastering Unity 2D** and give it the following properties:

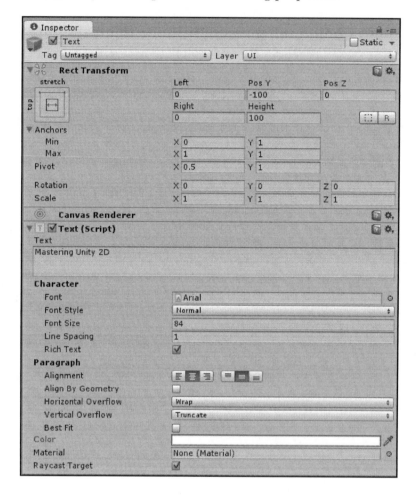

To make it a little more attractive, give it a drop-shadow, by selecting **Add Component | UI | Effects | Shadow**. Change the properties as shown in the following screenshot:

Now, we just need a button that will navigate the player from this screen to the `Town` screen. Create a UI button on the screen, and center it. Change its text to display the word **Play**.

Your scene should look as follows:

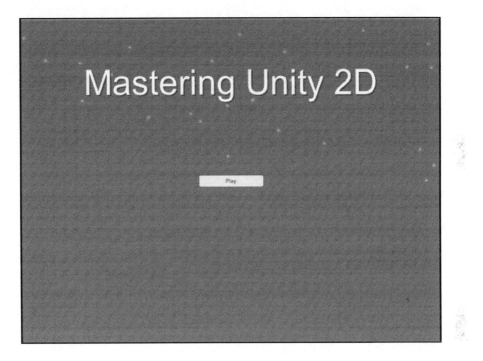

Now, create a script called `LevelLoader` in the `Assets/Scripts` folder. This will be a simple script that will transition to the next scene when the Play button is pressed. Replace its code with the following:

```
using UnityEngine;
using System.Collections;
using UnityEngine.SceneManagement;

public class LevelLoader : MonoBehaviour {

    public string levelToLoad = "Town";

    public void LoadTheLevel(){
        SceneManager.LoadScene(levelToLoad);
    }
}
```

Attach this script to the button and have the button run the `LoadTheLevel` function when it is clicked, as shown in the following screenshot:

Return to the `SplashScreen`, and play the game. You now will be taken to the `StartScreen` after 3 seconds and can enter the town upon hitting the lay button.

# Extending the editor

Now that we have the basic functionality of our game set up, let's look at some interesting things we can do to make further development easier.

Everyone who uses Unity knows about the editor. It's the core place where you will spend a great deal of time putting your game together. You will spend the rest of your time in your code editor, patching things together, adding values, and working around with what most see as limitations of the editor itself. This, however, is not the case.

The people at Unity realized early that they couldn't do everything, since everyone wanted something different or little tweaks here and there; if they had tried to do everything, nothing would have ever left their doors.

So, from the ground up, Unity was designed to be extensible, and they exposed much of what is needed to build your own editor in effect within Unity itself.

If you browse the **Asset Store** (`https://www.assetstore.unity3d.com/`), you will see a lot of assets that take advantage of this, and they have produced some really snazzy bolt-ons for the editor. These can reduce the need to code and just build things using the editor GUI.

These aren't magical things and most don't even require low-level C++ coding to achieve (although some do). You can update your editor to fix your game very easily, and you can do this in any of the languages that Unity supports.

The scripting framework behind the editor is broken up into several distinct layers that can be combined to give you almost any effect you need to build your content.

# The property drawers

The editor only has a basic way of looking at properties in the **Inspector** pane based on the classes and objects used in your game. If you are using an existing Unity class, such as a string, color, or curve, Unity already has ready-made property drawers (or visual handles) to manage these with their own editor windows in some cases (such as the curve editor). The majority of these are also built on the extensible framework that Unity exposes and is available to you as well.

Other classes such as vectors and numbers have a basic implementation, which is usually fine, but sometimes you just prefer it in a different way.

This is where the property drawers come in. They can either replace the existing property viewer for a single field or for a type of object entirely. If you want a slider to alter a value between two values, add a `PropertyDrawer` attribute to the property to show a slider instead of just `int` or `float` as follows:

```
[Range (0, 100)]
public float health = 100;
```

The preceding code example shows a range slider instead of a single `float` value as you can see in the following screenshot:

 For a more advanced example, check out the post on the Unity blog, which shows several different patterns to use your property drawers and even create them. The post is available at `http://blogs.unity3d.com/2012/09/07/property-drawers-in-unity-4/`.

While building the property drawers, you will use the `EditorGUI` controls to draw the elements on the screen. The `EditorGUI` class provides a rich collection of controls that can be used. For a list of available controls, visit
`https://docs.unity3d.com/Documentation/ScriptReference/EditorGUI.html`.

> The property drawers can only use the default layouts in the `EditorGUI` class. For performance reasons, they cannot use the automatic controller found in the `EditorGUILayout` class, which is used in `EditorWindows`.

For more information on property drawers, see the Unity reference guide at
`https://docs.unity3d.com/Documentation/ScriptReference/PropertyDrawer.html`.

> If you want to see some more creative uses for property drawers, check out the simple little GitHub repository at
> `https://github.com/tenpn/ChestOfPropertyDrawers`.

# Examples property drawers

Using the `NPC` script in `Assets\Scripts\Classes`, let's see the effect of adding some simple property drawers to our NPCs in the **Inspector** pane.

## Built-in property drawers

Starting simply, we can decorate some of the properties of the `NPC` class in our game with the `Range` attribute by adding the following code:

```
public string Name;
[Range(10, 100)]
public int Age;
public string Faction;
public string Occupation;
[Range(1, 10)]
public int Level;
```

Now if you look at the `Mayor` class's **Inspector** (remember, he's in the `Town` scene), the preceding code has the following effect on the editor Inspector:

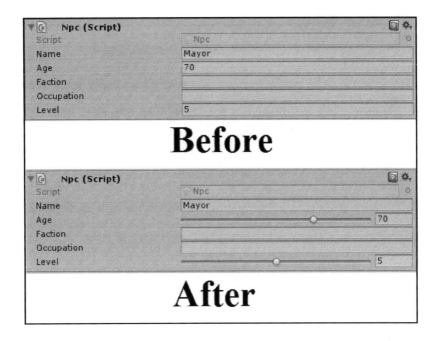

This just makes it easier to manage your settings and makes it a little prettier to look at. Now, let's look at something a little more complicated.

## Custom property drawers

Creating your own property drawer is certainly a bit more advanced. However, once you have learned the basics, it is quite easy to build your own.

For this example, we will create a simple pop-up that takes an array of values for possible selection, as shown in the following screenshot:

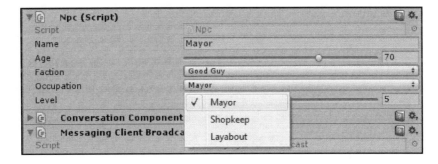

First, we need a property type or attribute that we want to control. This could be a set of parameters (such as the `Range` property, which has a beginning and an end), a validation string, or even an enumeration.

 The property type or attribute you want to control has to live in your project folder and **not** in the special `Editor` folder. Unity's documentation is not clear enough on this.

So, create a new folder named `Properties` in `Assets\Scripts\Classes`. Then, create a new C# script named `PopUpAttribute` in the `Properties` folder and replace its contents with the following code:

```
using UnityEngine;
public class PopUpAttribute: PropertyAttribute
{
  public string[] value;
  public PopUpAttribute(params string[] input)
  {
    value = input;
  }
}
```

Note that your `property` class must be derived from the `PropertyAttribute` class, and it must have a constructor with the same number of parameters required for your attribute (for example, the `Range` attribute has two `int` values).

 In a strange (I suspect reflection) circumstance, you can either call your class by its name or suffix it with the word `Attribute` (as shown in the preceding code); both will be recognized by the name alone.

For example, `PopUpAttribute` can be recognized as `PopUp` or `PopUpAttribute`.

With the property in place, we can now add our custom property drawer code. Unlike the property we just created, this does have to live in the special `Editor` folder.

So, create a new folder named `PropertyDrawers` in the `Assets\Scripts\Editor` folder and create a new script named `PopUpCustomPropertyDrawer`, replacing its contents with the following code:

```
using UnityEditor;
using UnityEngine;

[CustomPropertyDrawer(typeof(PopUpAttribute))]
public class PopUpCustomPropertyDrawer : PropertyDrawer {

  PopUpAttribute popUpAttribute {
    get { return ((PopUpAttribute)attribute); } }
}
```

The preceding code gives us the basic framework for our custom property drawer (the `public` property I've added isn't mandatory, but provides quick and easy access to the underlying property type we are enabling). Next, we need to add the `OnGUI` function, which will draw our custom property UI using the following code:

```
public override void OnGUI(Rect position, SerializedProperty prop,
GUIContent label)
{
  if (prop.propertyType != SerializedPropertyType.String)
  {
    throw new UnityException("property " + prop + " must be string
to use with PopUpAttribute ");
  }

  var popupRect = EditorGUI.PrefixLabel(position,
GUIUtility.GetControlID(FocusType.Passive), label);

  var currentItem = prop.stringValue;
  var currentIndex = popUpAttribute.value.Length - 1;
  for (; currentIndex >= 0; currentIndex--)
  {
    if (popUpAttribute.value[currentIndex] == currentItem)
      break;
  }

  int selectedIndex = EditorGUI.Popup(popupRect, currentIndex,
popUpAttribute.value);
  prop.stringValue = selectedIndex < 0 ? "" :
popUpAttribute.value[selectedIndex];
}
```

Walking through the preceding script is quite simple; it is described as follows:

- The class is decorated with a `CustomPropertyDrawer` attribute and the type of class it is targeted at.
- As stated, the class is derived from the `PropertyDrawer` class.
- A helper property (`popUpAttribute`) gets the correct type of class from the attribute property of the `PropertyDrawer` base class (optional).
- We override the `OnGUI` function for the property drawers.
- We then check whether the target property (the variable you will attach this to) is of the correct type (in this case, a string). It returns `UnityException` if it is not correct.
- A `Rect` variable is defined for where we want to draw the output from our property drawer (a requirement for using the `EditorGUI.Popup` control).
- We get the current value for the property we are attached to and compare it with the possible values for the item. We do this only because we have a list of options and need to know which is the current one. For other types, this may not be needed.
- We draw a pop-up control using the `EditorGUI.Popup` control.
- Lastly, we set the property we are attached to with the value the user has selected.

 We could have used an `enum` object instead of an array to give us a more programmatic approach, in which case the preceding steps would be very similar. However, this approach allows us to set the scope of the selection for each property.

With the property and our custom property drawer in place, we can decorate the variables in our NPC class to achieve the result I pictured earlier, as follows:

```
public string Name;
[Range(10, 100)]
public int Age;
[PopUp("Good Guy", "Independent", "Bad Guy")]
public string Faction;
[PopUp("Mayor", "Shopkeep", "Layabout")]
public string Occupation;
[Range(1, 10)]
public int Level;
```

It may seem like a lot of fuss. However, once it's complete, you can tune the Unity editor to work for you more efficiently.

# Custom editors

Say you want to control the entire scope of a single class or `ScriptableObject`; this is where `CustomEditor` scripts come in.

They can be used against any script that can be attached to a game object to alter how it works in the Unity editor Inspector.

As an example of these (the best way to show custom editors is through code), we will add some functionality to a camera to provide us with better control over it in a scene. This is just an example, and won't be implemented in our game.

First, we'll need a very simple camera script that will point the camera at a specified target, starting at 0, 0, 0. So, create a new script named `CameraLookAt` in `Assets\Scripts` and replace its contents with the following code:

```
using UnityEngine;

public class CameraLookAt : MonoBehaviour
{
    public Vector3 cameraTarget = Vector3.zero;

    void Update()
    {
        transform.LookAt(cameraTarget);
    }
}
```

We can then define a `CustomEditor` script that will be run by the editor whenever it detects a game object with the script attached to it.

 As with a lot of editor features, remember (as a good rule of thumb) that, if a class requires the `UnityEditor` namespace, it will need to live in the special `Editor` folder in your project.

So, create a new C# script called `CameraTargetEditor` in `Assets\Scripts\Editor` in your project and replace its contents with the following code:

```
using UnityEngine;
using UnityEditor;

[CustomEditor(typeof(CameraLookAt))]
public class CameraTargetEditor : Editor
{
    public override void OnInspectorGUI()
```

```
    {
        CameraLookAt targetScript = (CameraLookAt)target;
        targetScript.cameraTarget =
          EditorGUILayout.Vector3Field ("Look At Point",
            targetScript.cameraTarget);
        if (GUI.changed)
            EditorUtility.SetDirty(target);
    }
}
```

This script doesn't do much yet; we now have a `Vector3` handle in our script that displays the position of the camera's target (the specific point it is looking at). What is very nice here is that you can edit the values and the camera will automatically transform itself to look at the new point. To demonstrate this, create a new scene named `EditorDemos` in `Assets\Scenes` and attach the `CameraLookAt` script to **Main Camera**. If you then select the **Main Camera** game object in the Hierarchy, you will see the following settings in the **Inspector** pane:

This is a lot easier than messing with the rotation values of the ordinary camera. Let's continue to add more functionalities that will blow your mind.

> If the custom editor script depends on certain properties or components being available on the game object you attach it to, then be sure to use the `RequireConponent` attribute on the base class (not the `CustomEditor` script).

To make it even more useful, we can also represent this selection in the scene view as a control handle. To do this, we simply add another function to our `CameraTargetEditorCustomEditor` script; add the following `OnSceneGUI` function to the script:

```
void OnSceneGUI()
{
    CameraLookAt targetScript = (CameraLookAt)target;
    targetScript.cameraTarget = Handles.PositionHandle(
            targetScript.cameraTarget, Quaternion.identity);
    if (GUI.changed)
        EditorUtility.SetDirty(target);
}
```

Just as the OnGUI method draws in to your game, this function will draw in to the editor scene. Using the Handles.PositionHandle control, it will draw a regular handlebars control in the scene at the point you have specified, in this case, the camera's look-at target, as seen in the following screenshot:

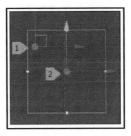

Camera Target (1) and Camera Transform (2)

Want more? You can then alter how the handlebars will look on the screen with the following code:

```
void OnSceneGUI()
{
    CameraLookAt targetScript = (CameraLookAt)target;
    targetScript.cameraTarget = Handles.PositionHandle(
targetScript.cameraTarget, Quaternion.identity);
    Handles.SphereCap(0, targetScript.cameraTarget,
Quaternion.identity, 2);
    if (GUI.changed)
        EditorUtility.SetDirty(target);
}
```

As shown in the following screenshot, this simply alters the handlebars we are drawing, decorating them with a sphere. There are several other options as well should you choose to explore them:

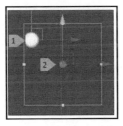

(1) Camera Target Sphere, (2) Camera Transform

For more information about custom editors, see the Unity reference guide at
`http://docs.unity3d.com/Documentation/ScriptReference/Editor.html`.

For more information about handles and what you can do with them, see the Unity reference guide at
`http://docs.unity3d.com/Documentation/ScriptReference/Handles.html`.

# The editor window

Quite simply, Unity editor windows are just separate containers for collections of editor GUI controls. These windows are a more advanced version of the property drawers described previously, and as such use a different set of custom controls.

The **Inspector**, **Game**, and **Scene** windows, and pretty much every other dockable window in the Unity editor, are editor windows. In fact, they are all built in the same way using the same scripting framework.

As stated previously, remember that any script that uses the editor functionality or the `UnityEditor` namespace must be placed in a special project folder titled `Editor`.

To implement your own editor window, you simply need to create a class derived from `EditorWindow` instead of `MonoBehaviour`. The script must also live in the special `Editor` folder within the project structure, so create a new script called `MyEditorWindow` in `Assets\Scripts\Editor`, as follows:

```
using UnityEditor;
using UnityEngine;

public class MyEditorWindow : EditorWindow
{
string windowName = "My Editor Window";
bool groupEnabled;
bool DisplayToggle = true;
float Offset = 1.23f;

}
```

I've added some properties to give some depth to the example.

With your new window in place, you then need to implement a function to display the window when it is called inside the new `MyEditorWindow` class:

```
[MenuItem ("Window/My Window")]
public static void ShowWindow ()
{
    EditorWindow.GetWindow(typeof(MyEditorWindow));
}
```

 It doesn't matter what the preceding function is called; it's just an editor reference attribute attached to the function to show where the option will appear in the Unity editor menu.

If you want more control over the size and position of your editor window, instead of using the preceding `GetWindow` function, you can use the following `GetWindowWithRect` function:

```
[MenuItem ("Window/My Window")]
public static void ShowWindow ()
{
    EditorWindow.GetWindowWithRect(typeof(MyEditorWindow),
      new Rect(0, 0, 400, 150));
}
```

This will set the position and size of the window to a fixed point on the screen but, as with all other editor windows, it can then be resized and docked like any other window. This method is more useful for displaying a collection of properties in the scene view to edit nodes or other position-based visual configuration.

Lastly, you need some GUI code. This is pretty much the same as the normal GUI code, but with a few editor extensions because it is being drawn in the editor. This goes in to an `OnGUI` method, for example:

```
void OnGUI()
{
    // Your custom Editor Window GUI code
    GUILayout.Label("Base Settings", EditorStyles.boldLabel);
    windowName = EditorGUILayout.TextField("Window Name",
      windowName);
    groupEnabled =
      EditorGUILayout.BeginToggleGroup("Optional Settings",
        groupEnabled);
```

```
    DisplayToggle =
        EditorGUILayout.Toggle("Display Toggle", DisplayToggle);

    Offset = EditorGUILayout.Slider("Offset Slider",
        Offset, -3, 3);
    EditorGUILayout.EndToggleGroup();
}
```

The preceding example will show the following menu window:

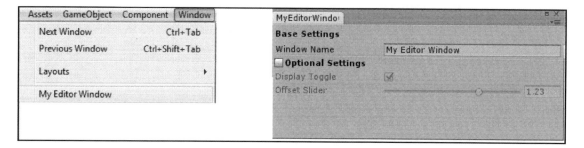

When you put GUI elements together in an editor window, you can use either the basic `EditorGUI` controls or the more advanced `EditorGUILayout` controls, which implement some additional automatic layout features on top of the basic controls.

> For more details about the controls available with `EditorGUILayout`, check out the Unity reference at
> `https://docs.unity3d.com/Documentation/ScriptReference/EditorGUILayout.html`.
>
> For more information on editor windows, see the Unity reference guide at
> `https://docs.unity3d.com/Documentation/ScriptReference/EditorWindow.html`.

# Gizmos

With custom editors, you could also have handles to represent a control in the scene view, extending the **Inspector** features in to the scene.

We also have another way to have class-based features that are only available in the editor through the use of **Gizmos**.

Gizmos offer a much richer graphical way to add visual elements to the scene to aid the use of a class, unlike custom editors; which are only added to your base class, which the editor will then make use of.

 The `OnDrawGizmo` functions are only available on classes that are derived from `MonoBehaviour`, **not** the `Editor` classes.

For example, we can amend the `CameraLookAt` script we created earlier and make it draw a Gizmo line from the camera to the target's look-at point by adding the following code to the script:

```
void OnDrawGizmos()
{
    Gizmos.color = Color.yellow;
    Gizmos.DrawLine(transform.position, cameraTarget);
}
```

The code produces the following result:

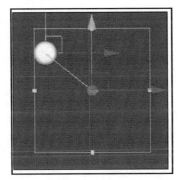

Now, when you return to the editor and move the look-at point or the camera, there will be a yellow line drawn between them.

 If you collapse the script in the **Inspector** pane, this will turn off the Gizmo. This is handy if you want to just hide it.

If you don't want the Gizmo drawn all the time, you can also track when the user has the Gizmo selected using the `OnDrawGizmosSelected` method, as follows:

```
void OnDrawGizmosSelected()
{
    Gizmos.color = Color.red;
    Gizmos.DrawLine(transform.position, cameraTarget);
}
```

Now when the GameObject the script is attached to is selected in the editor, the line will be drawn in red instead of yellow. Alternatively, just use the `OnDrawGizmosSelected` function on its own to only draw a line when selected.

For more information on Gizmos, see the Unity reference guide at `http://docs.unity3d.com/Documentation/ScriptReference/Gizmos.htm l`.

For fantastic additional resources and tutorials, check out the article on CatLike Coding's blog at `http://catlikecoding.com/unity/tutorials/editor/star/`.

Or, you can check out the excellent Gimzo-driven design tutorial at `http://code.tutsplus.com/tutorials/how-to-add-your-own-tools-to-unitys-editor-active-10047`.

# Building your editor menus

Another way of extending in to the editor is to customize it by adding your own menus. We covered little bits of this in previous chapters by adding extra options to create your assets; however, there's much more to it than that.

The `MenuItem` functions must be declared as a `Static` functions, otherwise they will not be recognized. Scripts must be placed in the special `Editor` folder.

# Adding a MenuItem attribute

The main way to add a new menu item is to define a script in `Assets\Scripts\Editor` and append the `MenuItem` attribute to a static method within it. So, create a new script called `MyMenu` in this folder and replace its contents with the following code:

```
using UnityEditor;
using UnityEngine;
public class MyMenu
{
    // Add a menu item named MenuItem1 to a Menu option called
    // MenuName in the menu bar.
    [MenuItem ("MenuName/MenuItem1")]
    static void EnableMyAwesomeFeature ()
    {
        Debug.Log ("I am a leaf on the wind. Watch how I soar.");
    }
}
```

This code simply creates a new top-level menu option called `MenuName` with a single item called `MenuItem1`, as shown here:

From here, you can execute whatever you need to.

When you return to Unity after adding a menu script, it may sometimes not show up immediately. You can either click on the menu bar or restart the editor to make it appear (it just needs a nudge).

# Enabling/disabling a MenuItem attribute

We can extend this further by adding a validation logic method to support a `MenuItem` attribute. This controls whether the menu option is enabled or not.

For this, you need to create a pair of the following items:

- A menu item
- A menu item validator

The menu item and the menu item validator must have the same menu path. So, if the menu item (as declared previously) is [MenuItem ("MenuName/MenuItem1")], the validator must have the same menu definition as follows:

[MenuItem ("MenuName/MenuItem1", true)]

Validators do not add menu items. They only extend or validate existing menu items.

So, using the menu item we just added earlier, we can add a validator menu function. It must have a return type of bool and an additional flag set against the function attribute, as follows:

```
[MenuItem ("MenuName/MenuItem1", true)]
static bool CheckifaGameObjectisselected() {
    // Return false if no transform is selected.
    return Selection.activeTransform != null;
}
```

This simple validator just checks whether you have a game object selected in the editor; if not, then MenuItem1 is disabled.

This new validation function is evaluated by the editor whenever it displays the menu item of the same name. Setting the bool flag at the end of the MenuItem attribute tells the editor that this function provides the validation logic for a MenuItem attribute of the same name. Then, the editor will enable or disable that MenuItem attribute based on the return of the validator function.

## Adding shortcut keys to a MenuItem attribute

If you add % and a letter to the end of your MenuItem attribute, Unity will also enable a shortcut key for that letter.

So, %g would enable a shortcut of *Ctrl* + *G* on Windows and *cmd* + *G* on a Mac.

For example, add a new function to our `MyMenu` script as follows:

```
[MenuItem ("MenuName/MenuItem2 %g")]
static void EnableMyOtherAwesomeFeature()
{
    Debug.Log ("Find my key and win the prize - g");
}
```

This will show us an additional option with the shortcut defined, as you can see here:

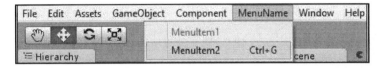

## Adding contextual MenuItems

The last bit of trickery you can perform is to add menu items to the existing features of Unity, even **Inspector**.

You do this with a custom name for the `MenuItem` attribute and a different signature for the function. So, we add the following method to our `MyMenu` script:

```
[MenuItem("CONTEXT/Transform/Move to Center")]
static void MoveToCenter(MenuCommand command)
{
    Transform transform = (Transform)command.context;
    transform.position = Vector3.zero;
    Debug.Log("Moved object to " +
      transform.position + " from a Context Menu.");
}
```

The preceding script attaches itself to any transform component (in this case, the **Inspector** pane). Then, when it is run, the parameter on the function receives the instance of the object it was run on and lets you interrogate or alter it, resulting in the following screenshot:

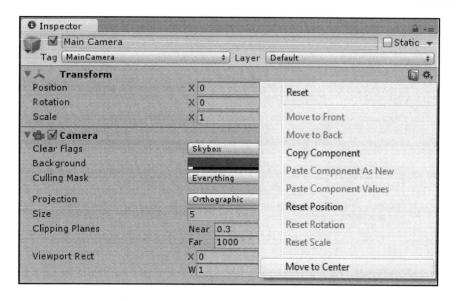

The structure of the special `MenuItem` name is as follows:

- **Context**: This is a fixed item to identify the menu as a contextual item
- **Object**: This is the type of object this context menu will be available on
- **Name**: This is the name of the menu item

You can just add extra dimensions/children to context menus by adding additional `"/"` characters.

However, if there is an error or your menus are too deep, Unity won't show the error; it just won't display the menu item (leaving you scratching your head). If this happens, try setting a shorter or different menu name.

Context menus can be added to just about any object/component in the Unity editor, including your own objects.

For more information on the `MenuItem` class and its use in Unity Editor, see the Unity scripting reference guide at `https://docs.unity3d.com/Documentation/ScriptReference/MenuItem.html`.

# Running scripts in the Editor folder

The last little tidbit you should be aware of surrounds scripts and their execution.

If you put a script in the `Editor` folder, it will be executed when you are in the editor. However, what about all your other scripts?

You can certainly run the game and see the script running, but that doesn't help you when you are in the editor. What if you want to see the effect of your script while manipulating game objects in your scene?

Thankfully, there is a way to force the editor to run your script, and all it takes is yet another attribute called `ExecuteInEditMode` added to your class. To do this, simply add the following line above the class definition of the script you want to affect:

```
[ExecuteInEditMode]
```

If you are applying this to the GUI that repositions itself to the scene, the visual aspect you see in the editor may not be the same as when the game is running. So, things may position differently. You either manage it in the code or live with it in the editor; it's up to you.

If you have portions of your script that rely on other components that may not be active in the editor, be sure to check for null references in your code to avoid nasty errors in the console, which may lead you down a dark path.

Also, any calls to the `Static` classes in the `OnDestroy` method may generate errors/warnings when they are run in the editor; so just be aware!

# Alternative approaches

There is always more than one way to cut the cheese as they say, and so too it is with Unity. Some more advanced options to run the scripts in the editor include the following methods.

### The [InitialiseOnLoad] attribute

Another advanced feature with the editor is to make use of the `[InitialiseOnLoad]` attribute. What this attribute does is run whatever class or script it is attached to when the editor opens or when a build event occurs (such as after you edit a script or run the project). Most developers use this for tracking purposes or to have background processes run whenever something has changed. This is especially useful if you have some level data stored in a custom file and need to regenerate a scene or level based on that configuration.

Unlike [ExecuteInEditMode], the [InitialiseOnLoad] attribute is an editor-only feature, and the scripts using it must be placed in the special Editor folder in your project.

It is recommended that you combine the use of the [InitialiseOnLoad] attribute together with a static constructor to ensure the script will run before any other scripts in the scene or project.

If you are loading resources in an [InitialiseOnLoad] class, beware that the file system may not be initialized when the script starts. It's recommended you delay it until the first editor update (using the following method). For more details, check out the detailed post at http://bit.ly/InitiliseOnLoadResources.

## Editor application callbacks

The editor, like a lot of things in Unity, also comes adorned with several callbacks to mark when things happen. Exposed through the EditorApplication class, you can gain access to the following events:

| Event/delegate | Description |
| --- | --- |
| update | **This event is called every time the editor window is updated or refreshed. Note that this is more often when the game or scenes update calls.** |
| projectWindowItemOnGUI | This event is called for each project item in the view of the Project window when it is drawn to the screen. |
| hierarchyWindowItemOnGUI | This event is called for each item in the Hierarchy window when it is drawn to the screen. |
| projectWindowChanged | This event is called whenever an item is changed in the Project window. |
| hierarchyWindowChanged | This event is called whenever an item is changed in the Hierarchy window. |
| playmodeStateChanged | This event is called when you start or stop the game in the editor. |
| searchChanged | This event is called whenever search criteria are changed in any Editor window. |

| Event/delegate | Description |
|---|---|
| modifierKeysChanged | This event is used to track when a modifier key (*Alt*, *cmd*, *Ctrl*, and so on) is pressed. So, you need to change a view when a modifier key is pressed, and you need to watch for this event/delegate. |

These events can be added to any class/script in your `Editor` project folder, so you can hook up a functionality to run when these events occur using the following syntax. For example, let's employ the following methods in an editor script to fire whenever we change the project's Hierarchy:

```
void OnEnable()
{
    // Event / delegate registration, usually put in the OnEnable
    //or other function
    EditorApplication.hierarchyWindowChanged +=
HierarchyWindowChanged;
}

//callback function for when event occurs
void HierarchyWindowChanged()
{
    //Scan hierarchy for new items
    //If found add something to the editor window
}
void OnDestroy()
{
    // Don't forget to unregister the delegate when it goes out of
    //scope or is not needed
    EditorApplication.hierarchyWindowChanged -=
HierarchyWindowChanged;
}
```

This gives your editor scripts the ability to react to whatever the editor does by attaching to the `hierarchyWindowChanged` event when the script is enabled (make sure you unattach it when the script is disabled).

## Mixing it up

In more advanced cases, you can build a framework that combines with the previous approaches effectively to create a complete editor manager. This needs to be implemented in a class with a static constructor so that it is initialized as soon as the editor starts.

To demonstrate this, let's create a simple script that will save the scene for us when we hit the Play button. First, create a new script called `SaveSceneOnPlay` in `Assets\Scripts\Editor` and replace its contents with the following code:

```
using UnityEditor;
using UnityEngine;
[InitializeOnLoad]
public class SaveSceneOnPlay
{
    // Static class constructor,
    // this is initialized as soon as Unity Starts
    static SaveSceneOnPlay()
    {
    }
}
```

This gives us the framework for an `[InitializeOnLoad]` script that will run when Unity starts. Then, we add our static function to do the work of saving the scene:

```
static void SaveSceneIfPlaying()
{
    if (EditorApplication.isPlayingOrWillChangePlaymode &&
      !EditorApplication.isPlaying)
    {
        Debug.Log("Automatically saving scene (" +
          EditorApplication.currentScene +
            ") before entering play mode ");
        EditorApplication.SaveAssets();
        EditorApplication.SaveScene();
    }
}
```

This method checks whether the editor is about to change the play state and is not being played currently; if this is the case, then it saves the current changed assets and the current scene.

Next, we hook up this function with the `playmodeStateChanged` event delegate in the static constructor as follows:

```
static SaveSceneOnPlay()
{
    EditorApplication.playmodeStateChanged += SaveSceneIfPlaying;
}
```

Now, with this script in our project, whenever we hit Play, the script will automatically save the project for us.

# Working with settings

Saving data is always important, especially in games where you need to keep track of the player's progress or at the very least maintain a track record of scores, plays, and other important data.

Within Unity, there is only one method of storing data natively, and that is `PlayerPrefs`. It is very simple to use and very flexible, although it does have a hard limit of 1 MB of storage for the web player. It is possible to serialize data into `PlayerPrefs` (and some developers do this), but generally if you need to serialize, most developers build their own system.

# Using PlayerPrefs

`PlayerPrefs` is simply a key dictionary to store individual variables as a key in the Unity runtime data store. On its own, it has to read each and every scene at runtime, which is why most games use a static class to keep the state stored in `PlayerPrefs` and only use it between scenes for scene-specific configuration.

Using `PlayerPrefs` is very easy and simple. The process is the same as any other dictionary to save a setting for your call:

```
PlayerPrefs.SetInt("PlayerScore", currentScore);
PlayerPrefs.SetFloat("PlayerDamage", currentDamage);
PlayerPrefs.SetString("PlayerName", currentPlayerName);
```

Loading it back again when you need it again involves the following code:

```
currentScore = PlayerPrefs.GetInt("PlayerScore");
currentDamage = PlayerPrefs.GetFloat("PlayerDamage");
currentPlayerName = PlayerPrefs.GetString("PlayerName");
```

You can also supply defaults to values with a second parameter if the setting does not yet exist, as follows:

```
currentScore = PlayerPrefs.GetInt("PlayerScore", 0);
currentDamage = PlayerPrefs.GetFloat("PlayerDamage", 0);
currentPlayerName = PlayerPrefs.GetString("PlayerName", "New Player");
```

By default, Unity will save the settings to disk when the application is closed. However, it's recommended that you save them intermittently when possible by calling the following:

```
PlayerPrefs.Save()
```

Saving settings in Unity isn't necessarily a given and should not be treated as safe. The settings file has a hard limit of 1 MB of storage on the web player. If this is exceeded, it will throw an exception. This limit is for each application.

So, you can either drastically limit what settings you store (recommended) or wrap your `SET PlayerPrefs` calls in a `try/catch` statement to be safe if you plan to deploy to the web player.

Other platforms do not have this limitation.

There are also `delete` functions to remove either a single key or to clear the cache completely.

For more information about `PlayerPrefs`, see the Unity reference guide at `https://docs.unity3d.com/Documentation/ScriptReference/PlayerPrefs.html`.

# Serializing your data

To store any kind of complicated data or structure, you need to serialize it into a concatenated format. The result can then be stored in `PlayerPref` as mentioned previously or saved on a disk or the web.

There are several types of serializer you can use, including the following:

- **Binary serialization**: This is binary-formatted output and is non-human-readable
- **XML serialization**: This is the basic text output formatted into XML and is human-readable
- **JSON serialization**: This is a compressed standalone output in XML format; it is human-readable and allows you to have a manual implementation
- **Custom serialization**: This is DIY and is used to build your own serialized output

Each serializer has performance or security gains. There isn't a one-size-fits-all; just choose the serializer that fits your purposes.

To learn more about generics (a fairly advanced topic), check out the MSDN documentation at `http://msdn.microsoft.com/en-gb/library/512aeb7t.aspx`.

Not all platforms support all serializers; also, some classes (such as
`MemoryStream`) are not available on all platforms. You will sometimes
have to tailor the approach you use to work with other platforms. If you
do, however, make sure you do it within the helper classes so that all the
platform-variant code is in one place and does not clutter up your game.

Serialization is important as it can be used anywhere you need to package data to be saved
or even transmitted over the wire for a cloud backup or even network play.

For more information about serialization, see the MSDN .NET reference guide at
`http://msdn.microsoft.com/en-us/library/ms172360(v=vs.110).aspx`.

# Saving data to disk

Another way to manage the way your games save data is to serialize it to disk; there is a
method you will use to determine how fast and secure this is.

Instead of using `PlayerPrefs`, it is better to manage the saving and loading of your player
data to a disk (or the Web; see the following sections). Thankfully, **MonoDevelop** (the C#
engine behind Unity3D) provide common functions to access the disk across all the
platforms that Unity supports.

There are exceptions, however, due to platform limitations or
specializations in some platforms. In these cases, Unity provides special
classes to access platform components, for example, the
`UnityEngine.Windows` namespace.

You can also write disk access routines that are more platform-specific if you wish to make
them more performant, but this requires you to write an interface and your platform-
specific code for each routine.

# Backing up to the Web

As an alternative to the basic way of saving data to a disk, a lot of games now (especially if
they are targeting multiple platforms) support a web backend to store a player's data. It
doesn't need to be heavy; just use a player name/ID key and store the serialized data.

The benefit of this approach is that the player can continue playing on any device,
regardless of which device they were last playing on.

Implementing this approach depends on the backend service you use for your data.

The simplest approach is to use the serialization methods described previously and post your data to a backend web service using the Unity WWW class. As a full example would be too complex to demonstrate; what follows is just some code snippets of the available Unity functions.

 To back up on the Web, you will have to write your web service on a server to accept this data, which is beyond the scope of this book, but if you search on www.codeproject.com or stackoverflow.com, you will find many good examples of such implementations.

For more information about the WWW class, see the Unity scripting reference guide at https://docs.unity3d.com/Documentation/ScriptReference/WWW.html.

# Going further

If you are of the adventurous sort, try expanding your project to add the following features:

- Expand on the SplashScreen and StartScreen by adding more interesting art, effects, and menus.
- Either add property drawers or even a complete custom editor for the dialogs in the conversation system covered in Chapter 6, *NPCs and Interactions*.
- Extend the Enemy classes in Chapter 9, *Getting Ready to Fight*, to better configure them in the editor.
- Build your menus either in a single scene or multiple ones. Manage the transition between each menu state/view.
- Research the various saving techniques and implement save functionality in your game.
- Take one of your own game ideas and plan the flow of the game from end to end using a Mindmap tool. Go beyond just the menu and sketch out the entire game.

# Summary

We started this chapter by looking into what is involved in finishing and packaging the game itself with menus and important touch points if you want to stand out.

To make best use of the editor, we extended and expanded on the default views that the Unity gives us.

Through the course of this chapter, we looked at all of the capabilities that Unity gives us to make best use of these features. With these tools in hand, we can keep building our games a lot easier and customize Unity to fit our game (rather than the other way around). The editor is there to help us build our game, so why not improve it?

Several developers graciously share their editor scripts and work in open source libraries, so be sure to look around; in many cases, you don't need to start from scratch.

We covered editor customization, property drawers, custom editors, editor windows, and Gizmos. We also covered architecting the game package with screens and menus and working with saving and loading data.

In the next chapter, we look at packaging the game on to several platforms, extending our game out on to the platform itself, and providing platform-specific features in the game.

# 14
# Deployment and Beyond

Building a game is one thing, and showing it to your friends and family is another. However, eventually, you are going to want to ship and sell your game in one of the most challenging markets: games!

Your title has to shine; it has to enable features that other titles don't have to stand out and be noticed.

In this chapter, we will look at the various bonus features you can add to your game as well as the differences in developing for different platforms.

The following topics will be covered in this chapter:

- Handling platform differences
- Building your asset projects (and making a fortune on the asset store)
- Distributing to mobile
- Social network integration
- Monetization

## Handling platform differences

Unity does a lot for developers to abstract us from the many platforms you can deploy to. Most of the common functions, such as memory management, audio, controller inputs, purchasing, and so on, are all implemented with a single generic interface with Unity3D. This means you do not need to write separate code to play an audio file, or draw to the screen for each and every device or platform that you want to support and deploy to. It really is a big time-saver (ask anyone who has written their own engine just how much fun they had doing everything multiple times for each platform).

Unity does a lot, but it doesn't do everything. For the following fringe areas, you will have to do the leg work to get these features implemented:

- Social integration (Facebook and others)
- In-app purchasing
- Alternate physics or networking implementations

The list goes on. In a lot of cases, there are already pre-made assets on the Unity store that have done the hard work to build these implementations. A fair few, you will note, do not support all platforms. In these cases, it will get you most of the way, but you will either have to wait for them to support platform *X* or write it yourself.

In all cases, assets need to integrate tightly with the underlying platform. Some are simple to perform, others not so much. Also, in some cases, you will have to work with the Unity platform build system to push your changes onto the platform (though not absolutely necessary, this will save you from having to repeat every build or if you want to create your assets).

In general, the patterns you need to support are as follows:

- Using different code paths with directives
- Accessing native platforms from Unity
- Calling platforms from Unity
- Implementing reusable libraries that are natively compiled to work on all platforms

# Preprocessor directives

When you want the code to run in a particular way on one platform and in a different way on another, you can use the pre-compiler directives to tell Unity to pick one section of code over another (when it builds the project), or to simply ignore the sections of the code. This is also true for the editor, which Unity considers a platform, just like any other. So, we can have code to run and deploy in the editor, but restrict its execution when it's deployed to another platform. You could use the special editor classes to do this, but you may also want to do this with any other code.

A few of the preprocessor directives (or the platform defines) that Unity recognizes are listed in the following table:

| Statement | Description |
|-----------|-------------|
| UNITY_EDITOR | **This code will run only in the editor, not on a platform** |
| UNITY_EDITOR_WIN | This code specifically targets the editor on Windows (if you have the code that runs differently than on a Mac) |
| UNITY_EDITOR_OSX | This code specifically targets the editor on Mac (if you have the code that runs differently than on a PC) |
| UNITY_STANDALONE | This code targets desktop platforms (Windows/Mac/Linux) |
| UNITY_STANDALONE_OSX | This code targets Mac OS X only (this includes Universal, PPC, and Intel architectures) |
| UNITY_STANDALONE_WIN | This code targets Windows desktop only (excluding Windows 8) |
| UNITY_STANDALONE_LINUX | This code targets Linux desktop clients only |
| UNITY_WEBGL | This code targets WebGL |
| UNITY_IOS | This code targets the iOS platform only |
| UNITY_ANDROID | This code targets the Android platform only |
| UNITY_WP_8 | This code targets the Windows Phone 8 platform only |
| UNITY_WP_8_1 | This code targets the Windows Phone 8.1 app or Universal projects on Windows Phone 8 |
| UNITY_WII | This code targets the Wii platform only |
| UNITY_PS3 | This code targets the PlayStation 3 platform only |
| UNITY_PS4 | This code targets the PlayStation 4 platform only |
| UNITY_XBOX360 | This code targets the Xbox 360 platform only |
| UNITY_XBOXONE | This code targets the Xbox One platform only |

For a full list of platform directives, visit:
`http://docs.unity3d.com/Manual/PlatformDependentCompilation.html`
.

It's worth noting that you are not limited to just the Unity preprocessor directives. You can use Visual Studio's directives or even create your own by adding the following class to the top of your `#define MyDirective` class (no semicolon). Then, you can block out sections of your code by enabling or disabling this line. If a directive does not exist, it will always be skipped.

To use these directives, we will simply declare them with an `#if` statement to surround the code we want to target.

# Pushing code from Unity

Unity provides several post-processing capabilities that allow you to both intercept and override and also add your own processing to just about anything in the asset pipeline: assets, scripts, and even the build process itself.

## Processing assets

Post or pre-processing of assets is very useful if you have custom-made or complex assets that need additional work once they are imported in Unity. In most cases, this is not needed as Unity already does a lot of work for you by processing assets.

If you do create any asset-processing scripts, remember they need to be placed in `Assets\Editor`.

We won't go into too much detail here as it is a very large area; this section is mainly to highlight its existence for those who were not aware. It is well-worth reading and checking up on.

For more information about asset processing, refer to the Unity scripting reference guide at
`https://docs.unity3d.com/Documentation/ScriptReference/AssetPost processor.html`.

For a nice, clean example of an asset processor, see the post on using Unity to make a simple FBX model post processor at
`http://forum.unity3d.com/threads/53179-Simple-AssetPostprocessor -example`.

# Processing the build

A more interesting area for study, especially if you are working with many platforms and find yourself doing repetitive tasks on each platform (or when you create your Unity assets and need to copy files to a platform), is the ability to extend Unity3D's own project build process.

Simply create a normal class script in `Asset\Editor`, and then create your build action function with the `[PostProcessBuild]` attribute and the build function signature, as follows:

```
using UnityEngine;
using UnityEditor;
using UnityEditor.Callbacks;

public class MyBuildPostprocessor
{
  [PostProcessBuild]
  public static void OnPostprocessBuild(BuildTarget target, string
pathToBuiltProject)
  { }
}
```

The attributes from the build processing give you the following information:

- `BuildTarget`: This tells you which platform is currently being built using the `BuildTarget` enumeration.
- `Path`: This gives you the output path where the build project is being written. This is useful if you want to copy additional files to it.

You can also control the order in which this function is processed by adding parameters to the `[PostProcessBuild]` attribute as follows:

```
[PostProcessBuild(10)]
public static void OnPostprocessBuild(BuildTarget target,
  string pathToBuiltProject)
{ }
```

The order number is a definition of priority: the higher the number, the lower the priority. By default, all scripts have a priority of 1. Scripts with lower numbers are executed first (even negative numbers such as -10 are allowed for ultimate priority), whereas scripts with higher numbers are executed last.

This is especially useful if you want to have several actions execute on a successful build and want to control the order in which they are executed.

You can also copy code files directly to the target solution, if you wish, from your Unity project. If you do not want those files to be read or executed by Unity, then simply suffix them with .ignore, and Unity will ignore them. Just remember to rename them when copying them to a platform.

For example:

```
MyPlatformClassFile.cs.ignore
```

For more information about build processing, see the Unity scripting reference guide at http://docs.unity3d.com/412/Documentation/ScriptReference/PostProcessBuildAttri bute.html.

For a very full-featured example of highly customized build processing, check out the AdRotator Unity plugin, which is open source, on GitHub at:
https://github.com/Adrotator/AdrotatorV2/tree/master/AdRotatorUn ityPackage

Just check in the AdRotatorUnitySDK.Assets\Editor\AdRotatorPostBuild.cs script.

# Building your assets

What may seem daunting is actually one of the simplest tasks to perform in Unity because it is just a two-click job.

If you recall in `Chapter 2`, *Building your Project and Character*, I said you will create a package that contains all the default folders you can use for any project; so, let's do that.

First, create a new project (just because it's best to start from scratch) and then add in whatever folders, assets, scripts, and other things that you need in your asset package. In this case, just all the folders we will commonly use in any Unity project are shown here:

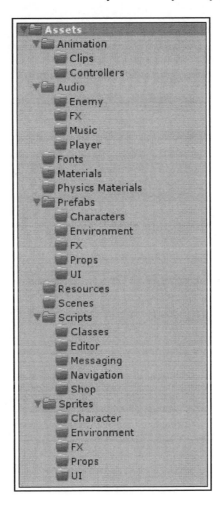

With that in place, just navigate to **Assets** | **Export Package** from the Unity editor menu, and you will be presented with the following window:

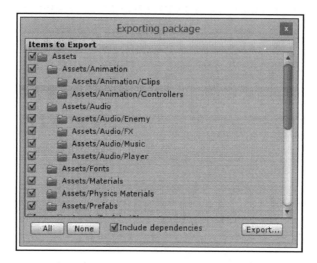

Here, you can select all the assets currently in your project that you want bundled up in your own reusable Unity asset package. Once you are happy with your selection, just click on **Export…**. Then, Unity will simply ask where you want your package to be created:

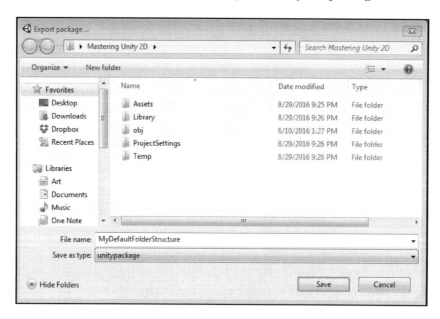

There you have it! Once saved, you will simply have your new asset package, which you can reuse on every project or even publish to the asset store and make millions (well probably not if it's just a bunch of folders; you might need a bit more than that). This package can be named as follows:

```
MyDefaultFolderStructure.unitypackage
```

# Packaging gotchas

You have your game running fine in the editor, and you finally come to start testing it on a platform. Life is good and surely you must be ready to deploy; sadly, this is just the point where your next journey begins.

Actually, shipping your title brings to light a whole raft of new challenges. What follows is a list of tips, tricks, and gotchas I've encountered while working with many different teams and events as follows:

- Just because it runs in the editor DOES NOT mean it will run on a platform:

  I've come across too many teams that finish their game in the editor without even trying to run it on at least one target platform. This can cause serious rework later on as you may find that the code will simply not run on some platforms.

  Another issue that can sometimes rear its head is when you have written code that depends on the editor but you have not placed it in the Editor folder. When you run it in the editor, it will work fine, but on a platform it will either crash or give you a spurious message (worse on some platforms than others.)

  The best advice is to build to a platform at regular intervals, and make sure that it actually compiles and will deploy to a device.

- Just because it works for one platform DOES NOT mean it will work for all:

  Unity obviously supports many different platforms, and each has its own peculiarities. If you mean to target multiple platforms, always check periodically whether you can build and deploy to the various platforms. It doesn't have to be too often, just find the right balance for you. See whether you can automate it through the Unity command-line tools.

- For maximum exposure, try to focus on the lowest common denominator:

  It's always attractive to build to the highest resolution and target really high-spec machines; however, this is going to really limit your target audience.

  When working with mobile projects, it is better to test and target minimum specifications or devices, and make it run acceptably on that device. Any higher-spec device, and it will just fly.

  If you are feeling adventurous, then build your game to turn on higher spec features/assets when a high spec machine is detected. However, this will also potentially increase the size of your final download, which may also put your game out of budget for low-spec devices.

  This is a hard challenge and requires a different approach for each game you make, so think hard about it.

  A last resort (which most developers shy away from) is to build two versions (a PRO HD version and a Basic low-res version). There is no one right answer, so just pick a path that fits your game, budget, and time.

- Assets from the store can be your savior; they can also be your downfall:

  Be aware of what assets you are downloading in the scope of your title; check what platforms it supports and make sure it's maintained.

  There have been quite a few horror stories about not being able to move to platform X because the plugins won't even compile, and finding an alternative is very difficult because of the particular plugin that is integrated in a project.

  It all comes down to balance-ask why you are using a certain asset, make sure you understand why you are using it, and assess its long term fit before committing yourself to it.

- Beware of the platform requirements:

  Certain platforms have very specific requirements when it comes to games and/or apps. Some have limits on project sizes, others (such as Windows Phone) have certain operating restrictions (Windows Phone has a hardware *Back* button, which must always *Go Back* for example).

  Others have restricted device capabilities or require enforced policies to be in place before you can target certain markets.

In the end, it comes down to assessing your titles fit for a certain device/market or operating system, and making plans before you go all-in to adopt it. Make a plan, understand what you are getting into, and then move forward.

# Distributing to mobile

The three major mobile platforms are iOS, Android, and Windows Phone. Each platform has its strengths and weaknesses in terms of performance, distribution, and marketing.

Before you begin publishing, make sure you have all UI elements scaling correctly at various resolutions. Using a canvas with the anchor and pivot points properly placed helps with this. Android has many more screen resolutions than any other mobile platform and it is impossible for you to test on all resolutions, so making sure everything scales appropriately is essential.

To publish on iOS, you final game must be built on a Mac. To publish on Windows Phone, you final game must be built in Windows 10. To publish on Android, your final game can be built using either a Mac or Windows operating system. So, to build to all three platforms you need both a Windows 10 machine and a Mac with a current OS.

Each of the mobile platforms require you to sign up for their storefront; none of them allow you to do so for free. Android development costs the least amount of money upfront, with the total cost of a Google Play account only being $25 for a lifetime. Developing for iOS is the most expensive. You have to pay $99 a year to get an Apple Developer account. Microsoft is right in the middle in pricing. Its pricing varies by country, but it is around $20 per year for an individual account.

# Social network integration

There is a lot you can do to add social network integration into your game. You can go as simple as adding a Facebook **like** button or Twitter **share** button. Or you can get more complicated and integrate Facebook friends lists to allow for multiplayer gameplay, for players to give each other items, or for players to compete through leader boards. Even something as simple as allowing players to share their high score is valuable.

Including incentives for using social networking options is a good way to raise awareness for your game. Often, games will offer bonuses for pointing others to a game, or offer additional bonuses for playing with others by way of social media.

Some games take it a step further. The 2015 game #IDARB actually allowed players to tweet specific hashtags at games being publicly streamed online in order to make things happen that both hindered and helped those playing. The 2011 mobile game, **Superbrothers: Sword & Sworcery EP** allowed players to tweet out specific lines of dialog from the game without clearly identifying the source of the text, which helped to build an air of mystery around the game.

You can find many different assets on the Unity **Asset Store** to assist you in adding social network integration into your game.

# Monetization

One of the hardest decisions we have to make with our creations is how to get paid. It is true that we love our creations and they are a part of us, but there should always be some sort of reimbursement for our effort.

Some of the most common patterns for monetization in games are paid, paid with trial, ad-supported, in-app purchase, and in-game currency.

# Paid

Games are usually sold at a fixed price. For big game studios, this is generally the only option, especially with disk-based delivery and some marketplaces.

The emphasis on a paid-only pattern means that you need a high-quality sales portfolio for your game and outstanding game-marketing assets (logos, screenshots, videos, and so on).

What is also just as important is the blurb about your game. It really has to stand out and draw the player in to make them part with their hard-earned cash.

# Paid with trial

Offering a trial with your game is a great way to entice the players in. Obviously, it gives them a taste of your game before they commit to paying for it.

 Be honest about the trial though; there have been many cases of annoyed players where games were published for free but were actually limited trials. Do not upset your potential buyers; be upfront about it.

You still need a good presence with your marketing and storefront, but the trial is also another great option to draw them in.

When going down the trial route, be sure to pick a single path and stick to it, either by limiting the game, offering so many levels, or even having a time-limited play. Just don't mix them!

Another factor in offering trials is that each platform you deploy to may have a different way of providing it, either directly from the marketplace or through marketplace APIs. It's best to design how your game will behave in a trial and link that to a flag or option. You can then control the game separately from the menu or check the game on startup.

# Ad supported

Often, the ad-supported option is the route for a lot of free-to-play mobile titles. This is one option that can be difficult to get right. If there are too many ads, the player will just get annoyed and uninstall it. Alternatively, if there are few ads, you are not going to get much back from it.

A key thing to remember about ads is that it's all about presentation and numbers. You need thousands of ads presented through your titles to make any kind of money back from the ad providers. It will be better if the player also clicks on the ad, as this generates better revenue; however, you cannot guarantee that the player will do this.

**Warning**

Do not attempt to fake or force the player to click on ads. It's a very bad experience and will most likely force the player to uninstall your game quickly. Also, ad providers are clever enough to work out whether you are faking the clicks; if so, they'll simply not pay you.

I have seen cases where developers have layered ads on top of each other to maximize their presentation or have use GUI controls in close proximity to the ads, tricking the player to click on them. These are very bad practices and should be avoided. At best, you won't get paid for your ads; at worst, it will significantly get you bad reviews and lower your number of players.

A few actions that generally work are as follows:

- Displaying ads in a non-UI blocking portion of the screen in the gameplay
- Displaying ads only in the menu or non-game screens (for example, the inventory and the pause screen)
- Displaying ads only in the loading screens
- Pop-up ads that appear when an event occurs
- Ads that players elect to play to receive an in-game currency or reward

You can mix-and-match the preceding patterns, but remember there is a fine line between background annoyances that the player can just ignore if they don't want to look and screens that are too intrusive and overbearing. Test with a selected audience and alter your implementation based on their feedback *before* you publish it.

The terms used by the ad providers aren't meant to befuddle you, but they do take some getting used to. Some of the terms and their meanings are described as follows:

- **Fill rate**: This term is the percentage rate at which ads will be sent to your game. If the provider has run out of ads or has none for your ad settings (age, region, language, and so on), this can drop to zero, meaning no ads.
- **Impressions**: This term denotes the number of successfully shown ads in your game. Beware of the same ad shown several times; some ad providers count this as the same impression. Just check against your own experience.
- **Click through rate** (**CTR**): This term is the higher paid option with ads; it denotes that the players are actually clicking on the ads to look into them.
- **eCPM**: This term is basically a unit of measurement of how much you will be paid per click or impression. Usually, you just need to multiply this figure by the number of impressions to see how much you will get. Note that this figure will go up and down based on just about anything, including the weather.
- **AdTypes**: There are various ad types and sizes supported by each provider with different capabilities. Banners are the simplest. They take up the entire screen while displaying the ad. Others such as interspatial are interactive and generally take up the entire screen. Check each provider to know what they support and which you want to use.

Another factor to keep in mind is publishers. They will all perform differently in different markets and languages. Generally, ad publishers focus on a few selected markets or only take advertisements in certain languages, and so on.

Some of the publishers are as follows:

- **Unity Ads:** Unity Ads is great for beginners as it is easy to implement, but it only works on a few platforms
- **Smaato**: This publisher is strong in central Europe and the US but poor in non-English countries
- **Inneractive**: This publisher provides a good mix of support and ads across the globe but suffers from low or poor fill rates in practice (something they are working on)
- **Google AdMob**: This publisher is strong across the globe, but you need millions of impressions to make any real money

There are many more publishers out there that have their strengths and weaknesses. You will be able to determine which publisher works best for you in which countries by personally testing them.

 When using advertising, it is very important to add your own instrumentation to your title to track how the adverts are doing. Don't just use the ad publisher's figures from their respective dashboards. This way, you can work out with what works best for you and alter your plans accordingly. Don't just publish and let go; manage effectively to improve your returns.

While implementing ads, there is no rule that says you have to use only one provider. Always hedge your bets with ad providers and implement as many as you are comfortable with; structure your ad presentation in a framework so that you always show the best-performing adverts first; and use another ad network if the current one isn't delivering.

If this seems a bit much to do by yourself, there are several frameworks out there that will do this for you. **Ad-rotating** solutions are fully featured to work with a number of ad providers and ensure that you always display ads.

# In-app purchases

A common feature implemented in most games these days is in-app purchases. This feature is simply your paid shop front within the game to unlock levels, purchase rare items, or remove unwanted features such as ads.

In some cases, in-app purchases have been used to implement trial functionality: publishing the title as free and then offering an in-game unlock option.

 Note that, with the trial system, be upfront if your game is sold as a trial. Players do not like this and will aggressively mark down and slam titles that appear free until they are forced to pay to play!

In-app purchases on most platforms come in the following two forms:

- **Durable/nonconsumable**: These are in-game items that the player can purchase (such as a sword, an unlockable area, or even the ability to turn off advertising if your game is ad-supported). These are generally single-use items, and you can verify with the marketplace of the platform to check whether the player has purchased them or not. It is advised that you also manage the information locally to ensure that you don't slow the game down on startup while checking. You can also keep this information on a backend service, just in case the user resets their device or transfers to a new one; this is not mandatory however.

  These can only be purchased once.

- **Consumable**: Effectively, consumables are in-game currency, items that are meant to be recharged and replenished over time.

  The big difference between consumables and durables is that consumables are not tracked on the server (other than in the payment history, but the payment history is not available in apps/games).

  These can be purchased many times over.

Besides the store/marketplace for each platform, there are some online services that will create payment systems for you, saving you from recreating everything for each platform you support. You still, however, have to publish your app to each platforms' store.

**Warning**

 If you are using in-app purchases, beware that *Big Brother* is watching. Employing unethical or illegal practices when implementing these systems could bring you a whole heap of trouble.

# In-game currency

Virtual currency, as a practice in games, has been rising steadily. The basic premise is that the game is generally free to play and uses some kind of in-game currency, which the players can earn in the game. This currency usually takes two forms; the basic coin, which can be earned in-game, and the premium coin, which can only be bought with cash (or as a result of completing rare and special events).

The idea is simple; play through the game slowly and normally. However, if you want to advance quicker or get ultra-rare items, you need to buy and spend the premium coin for those items. In some cases, you can also convert the premium coin to the basic coin to get the in-game currency quicker.

Although this makes a steady profit in single-player or offline games, it really comes into its own with the multiplayer option online. It seems there is a growing market for people to advance quicker than others or just to beat their friends quicker.

Implementing coin systems is generally harder than just implementing in-app purchases but makes for an easier-to-manage ecosystem.

Also, see the warning about in-app purchases, as this applies heavily to in-game currency/bitcoin systems as well, if not more.

# Going further

If you are the adventurous sort, try expanding your project to add the following features:

- Make your dream a reality and ship a game
- Market your game through social media, a blog, and other venues
- Implement social media in your title

# Summary

Rounding out our last chapter, we have been through an interesting ride to finally complete and get your project out there. We covered extending your Unity project onto the platform, plugins and their extensions, building your very own reusable assets, social media integration, and monetization.

Something you can try when you engage with a platform is to look at engaging across platforms, building titles that work cooperatively, enabling either a true multi-platform, multiplayer experience, or even building cooperative apps/games (where the phone version of a game can act as a second screen for your tablet/console version), as this is where dreams truly come alive!

# Index